Chronology

Roman Expansion 350 B.C.

Roman Empire 27 B.C.–A.D. 476

Germanic Invasions 375–525

800 Charlemagne H.R.E.

1073 Hildebrand = Pope Gregory VII   Emerging city-states in Nigeria

1138–1250 Hohenstaufen H.R.E.
1272–1806 Habsburgs H.R.E.
1348 Black Death

1434–1494 Original Medici rule in
          Florence
1494 French invasion of Italy   ca. 1500 Great Walls of Zaria

1618–1648 Thirty Years' War   ca. 1600 Songhay empire
                                          defeated; Bornu empire
1769–1821 Napoleon   weakened
                                       1804–1812 Fulani Caliphate at
                                          Sokoto established

The City-State in Five Cultures

THE CITY-STATE IN FIVE CULTURES

Edited and with an Introduction
by
Robert Griffeth and Carol G. Thomas

ABC-Clio

Santa Barbara, California   Oxford, England

Library of Congress Cataloging in Publication Data

Main entry under title:

The City-state in five cultures.

   Bibliography: p. 209.
   Includes index.
   Contents: Sumerian city-states/Song Nai Rhee—
The Greek polis/Carol G. Thomas—The Italian city-
state/Gordon G. Griffiths—[etc.]   1. City-states.   I. Griffeth, Robert.   II. Thomas,
Carol G., 1938–
JC352.C57   321.06   81–7897
ISBN 0–87436–316–0   AACR2

Illustration Credits

All maps and figures 3 and 5 drawn by Alice Alden.
Figure 1: C. J. Gadd, *History and Monuments of Ur* (New York: E. P. Dutton and Co.,
     1929), frontispiece.
Figure 2: H. R. Hall, *A Season's Work at Ur* (London: Methuen and Co., 1930), p. 85,
     fig. 70.
Figure 4: George Grote, *History of Greece,* 2d ed. (New York, 1899), facing p. 216.
Figure 6: Ambrogio Lorenzetti, ''The Effects of Good Government in the City (1337–
     1340). Siena, Communal Palace. Reproduced in Emilio Cecchi, *The Sienese
     Painters of the Trecento,* translated by L. Penlock (London: Frederick Warne
     and Co., 1931), plate CXCVII.
Figures 7 and 8: B. Matth and J. Merians, *Topographia Saxoniae Inferioris* (Frank-
     furt, 1653), Hamburg facing p. 124; Lubeck facing p. 154.
Figures 9 and 10: Dixon Denham, Hugh Clapperton and Doctor Oudney, *Narrative of
     Travels and Discoveries in Northern and Central Africa, in the Years 1822,
     1823 and 1824* (London: John Murray, 1826), town facing p. 36; plan of Kano
     p. 56.

ABC-Clio, Inc.
Riviera Campus
2040 Alameda Padre Serra, Box 4397
Santa Barbara, California 93103

Clio Press Ltd.
Woodside House, Hinksey Hill
Oxford OX1 5BE, England

Manufactured in the United States of America

Contents

Maps and Illustrations

Preface

Deep in the middle of winter teaching term, Carol Thomas, returning from her course in Greek history, stopped by Robert Griffeth's office to chat. When casually asked what topic she had addressed in her class that day, she replied, "The Greek *polis*." This prompted her to go on and ask, in the manner of all historians interested in comparisons, whether the history of Africa had ever produced anything similar to the Greek city-states. Griffeth's immediate, if cautious, response was, yes: certainly, at various times and places in that vast continent, there had been entities usually described by that term; but whether or not they were comparable to the famed Greek *poleis* would require a more precise definition of the term *city-state*.

In due course this modest question was carried to other historians whose specialized areas of interest included places to which the city-state label was normally applied: various civilizations of the ancient Near East; late medieval and early modern European states; commercial colonies of trading peoples that had developed into small, independent replicas of their parent cultures; and other examples from Asia and elsewhere. In fact, the possible range of examples seemed boundless—widely distributed in both time and space, and across great cultural frontiers. Nearly every civilization, it seems, provides some evidence of small independent or quasi-independent polities with urban cores.

Thus it became clear to us that historians—and social scientists from many other disciplines—had taken to using the simple, hyphenated term *city-state* to classify identifiable units or perhaps a stage in the life of certain units within the societies they studied. But the second part of the question put by Thomas to Griffeth was not so easily answered: were city-states, viewed across time, space, and cultural divides, really alike? Can we speak of a defined and particular form of human organization called the city-state which sets it apart from other kinds of states and cities in the world's history? And if we can specify a typical form, upon what grounds might we make comparisons between their different historical expressions?

vii

Discussions of this simple question now grown intriguingly more complex were soon joined by Gordon Griffiths, an historian of the European Renaissance and Reformation, and subsequently by two other scholars, Christopher Friedrichs, a student of German history, and Song Nai Rhee, a specialist in the history and archaeology of the ancient Near East. Surely our discussions would have been greatly enriched (and perhaps modified) through insights provided by students of other cultures. But we five quickly reached general agreement on the key issue—that the city-states of the places that we individually study from an historical perspective possess and share basic characteristics. They are, clearly, fit subjects for comparison. The task of demonstrating the validity of our consensus is the work that follows.

Foreword

Tom B. Jones

The second half of the present century has seen the development of a lively and sustained interest in urbanization. Not only have the origins, characteristics, problems, and future of cities been the objects of study and speculation, but the field has also widened to embrace related topics, such as the city-state, which is the focus of this volume.

A chronological survey of the extensive literature generated by contemporary concern with urbanization reveals an evolution in ways of thinking about the subject. At the outset it was only natural to assume that the whole matter was not overly complex, that a fund of information was already available, and that a few broad and facile generalizations would suffice to deal with the subject and its ramifications. Before long, however, it became apparent that we were trying to run before we had learned to walk or even to crawl. Diversity was discovered where unanimity had been taken for granted, and unsuspected complexities came to light. Terms used loosely and confidently at first were found to require tighter definitions. It became essential to know whether the terms "urbanization," "city," or "city-state" had the same meaning for Professor X as for Dr. Y. Frequently they did not, which inhibited communication and promoted controversy. It became evident that one must also ask what elements were truly basic and common to this or that situation in various places or at different times, or whether seeming similarities were superficial and of little significance.

In short, ideas thought to be obvious and well established were often found to consist more of fancy than of fact. After three decades of investigation and debate the older illusions of certainty have been fairly well dispelled, but the small hillock of current fact and understanding is vastly overshadowed by a mountain of ignorance that can only be leveled by careful, painstaking research, its bulk reduced stone by stone or even pebble by pebble.

The City-State in Five Cultures bears the stamp of a reasonable, thought-provoking, and potentially useful venture. Avoiding dogmatism, it presents its conclusions modestly, and solicits criticism, further investigation, and additional comparative studies. The fact that this work was the product of proximity—the five contributors live almost within shouting distance of one another—provided an advantage seldom enjoyed by such cooperative projects. A frequent exchange of views among the participants was possible, instead of being inhibited by distances involving great travel expense, fewer meetings, and less opportunity to reconcile differences of opinion. Granted that another group of specialists with other backgrounds would not have chosen the same city-states for study, there is no reason to think that a different alignment of states would have been more successful. The assemblage as it stands may be novel, but that is one of its virtues. The contributors give us a sample that has variety in space, time, and content, and has the further advantage that each author is conversant with his own material.

The editors have been careful to establish for their readers a specific definition of city-state. This term has always been an awkward one for which, regrettably, there is no acceptable alternative. *Polis,* as the editors warn us, will not fit every case. Part of the difficulty with city-state is that one must include in this category small towns that cannot qualify as cities in the modern sense. Further, citizens of city-states were not in every instance residents of the population centers where the governments were housed, nor did such cities or centers of government always rule the surrounding countryside. Even worse, city suggests to many persons urbanization as we know it today in the contemporary megalopolis, when in fact our kind of urbanization was a late phenomenon in antiquity. Positive and abundant evidence for urbanization is lacking before ninth-century Nimrud (Kalakh) or Neo-Assyrian Nineveh two hundred years later; after that come Periclean Athens, the great Hellenistic cities, and Rome.

Four common features may have determined the evolution of the earliest city-states (those states that developed independently of any foreign or previous mode). First, just as the change from nomadism to life in a settled agricultural community necessitated political, social, economic, and religious alterations—new responsibilities for the village chief, old gods made over and new ones conceived, and the like—so also the creation of a city-state posed new problems leading to further adjustments. A greater concentration of population in a small space called for an extension of authority and possibly the establishment of new officials to cope not merely with the aggravated problem of people trying to live harmoniously with one another but also other more complex matters involving the welfare of the community as a whole: relations with neighbors and the gods, provision for defense, an adequate supply of food, and so on.

Second, the actual form of government that would develop as the group passed from one stage to another would ordinarily depend upon traditional concepts of sovereignty. Among the Greeks and Romans and most other Indo-European groups we find that sovereignty was invested in the people (citizens), originally the warriors, who constituted an assembly which in turn delegated to the king powers they wished him to have. The king, essentially a war leader, was advised by a council of the elders, from which, among the Greeks and Romans, eventually developed a council of aristocrats (representing the noble clans), and a group of officials, recruited from the same landed nobility, elected by the assembly. At this point, the kingship had been abolished and the functions of the king divided among the elected officials. The final step in most cases was a liberalization that brought timocracy, which in turn had been created by economic changes that conferred wealth upon others besides the aristocratic landowners. In any event, the assembly of the citizens, however defined, retained its legislative and electoral functions.

The Sumerian concept of sovereignty remains obscure. The primitive democracy deduced for the Sumerian city-states comes from the single example drawn from a ballad and the very large assumption that the Sumerian and derivative Babylonian epics originated as the product of a heroic age in which traditional institutions resembled those of the Greeks and Romans. This scanty evidence inspires skepticism rather than confidence. When we remember how little the poet of the Iliad knew about Mycenaean kingship, we refrain from jumping to conclusions about the Sumerians. Anachronisms are common in epics of all periods and regions.

In trying to discover possible Sumerian concepts of sovereignty, an older theory is worth keeping in mind. Simply stated, we moderns see the world differently than did the Sumerians or the Egyptians. We tend to minimize or even overlook the atmosphere of supernaturalism in which the ancients lived. It is hard for us to comprehend how they understood the world and the obvious (to them) way in which it worked. From the very earliest times of which we have any knowledge, the Egyptian and Mesopotamian states were theocracies administered either by god-kings or by persons considered the viceroys of the gods. Sumerian *en,* high priest, occurs in the documents centuries before *ensi.* Just as religion was the main source of inspiration for art and literature, so also it may have been the original basis for the power of the governing authority and thus the theocratic tradition would be older than the earliest Sumerian city-states.

A third factor which appears to have influenced the future of a city-state was the geography of the territory in which a city-state was situated. The Greco-Roman city-states arose in small topographically delineated areas, while in Mesopotamia each state occupied only a small portion of the lower Tigris-Euphrates valley, which itself constitutes a single geographical unit. It should therefore occasion no surprise that the political unification of the whole came early to the lower valley (the first movements in that direction occurring in the Proto-Imperial period in the century and a half before Sargon of Akkad). This unification was the beginning of the end for the independent city-state in Mesopotamia. In Greece on the other hand, the compartmentalization provided by nature delayed unification for all practical purposes until the Roman conquest.

Finally, in both the Greek area and in ancient Sumer the natural geographic regions were dotted with many small villages scattered over the landscape in the pre-city-state era. Subsequently, the process the Greeks called *synoikismos* (setting up house together) began to take place as outlying areas were incorporated into a single city-state in which the major governmental functions were located in one center, which became the capital of the region. *Synoikismos* in Greece was often commemorated in local legends that ascribed the act to an individual: Theseus, for example, was supposed to have performed the *synoikismos* of Attica. In Mesopotamia a similar process of incorporation seems to be illustrated by the archaeological finds of the late fourth millennium, which show a decline in the total number of villages paralleled by the growth of a limited number of larger settlements.

This volume concentrates on the independent city-state, and clearly there is much more to be done with this topic. In conclusion, I would like to suggest a subject for additional future research—a sequel to the story told in this work. When the city-state lost its independence, it did not necessarily lose its essential vitality or its viability, though it became a cog in a larger machine. Frequently, as in the Hellenistic Age or in the days of the Roman Empire, it was employed as a unit of local government for purposes of taxation or for imperial administration below the provincial level. This is a subject that is far from exhausted and for which there is a mountain of evidence. The history of the city-state in Mesopotamia from the time of Sargon of Akkad onward has not been adequately explored, especially the late Assyrian and Babylonian periods when cities were blessed with royal charters that gave a large measure of independence and a certain freedom of choice. For the Greeks and Romans the task is also unfinished. Evidence for the classical period is still accumulating, and it would be useful to study more thoroughly the survival of the Greco-Roman city-state form into the medieval and early modern periods. *The City-State in Five Cultures* is bound to encourage further research on city-states, both in their independent earlier stages and their more dependent later forms.

Introduction

City-state is the term we use to describe a particular form of human social organization. The first well-documented appearance of this form occurred in southern Mesopotamia during the second half of the fourth millennium B.C. in ancient Sumer. While numerous other examples might be cited from this early period, the classical expression and principal model of city-state organization is provided by the Greek *polis* of which more than fifteen hundred came into existence between the ninth and third centuries B.C. City-states have flourished at other times and in different places well into the nineteenth century A.D. It might even be argued that city-states, dressed in modern garb but still possessing the basic attributes of the ancient *polis,* are with us still. Virtually the whole spectrum of possible political systems was represented by one or another of these polities, from strong centralized monarchy through aristocratic oligarchy to republican democracy. However, each has shared certain basic features.

These features include a defined core, the city, usually enclosed by walls or surrounded by water. Each also had a policy of striving for economic self-sufficiency, often achieved or promoted through the acquisition of an immediate productive hinterland under the city's control which supplied the basic needs of the city-dwellers. In every instance there was a fundamental sense of shared language, culture, and history with other units like it in the same general area or region. Perhaps most important of all, the city-state regarded itself as an independent, self-governing polity whether or not its claims to political autonomy were disputed by some higher legal authority.

Our use of the term *state* in this book encompasses the widest meaning associated with that word in a socio-political context. That is, a state is a definable geographical territory within which the ruling group claims a large and exclusive control over the political, social, and economic life of the inhabitants, both citizen and subject. This represents a *de facto* condition of state sovereignty, even though that concept does not enter the vocabulary of European political thought until the seventeenth century. The term *polis,* which in the Platonic and Aristotelian views contained the concept of an ideal,

xiii

self-governing, self-sufficient political community directed toward the aim of
moral development for its members, therefore differs from the usage we
employ here for the state. For that reason, *polis* is used only to refer to the Greek
city-states. Our use of the term *city* is meant to have equally broad meaning. It
does not attempt to achieve anything approaching the precision which the
analytical efforts of urbanists have sought to impart to it. For us, a city is a
demarcated physical space which contains a major concentration of population
within a state. In a city-state, the city serves as the political capital and the hub
of its social and economic affairs. The hyphenated term *city-state* thus desig-
nates such historical cases as generally contain the elements of the four-part
definition we offer here. Common sense dictates that this definition is not
exclusive to the city-state but applies to other forms of both cities and states as
well. However, other than smallness of scale, the key element required to
distinguish city-states from other state forms is expressed by the perception of
its citizens that they possess a substantial capacity to govern themselves
independently. This holds true even in such cases where city-state sovereignty
is in theory limited by another power (such as was true of the German city-
states). We shall proceed to argue that the city-state comes to an end as a
distinctive form of political association when the citizens' perception of their
independence is forcefully changed, by whatever means.

We use the term *polity* to refer to any type of political association—large or
small, state or groupings within states—and it appears in this text only for
purposes of stylistic variety.

The term *nation* (i.e., a community of persons who regard themselves as
sharing a common language, culture, and historical tradition—features that
differentiate it from other nations) does not apply to individual city-states
since in every case we examine here the sentiment called nationality included
more than one city-state belonging to a common "national" culture. Occasionally we employ the abstract coinage "city-state system" to indicate this matter.

It is our basic assumption that city-states conforming to our four-part definition arose in other times and places and bore striking similarities to the Greek
polis, although the historical circumstances of their origins and development
were, needless to say, very different from the Greek experience. Our efforts to
compare examples drawn from such a broad range of possibilities will thus be
handled in two ways. First, employing individual case studies, we set out to
describe and analyze the emergence of city-states in five different cultural and
historical settings. In addition to Greece, these settings are Sumer of ancient
southern Mesopotamia; the northern Italian city-states between, roughly, 1000
and 1500; the Swiss and German city-states from the late medieval period to the
age of the Napoleonic wars; and the walled cities of the African Hausa (of
today's Nigeria) which flourished between the fifteenth and eighteenth centuries A.D. We regard the city-states of each of these settings as possessing a
particular form of human social organization that set them apart from other
forms of either urban development or state creation. Having presented these

five case studies, our second goal will be to employ the concepts and tools of comparative analysis in an effort to discover the common denominators in the historical processes that brought each into being and of those conditions that characterized their demise.

A case could be made that other political organizations meet the criteria suggested here. While we do not claim the final verdict for the pre-modern city-state, we do claim to have isolated typical examples. Rome, for instance, began as a city-state but developed into an empire; the Greek *poleis* could never form an empire. The existence of city-states in China is a matter of ongoing debate, but no one denies the existence of the Italian forms. For the modern period the situation is somewhat different. Singapore, a territorially-compact sovereign entity, exhibits many features to be found in both early modern and ancient city-states. In a somewhat different sense, the tiny oil sheikdoms of the Persian Gulf—Abu Dhabi, Qatar, Kuwait—have parlayed their fantastically rich oil resources into bargaining counters on both the local and international levels that have resulted in a remarkable degree of political and territorial autonomy. And in still another sense, Hong Kong, though formally linked to its British imperial overlord as a colony, possesses many of these special characteristics which animated and sustained city-states of time past.

Yet all these examples of modern city-states, if one wishes to consider them that, owe their origins and continued existence to a single, dominant historical fact: they assumed their present shapes as the result of the creation of a complex, intricately interdependent global economy. That economy was itself the product of initiatives taken by an industrially mighty Western Europe in those few centuries leading up to the present day. For this reason, among others, our studies of the city-state, the comparisons and themes that we find appropriate to them, will be confined to the premodern, preindustrial period of world history. Ancient Sumer stands at the beginning of this vast time span, and the incorporation of the Hausa cities in a Muslim imperial system in the early nineteenth century will represent the end date of the "premodern" period.

The most salient characteristic of the city-state is surely that expressed by the notion of independence: the ability of its rulers and citizens to exercise control over their affairs, or at least the agreed-upon fiction that they possessed such control. This passion for political autonomy appears regardless of the special historical circumstances in which the actual territorial unit came into being. In some cases, the founding inspiration seems clearly associated with the need of a society to defend itself. In such cases the citadel (the acropolis) becomes both symbol and physical manifestation of the independent unit. Where the principal attributes of the core are associated with a sacred place, either a natural feature of the environment or a temple, this too reinforces the feelings of particularism and of independence maintained by the city-states' citizens. In other cases it has been argued that economic considerations were paramount in that social class formation and a division of labor based upon social stratification were invariable features of city life.

This last matter raises an important analytical issue. Major changes in the economic bases of any society—particularly those which reflect population growth and density—are often interpreted as the principal causes of the process loosely defined as political centralization. Surely the city-state is the product of political centralization. But the results of major economic transformations have only occasionally taken the form we identify as the city-state and this remains true whether the changes stemmed from an economic system in the process of growth or one that experienced disruption and decline. Political centralization and decentralization effected by major economic changes produced a great variety of political units—kingdoms and empires, feudal institutions and intensely localized village or tribal aggregates. Consequently, it is difficult to establish significant economic change as *the* central causal explanation of the origins and growth of city-states.

How, then, are economic factors to be taken into account? We offer the following suggestions. First, among the cases of city-states studied here, none developed as self-sustaining economies. All were dependent in important ways on trade and commerce with areas outside their control. Indeed, we would argue that city-states constitute *prima facie* evidence of much wider economic systems to which they belong. If those economic systems experience decline, so generally do the city-states which form important components of them. This is not to say that some city-states do not manage a continuing independent vigor during periods of general economic decline; such clearly was the case with Venice, Genoa, and Florence during Europe's calamitous fourteenth century when these centers of commerce and finance largely escaped the disasters that befell nearly all of their neighbors. However, in the reverse case—that is, during periods of general sustained economic growth over large regions— political centers that are better equipped to organize and control large-scale territories often circumscribe and then overwhelm the city-state. The city-state's wealth was its principal attraction to kings and emperors. This was the case of the Greek cities, as indeed it was in all the other examples presented here.

Second, and viewing the city-state's economy from an internal perspective, a city's success depends upon the degree to which it can exercise control over a substantial economic surplus. This is a prime requisite, for upon such control is based the high degree of occupational specialization so characteristic of city life. While much of the surplus (especially foodstuffs) might be produced within the immediate territory falling under the city's rule (Sumer, Greece, the Hausa, for example), in other instances (the Italian and North European city-states) commerce, and later finance, were the principal means by which the economic surplus was generated. In all our five cases the main point is clear: political independence was not matched by economic independence, by self-sufficiency. We must therefore turn to some other means of explaining the role of economic developments in the origins and growth of city-states.

One key factor seems to be tied up in a correlation between the size or scale of the political unit—city-states are small—and the aims of the rulers, or citizens, in using the economic surplus at their disposal. The political independence of the city-state gives it the capacity to control and dispose of its surplus, or at least a considerable share of its surplus, on matters that directly benefit the city and its ruling groups. In cities that belong to a kingdom or the tribute-paying lands of an empire, the ability to control that surplus is very much less. The issue is *not* whether the city-state's economic surplus is acquired through direct taxation imposed upon its workers, through the earning on its exported industrial output, commercial exchanges, or finance capital lending, or some combination of all these things. The ability to control that surplus within the territorially defined structure of the city-state is the central subject. That surplus may be spent on building temples, Doge's palaces, Renaissance churches, or sumptuous dwellings for rulers. Or it may be reinvested in ways that sustain growth in its economic system such as Florentine banking and Hanseatic commerce attest. But that surplus is not passed on to some higher sovereign. When it is, the political-economic unit we call the city-state has ceased to exist.

The discovery of the common elements, on the one hand, and of dissimilar features, on the other, may be the most important products of this collection. Yet the analysis rests on specific instances of city-state organization and, consequently, five individual studies are presented. Although the ultimate aim of the study is comparative, each essay attempts to describe the city-state as it would have been understood by inhabitants of that polity. The main topics are the circumstances that led to its development, the conditions that sustained its vigor and, ultimately, the factors that precipitated its end. One question is whether the city-state appears to have been a stage of development in the formation of a larger political entity; or, conversely, whether it emerged after the decline of a more complex system of organization. The evidence indicates that both patterns occur: Sumer and the Hausa give clearer evidence of the first pattern, a stage in what subsequently became larger political entities; the Italian and North European city-states show greater evidence of the second pattern; Greece appears to reflect elements of both processes.

The question of territory is thus a major concern. All city-states have been of relatively small size, particular communities occurring within larger cultural units. So one must inquire about the territorial configuration of the city-state. The city and its countryside interacted in a variety of ways that are difficult to explore since the connections were taken for granted by contemporaries. For our purposes, we must ask whether there were maximum limits to a city-state's size that were essential to its continued existence or, indeed, to its origin. Geographical conditions may well be basic to the initial formation of the city-state and the exploitation of some natural resource may have promoted the growth of a particular area. And just as the territory of the city-state had specific characteristics, so too did the city acquire certain regular features. Walls surrounded the Hausa cities; the ziggurat symbolizes the nature of the Sumerian city; acropolis, agora, and wall define the Greek *polis*. Each author examines the connection between form and function.

City-states are both communities of place and communities of people. Consequently, each study also focuses on the nature of the social structure of the population. The nature of population differentiation and the grounds for distinctions are equally important to an understanding of social orders (classes). In all city-states there were rulers or leaders, but they did not necessarily derive from a nobility set apart from the bulk of the population. In some of the five case studies it will be possible to describe a proletariat; in others such a description is totally inappropriate. One especially interesting comparison will emerge from a study of slavery. The economies of antiquity were founded on slavery, as the Greek city-states illustrate very well. The economy of the North European state had far different foundations.

In all cases there were certainly differences in the political rights and obligations of members of various social strata and these differences are encompassed in an examination of citizenship. Descent, ownership of a certain type or amount of property or other factors drew a firm line between citizens and outsiders; each group had a special relationship to the state, and the state, in turn, made a different set of requirements for citizens and non-citizens. The Greek *polis* commanded an almost fervent loyalty from its members while most inhabitants of the Sumerian city-states were members of the community by economic constraints. We have individually examined the relationship between an individual and his state to ascertain the reasons responsible for the responses.

Inasmuch as the city-state encompassed the entire life of its members (that is, the sovereign was the city-state), it had therefore to provide certain functions for them: it exercised a judicial function, was responsible for matters of defense and security, fulfilled religious needs and functioned as an economic provider or redistributor of goods and services. Each study treats the nature of the law, legal institutions, and the judiciary—if one existed; the character of the army; the role of specialized religious or economic authorities and/or corporations.

The totality of the city-state's functions and the means for their execution may be described as a reflection of its political form or, in short, its constitution. All five studies examine the organs of government and the eligibility or obligation for official service to the state. We have asked whether political groups coalesced to pursue special interests and whether they were recognized as playing significant roles in the political structure of the state; that is, whether it is proper to discuss parties and factions. An individual's continuing fitness to serve the state may change and each study is concerned with the recognition of rules which, if broken, resulted in the exile or death on charges of treason to the state. Since an individual city-state is part of a larger cultural, if not political, whole, it has been fruitful to inquire, where the evidence permits, whether constitutions varied between states and, if so, whether there were any major consequences for the well-being of the individual polities.

On the basis of the answers provided to these and other more specialized questions we move to the problem of the demise of the city-state form. If we were to consider the city-state form as basically a *stage* that normally occurs either in the process of growing political centralization or in times of terrible disruption of large political units such as empires, then the quest for an all-embracing theme might be readily answered. The city-state would emerge as no more nor less than that political entity—doomed to a finite half-life—that often appears in the form of a localized outburst of a community's desire for independence when larger governing authority is either absent or has been severely weakened. Such an interpretation is appealing since either one or the other of the two processes described is present in all our case studies. Moreover, the staying power of city-states seems positively limited to a time-span rarely exceeding four to five hundred years. But the major problem with such a sweeping thematic interpretation is that we can discover many circumstances in which either growing political centralization or decentralization takes place, and yet the city-state form is virtually absent. The history of Russia, of the great empires founded by nomadic warrior groups, or of the spread of farming groups into agricultural frontier lands, for example, all feature the ebb and flow of concentrated political power at governing centers at various points in their histories; but the definition of what took place at different stages of their development and decline reveals no city-state stage. Thus our effort to determine comparative themes that account for the end of the city-state form will be necessarily limited to those that are found in the specific cases studied here, and we shall leave to others the effort to construct a grander theory of where the city-state falls within the overall comparative analysis of civilizations. This point must be made emphatically. We have not attempted a compendium of examples or the definition of a universal model. The five examples represented are polities generally described as city-states and we have examined them both individually and comparatively.

Our comparisons are focused upon an analysis of the data presented in the five cases. To begin, we address the issue of origins: specifically, we identify whether a given case came into existence as a result of growing centralization of political power or, conversely, as the product of disruption of a major political unit. Second, we make an effort to identify what caused the city-state form of organization to prevail over other possible types of government in each area. Third, we draw from the wealth of descriptive data provided in the studies to take the measure of similarities and differences found in detailed comparisons of the institutions, social arrangements, economic systems, and constitutional character of our five examples. Fourth, we examine the historical circumstances leading to the decline and fall of independent city-states. And, we venture a word or two on whether the comparative themes that we posit might also apply to the study of other cultures than those used in this volume.

In conclusion, some mention should be made about the historical sources employed to construct this volume. Each of the authors has worked with the primary data relevant to the particular area studied in other scholarly works. However, for this volume, each uses the technique of making reference to the basic scholarly literature on the case studied. Since these literatures are both vast and replete with scholarly controversy over particular matters, no effort has been made to indicate them comprehensively in either the notes or the selected bibliography. Rather, where unresolved scholarly dispute goes on, this is appropriately noted. The suggested readings are meant to indicate the best sources (in English, wherever possible) that the interested reader might turn to for greater detail on any specific issue raised.

It should be equally clear that the primary sources of historical data differ substantially from case to case. Whereas a relative wealth of documentary evidence exists upon which historical reconstructions of the European city-states described here are based, archeology provides the principal source of evidence on ancient Sumer. The literary evidence that has survived from antiquity also tells us much about the societies of that period—as do the accounts produced by literate Muslims who resided among the Hausa—but these sources differ in both volume and character from the documentary material relating to medieval and early modern Germany and Italy. Therefore, the analysis of preserved oral traditions, speculative reconstructions from archeological evidence, and cautious use of ethnographic accounts have all figured in varying degrees as sources of evidence in the attempt to portray city-state organization and life in Sumer, Greece, and Hausaland. These fundamental differences in the kinds of evidence available to the historian naturally complicate the task of making detailed comparisons, but do not, in our view, preclude the possibility.

Chapter One

SUMERIAN CITY-STATES

Song Nai Rhee

During the last one hundred years, archeologists have uncovered scores of ancient human settlements in the desert lands of southern Mesopotamia. As a result, we know that in the now scorching, inhospitable sand dunes of the Tigris-Euphrates alluvial plain there once stood great fortified cities teeming with people, flourishing in trade and commerce, bustling with skilled craftsmen and merchants, dominated by majestic temples, and supported by fertile farms and intricate systems of irrigation canals.

As man's first civilization, Sumer is credited with numerous inventions without which modern civilization would not have been possible, such as a system of writing, wheels, codes of law, and schools. Historically, Sumer is particularly well-known for being the seat of the earliest city-states, a phenomenon that subsequently occurred in other parts of the world, each sharing features remarkably similar to the others. Through Sumerian cuneiform records and archeological surveys we know that during the early Dynastic period (2,800–2,350 B.C.) about a dozen independent, autonomous city-states dotted the landscape of the lower Tigris-Euphrates plain: Kish, Ur, Uruk, Lagash, Umma, Eridu, Shuruppak, Adab, Larsa, among others.

The processes which led to the emergence of city-states in ancient southern Mesopotamia are of considerable interest in themselves, but they become particularly important in a comparative study of similar polities. Sumerian civilization was primary; that is, it grew out of prehistoric roots and was not modeled on earlier civilized societies. The other cultures examined in this volume are secondary civilizations, that is, they were influenced by other contemporary or earlier cultures. There is, consequently, a uniqueness to the Sumerian polities which were the end products of developments from the onset of human prehistory more than a million years ago. Therefore, considerable attention will be devoted to the very emergence of civilization without which specific political orders of any sort could not have taken shape. On this base we will describe the Sumerian states emphasizing their essential components in terms of physical form, political structure, economic foundation, functions of

1

the state, social structure, and interstate relationships. And, finally, we must
analyze the causes of their ultimate decline.

Origin of the Sumerian City-States

The city-states of ancient Sumer were the culmination of socio-economic as
well as cultural developments of several millennia following the emergence of
agriculture in the Near East during the Neolithic period. As one of the major
events in human history the agricultural transformation brought about fundamental changes in population growth and density, settlement patterns, architecture, social organization, and the economic base of society. Increasing improvements in the technology of food production made the prehistoric inhabitants of the Near East depend increasingly on settled community life, paving the
way for the emergence of villages, towns, cities, and finally the economically
self-sufficient as well as politically independent city-states.

The emergence of agriculture resulted from a complex set of factors which
included certain preconditions such as availability of domesticable plants and
animals and man's knowledge of their traits and behavior, broad-spectrum
subsistence, controlled and selective hunting techniques, and technological
improvements in harvesting and food-processing (sickle blades, grinding
stones, roasting ovens, and storage facilities). Both external and internal
stimuli, such as post-glacial climatic change from colder to warmer and wetter,
and population growth and pressure were also important. These various factors
in the development of agriculture were closely interrelated and mutually reinforcing in what Charles Redman calls "positive feedback relationships."[1]
Archeological data from several Near Eastern sites such as Zarzi, Zawi Chemi,
Karim Shahir, and Tepe Asiab in the Zagros region as well as the sites of
Kebara, Nahal Oren, and Malaha in the Levant indicate that many of the
preconditions for agriculture had already appeared by the end of the
Epipaleolithic period (12,000–8,000 B.C.). And it is soon after 8,000 B.C. that
we start finding evidences of domestication of plants and animals in the Near
East.

It is impossible to pinpoint the exact locations and the time of domestication
of specific plants, but it is generally assumed that barley, the most important of
the ancient Near Eastern foodstuffs, was domesticated about 7,000 B.C., as
evidenced by the archeological remains of the Beidha and the Bus Mordeh
phase of Ali Kosh. Since its natural habitats were scattered throughout the arc of
the Fertile Crescent, it could have been domesticated anywhere between the
hilly flanks of the Zagros mountains and southeastern Anatolia and as far as
southern Negev in the Levant. Einkorn wheat, whose natural habitats were
primarily the regions of southeastern Anatolia and western Iran, appears to have
been first domesticated in southeastern Turkey by about 7,000 B.C., and emmer
wheat shortly thereafter in the Golan Heights as well as in the upper Jordan
watershed. Due to difficulty involved in distinguishing the domesticated peas
and legumes from the wild forms, it is not certain when they were domesticated,

but they appear to have been important parts of the diet in early village communities, as evidenced at Mureybit. Their primary habitats are roughly the same as those of barley and wheat, and it is probable that legumes were first domesticated in open oak forests.

Domesticated animals included dogs, sheep, goats, pigs, and cattle. These animals possessed certain characteristics that enhanced their domestication. Some animals such as sheep, goats, and cattle were consumers of cellulose (dry grasses, leaves, straw, twigs), not vital to human diet; some had natural sociability with man as in the case of dogs; others, like sheep, goats, and cattle, had a natural "herd instinct." They not only moved in groups but were easily led. Of these animals, the sheep was the first to be domesticated for food, followed by goats and cattle. Cattle appear to have been first domesticated in southeastern Europe about 7,000 B.C. and became an important domesticate of the Near East about 6,000 B.C., starting in central Anatolia, as clearly evidenced at Catal Hüyük.

Domestication of plants and animals, however, did not transform human subsistence patterns overnight. During the initial period of early villages (7,500–6,000 B.C.), only a small portion of human diet consisted of domesticated cereals. For the major portion of their food, the early villagers relied on hunting and gathering, as evidenced at prepottery Neolithic B sites of Beidha, Jarmo, and the Bus Mordeh phase of Ali Kosh. Inhabitants of Beidha still hunted wild animals, such as gazelle, aurox, and ibex, and also collected pistachio nuts, acorns, and various legumes. A similar picture emerges at the Bus Mordeh phase whose inhabitants appear to have migrated to higher elevations during summer for hunting. Hunting and collecting continued to be an important part of Near Eastern subsistence economy until as late as the Samarran phase of advanced farming villages, as evidenced at Choga Mami and Tell es-Sawwan and at Catal Hüyük in Anatolia.[2] Transition from dependence on hunting and gathering to substantial reliance on food production was a gradual process that was not fully realized until 4,000 B.C.

Despite its relative slowness, the emergence of agriculture did successfully initiate processes that became irreversible—greater dependence of the subsistence economy on farming, increasing sedentarism, and growing complexity of community organization. As food-production became an attractive alternative to hunting and gathering, Neolithic bands devoted more time and effort to agricultural pursuits and to the development of agricultural technology. Inevitably this process led to an increasing sedentary life inasmuch as agricultural activities tie the farmer to the land he works. To be sure, some early sedentary communities in the Levant, such as Mureybit, prepottery Neolithic A Jericho, Nahal Oren, and Malaha, had appeared prior to agriculture; but agricultural pursuits did intensify the process of permanent settlement to an unprecedented degree. Successful food production, in turn, contributed to the growth and stability of the population in the settled communities. Increases in caloric intake as well as decreases in strenuous physical activities required of mobile hunting life enhanced female reproduction cycles, an important factor in population growth. Growth in population, in turn, necessitated a more complex organization of the community for efficient economic activities. When community development reached the level of advanced villages and towns, social organization arranged itself in a hierarchical system centering on a chief and flanked by craft and farming specialists. The chief generally controlled the mechanism of collection and distribution of goods and resources. Such new forms of social organization not only enhanced the community bond but improved its agricultural productivity. Improved productivity, in turn, facilitated the growth of permanent agricultural settlements.

Permanent farming villages first appeared in southern Mesopotamia about 5,300 B.C. By this time, the transition to agriculture was well under way throughout the Near East. Agricultural settlements had sprung up in most regions of the Fertile Crescent: from the Levant into the Zagros mountains and north through northern Mesopotamia into Anatolia. And from about 6,000 B.C., many villages had reached a high degree of sophistication in architecture, technology, subsistence, community organization, and interregional trade.

The general architectural trend was a transition from earlier circular structures to rectilinear and multiroomed buildings, as evidenced in the upper levels of Beidha, and at Cayönü, Jarmo, and Ali Kosh. This transition is indicative of craft specialization and activity differentiation. Trade with distant peoples is indicated by the presence of non-native raw materials in the villages. Increasing numbers of artistic objects and jewelry further reflect craft specialization. The use of well-fired pottery was becoming common throughout the Near East; the first pottery appeared as early as 7,000 B.C. in either southern Anatolia or the Iranian plateau.

By 5,500 B.C. simple irrigation was being employed to increase productivity at certain sites like Catal Hüyük, Choga Mami, and Tell es-Sawwan. Cattle were becoming an important source of meat. Burial goods and ritual objects, found at Catal Hüyük and at Tell es-Sawwan in northern Mesopotamia, indicate that formalized religion had become an important part of Near Eastern farming villages by the middle of the sixth millennium. Anatolian obsidian at Jericho, 1,000 kilometers away from its source, and the presence of copper and turquoise at Catal Hüyük from eastern Anatolia or Sinai, 500 and 1,000 kilometers away, respectively, demonstrate that extensive trade networks had been developed throughout the Near East. Fortifications (walls, ditches, watch towers) at Tell es-Sawwan as well as Choga Mami reveal that warfare was part of village life, and defense was an important concern in Samarran communities of the early sixth millennium. Building of fortifications is evidence of another advance in effective community organization and cooperation. Precious burial goods in some infant graves at various Samarran sites are signs that by 5,500 B.C. social stratification had emerged. Finally, stamp seals at Catal Hüyük and potters' marks on Samarran pottery vessels suggest that private ownership had become an important factor in Near Eastern villages.

By the time the first colonizers arrived in the alluvial plains of southern Mesopotamia, the agricultural transformation was already well advanced in most regions of the Near East—especially in the fringes of the Mesopotamian Plains. The main reason for the relatively late appearance of farming villages in southern Mesopotamia was the time it took to develop cereal grains and animals that could survive the hot, dry environment of the lowlands. For nearly two millennia, following the first domestication of plants, agriculturalists settled at relatively higher elevations where rainfall farming was possible, i.e., in the areas not too radically different from the natural habitats of the domesticated plants. It was only after the farmers living on the fringes of the alluvial plains, such as the Deh Luran Plains, had successfully adapted the cereal grains to a hot, dry environment by using irrigation that colonizers moved into the hitherto inhospitable regions of the Mesopotamian lowlands.[3]

And yet it was precisely during this "late arrival" phase that the Ubaidian colonizers of southern Mesopotamia founded the first urban settlements. Entering a region surrounded by advanced farming villages, the Ubaidians drew upon their agricultural technologies in fostering the development of history's first cities. By definition, cities are centers of large and dense population concentration that exhibit social stratification, diversity of economic activities, complexity in administrative organization, and mechanisms of social control. They act as nodes or junctions of variegated, functionally-related networks within a civilization. Thus cities are intimately related to civilization itself, inasmuch as they become the nexus for the generalized set of cultural developments which, taken together, we term civilization.

Since southern Mesopotamia provides the first evidence of the urban phenomenon in human history, it is worthwhile pausing for a moment to survey the most important scholarly theories that have been advanced to account for the appearance of cities there.

One major group of scholars has favored stressing a single factor, or prime mover, approach to explain the origins of urbanism.[4] Among them, Karl Wittfogel and Julian Steward have singled out early farmers' need for large-scale water management as the primary cause in the rise of urbanism. Generally known as the Hydraulic Hypothesis, this view claims that the first great cities and states came into being in semiarid regions in response to the need for an effective system of irrigation and all that entailed with respect to the construction, maintenance, and protection of the water system. Somewhat in line with the Hydraulic Hypothesis, V. Gordon Childe suggested that large towns emerged near canals and waterways which, along with the employment of pack animals, served to create transportation networks.

Robert Carniero focused attention on the factor of population pressure and the consequent military conflicts related to such pressure on resources to help explain the origins of urbanism. According to Carniero, when populations reach their maximum subsistence capacity, they are forced to compete with their neighbors for available land and resources. This inevitably leads to warfare. In these conflicts, the victors become a wealthy upper class while the losers usually become the low class serving the former. Conflict may also arise as part of a class struggle between rich and poor, the rich having emerged as dominant through control of the irrigation system and the farms served by it. In the process of conflict, victorious communities increase in population size and organizational complexity as the vanquished are incorporated into them.

Henry Wright and Kent V. Flannery, among other scholars, see interregional and intraregional trade as the primary stimulus in the rise of urbanism. According to their theory, when a region lacks certain raw materials, an administrative organization emerges to manage efficient procurement and redistribution of the goods (trade). The presence of a managerial and controlling group enhances production and helps to diversify economic activity. This, in turn, causes settlements to expand. Trade, in this view, is assumed to have played the crucial role in the rise of cities and states, particularly in southern Mesopotamia which lacked many essential raw materials such as stone, metal ores, and timber.

Other scholars have found these various single-factor (prime mover) hypotheses inadequate to explain the early urban phenomenon. To them, a multifactor, systems approach to the problem is required to achieve adequate understanding. Charles Redman, for one, sees the rise of urbanism "as a series of interacting incremental processes that were triggered by favorable ecological and cultural conditions and that continued to develop through mutually reinforcing interaction."[5] He rejects the conventional approach which stresses sequential, linear developments with one primary factor leading to another. Redman goes on to emphasize that "none of these feedback relationships functioned for a long period in an administrative vacuum, with an administrative elite suddenly appearing 'full blown' to control the already developing institutions. Rather, each institution started at a simple level and increased by small increments."[6] Slowly, bit by bit, community life became more complex, each new development affecting all the others, culminating in the institutionalization of various economic and administrative strata which then shaped a hierarchically structured society.

Looking at the development of the Sumerian city-states in terms of Redman's theory, when farmers first settled in the semiarid lowlands of southern Mesopotamia around 5,300 B.C., the lowland alluvial plains were a "potentially productive ecological niche." The first colonizers, the Ubaidians, had the necessary technological knowledge, including an organizational strategy for developing these hitherto uncultivated lands. The settlers belonged to a culture that had used irrigation techniques in farming marginal areas of the northeastern Mesopotamian plains. They had successfully raised domesticated plants and animals in a harsh lowland environment made difficult by saline soils and a hot climate. Finally, labor specialization within an increasingly complex social organization had already appeared in their advanced farming villages such as Tell es-Sawwan. These ecological, cultural, and technological factors stimulated numerous socio-economic changes: increased productivity, rapid population growth, generation of a larger food surplus, specialization within craft and artisan trades, and development of long-distance trade to obtain essential raw materials. A more sophisticated economic system developed from these changes in which attention was necessarily focused on the redistribution of foodstuffs to non-agricultural workers. The village populations thus developed along class lines, a wealthy elite coming to dominate the whole. The upshot of these mutually reinforcing feedback relationships was the emergence of a complex, urban society.

Why southern Mesopotamia became the scene of these developments can only be a subject of conjecture. It may have been due to population pressures on the upland regions. It may have stemmed from soil depletion caused by long, intensive cultivation in the uplands and the best of the marginal areas adjoining them. Or it may simply have been the final stage of the gradual migratory movements of farming populations from the uplands to the lower elevations following the first successful experiments in plant domestication.

Following the initial settlement around 5,300 B.C. the traits of civilization began to emerge in southern Mesopotamia with amazing rapidity. By the end of the Ubaidian period (5,300–3,600 B.C.) great towns had already come into being: Eridu alone occupied an area of 10 hectares with a population of 2,000 to 4,000 people. By the latter part of the Uruk period (3,600–3,100 B.C.) the great city of Uruk appears to have had a population of 10,000 people and occupied an area of at least 80 hectares [800,000 sq. meters], and by the middle of the Early Dynastic period, ca. 2,700 B.C., Uruk was a great metropolis of 50,000 people and 400 hectares [4 sq. km] of city proper.[7]

The substantial increase in settlement size by the beginning of the Early Dynastic period, around 2,900 B.C., was largely a result of population redistribution brought on by military conflicts in the countryside, evidenced by the appearance of fortified cities. By the Late Uruk period (3,600–3,100 B.C.) settlements in the Uruk region had numbered as many as 123, whose average size was 1 to 2 hectares; but by the Early Dynastic period the number was reduced to less than 50, the average settlement occupying between 6 to 10 hectares.[8] In other words, increasing warfare caused rural populations to flee to the larger communities for protection leaving the countryside deserted and causing the urban centers to expand rapidly. Along with the increase in settlement size, significant innovations occurred in the socio-economic and the technological sphere. By the end of the Ubaid period and more widely during the Uruk period the fast wheel was introduced into pottery making, resulting in mass production of standard ware, such as the bevel-rimmed bowls and conical cups of the subsequent Jemdet Nasr period. In addition to the mass production of pottery, the Ubaid period is noted for having the first monumental buildings with more sophisticated architecture emerging during the Uruk and Jemdet Nasr periods, as exemplified by the massive temple complexes of Uruk. Sculpture, metal works, lapidary works, and stamp and cylinder seals show the degree to which craft specialization had developed, and the presence of non-

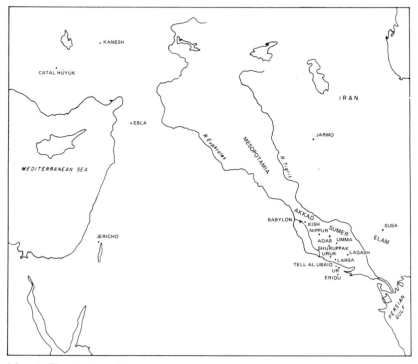

Map 1: *The Ancient Near East*

native metals, such as copper and silver vessels and flint blades, indicates that trade with distant lands—perhaps as far as Anatolia—had become an important feature of the Jemdet Nasr period.

In addition to the development of agriculture, crafts, trade, and the social organization to support them, three other crucial innovations emerged from urbanization: a system of irrigation, the invention of writing, and the introduction of the wheel-drawn cart.

In the region of the Sumerian city-states, the first glimmerings of irrigation began near settlements located along small water courses and marshes that could be effectively utilized for simple, short-range irrigation of limited areas. As the need to expand the settlements and cultivated lands arose (perhaps as early as the Jemdet Nasr period), people began settling along large stream courses in order to develop large scale irrigation systems. This resulted in what Robert Adams calls the "linearization" of settlements along major streams and canals. By the middle of the Early Dynastic period most of the settlements that were dependent on irrigation had been absorbed into nearby large urban centers, such as Uruk, Umma, Shuruppak, Kish, and Lagash.[9] The urbanization of these settlements brought about the efficient management of water throughout southern Mesopotamia. Intercity and interregional transportation, which acted as a stimulus to commerce, technology, and the spread of information and social organization, was greatly enhanced by the invention and diffusion of wheel-drawn carts and water-born vehicles that moved along the canals.

Even more important was the invention of a system of writing. The first attempts took place around 3,500 B.C. (during the Uruk period). Continually improved and simplified, the script employed wedge-shaped characters and is called cuneiform. Writing was largely the monopoly of the temple communities; it was used throughout southern Mesopotamia by the middle of the Early Dynastic period.

The temple was the most important organization to emerge within the Mesopotamian social structure; it served not only as a religious center but also as the center for the collection and exchange of goods and the redistribution of surpluses.[10] The temple elite, in addition to their spiritual activities, administered the distribution of goods for the region and, in many cases, they also supervised the production of foods and crafts; obviously they exercised enormous power. The architectural complexes at Eridu and Uruk not only occupied central positions but grew in size and complexity as their cities grew larger and more complex, illustrating the central and powerful position held by temples in the prehistoric Mesopotamian lowlands.

The development of urban centers as "temple cities" was an important factor in the rise of the Sumerian city-states. A fierce sense of independence is a distinguishing feature of city-states, and it was the loyalty to the temple and its god that generated and perpetuated a sense of independence.

The rise of city-states in ancient Sumer was thus facilitated by the growing power of the temple elite, who, in alliance with the city's wealthy nobility, controlled access to basic resources and demanded the loyalty and labor services of the common people. The temple-cities of the prehistoric period in Mesopotamia first emerged during the age of Sumerian dominance in the Early Dynastic period. They were the precursors of the dozen city-states which coexisted during the early part of the third millennium in an atmosphere of rivalry, competition, and incessant military conflict.

The origin and identity of the Sumerians remains a mystery.[11] On the basis of archeological data some scholars favor the view that the Sumerians were descendants of the Ubaidians, the first colonizers of southern Mesopotamia. They cite apparent continuity of cultural traditions as underlying evidence for their theory. Others suggest that the Sumerians were a people distinctly different from the Ubaidians. The chief evidence in favor of this view is their apparent linguistic differences. For example, many of the well-known Mesopotamian geographical names, such as the Tigris (Idiglat) and the Euphrates (Buranum), as well as the names of the most important Sumerian cities, such as Ur, Eridu, Larsa, Adab, Isin, Lagash, Nippur, Kish, and Kullab, are of non-Sumerian language. Also, some of the most basic Sumerian terms associated with agriculture and industry are non-Sumerian, which seems to indicate that the Ubaidians, who brought agriculture and other technology into southern Mesopotamia, were non-Sumerians.[12] Be that as it may, by the time the Sumerians appear on the historical scene at the beginning of the Uruk period (around 3,600 B.C.), urbanism, centering on temple cities, was well under way, and by 3,000 B.C. or shortly thereafter the Sumerian urban centers were becoming independent, autonomous city-states with their own tutelary deities, administrative mechanisms, economic activities, and systems of defense.

There is no ready explanation for the emergence of city-states in southern Mesopotamia while village life continued relatively unchanged in other parts of the Near East. One factor is surely the growth in complexity in the region of Sumer. Economic specialization in all sectors of the economy increased with attendant changes reflected in social structure and political organization. Another factor is the amazing productivity of the land so long as sophisticated techniques of irrigation, cultivation, and harvesting were employed. Such techniques could provide a surplus from a relatively few hundred square acres capable of supporting a population that was enormous by standards of the preceding Neolithic Age. In other areas of the Near East, there were not the incentives—perhaps—to develop and maintain the new levels of sophisticated, intensive cultivation. Whatever the final explanation, life in much of the ancient Near East continued to be centered on villages with populations in the hundreds rather than the tens of thousands of the Sumerian city-states. There was some specialization within villages and trade was an element in village life. However, there was nothing resembling the degree of economic specialization and social stratification that rose with the city-state structure.

Physical Form

Sumerian city-states each consisted of a city proper and its surrounding territory. In some cases a city-state, such as Lagash, comprised several villages and towns situated along a major irrigation canal or stream course that the main city controlled. The smaller communities within a city-state's territory were both politically and militarily dependent on the main city for protection and governance. While the surrounding territory supplied the city with grain, vegetables, meat, fish, and large numbers of manual workers, the inhabitants of the agricultural hinterland depended on the workshops of the city for manufactured goods.

It is difficult to define precisely the size of Sumerian city-states in the absence of the necessary geographic and demographic data. Their size and character no doubt varied with their geographic position and other natural factors. At least one city-state, Lagash, which has been studied in detail, is believed to have occupied an area of as much as 30,000 hectares, two thirds of which was naturally irrigated. Situated in the southernmost part of the Mesopotamian lowlands, Lagash had also the benefit of access to the sea. The city-states of

Illus. 1: *Aerial Photo of Ur*

Kish, Umma, and Isin, all located in the hinterlands, had no such natural advantage and were much smaller in size.

The countryside surrounding the city-states, a combination of ancient dunes and scorched alluvial plains, marshes, and swamps, was crisscrossed by an intricate system of canals and dikes. It was peopled with farmers, sheepherders, and fishermen living in small hamlets and inside mud-brick houses furnished with reed mats. The countryside itself and the people who lived there were jealously guarded by those living within the city. So were the irrigation networks. Much of the surrounding territory and its water courses were owned by the people residing in the city: the temple elite and the wealthy families usually owned the best farm lands lying close to the irrigation canals. Because of the mutual dependency for survival, generally there was a close relationship between the city and the surrounding territory under its protection. The people of the countryside tended to flock to the city in times of war.

One of the most important Sumerian ideas governing the social organization of their territory was the belief that all of the city-states' territory belonged to their chief deities, at least in theory. Thus, a strip of land over which two neighboring city-states, Lagash and Umma, had a war was called "the beloved field of Ningirsu," the tutelary god of Lagash. After their victory, the people of Lagash returned the field to their deity.[13] Despite the theoretical ownership of the city-state's lands by its gods, however, only a fracture of the territory *actually* belonged to the temple estates.[14] The land that belonged to the temple was of three categories: *nigenna* fields, cultivated for cultic uses and the economic maintenance of the temple itself; *kurra* fields, leased to temple personnel and to the cultivators of the *nigenna* fields as a part payment for their services; and *urulal* fields, which were worked by share croppers.

The largest part of the city-states' lands belonged to the nobility (wealthy families, high ranking officials of the states, and the members of the royal administration). The rest of the land was owned and worked by ordinary free citizens of the state. Except for the temple property, lands could be bought and sold. The bulk of the land owned by the nobility usually had been acquired from the poorer citizens.

Despite the economic importance of the surrounding territory, the heart of the Sumerian city-states was the city itself where the majority of the population resided. Begun originally as small villages built on mounds and natural levees near the Euphrates and the Tigris, they grew rapidly in size; by the beginning of the Early Dynastic period they had become walled cities. The walls were usually built of plano-convex bricks and were massive in size, as evidenced by the great city walls of Uruk which were 9.5 kilometers long with 900 to 950 semicircular towers. Nearly all of the south Mesopotamian fortifications date from the beginning of the Early Dynastic period, strongly suggesting that city-states had grown in number and had become land hungry. By the middle of the Early Dynastic period, ca. 2,700 B.C., Uruk, the largest of the Sumerian cities, occupied an area of 400 to 500 hectares while Nippur, about 150 kilometers to the north, covered an area of 323 hectares. The population of the Sumerian cities usually averaged between 20,000 and 25,000 people; Uruk had 50,000 people.[15]

By modern standards, the Sumerian city was quite primitive. Having evolved from prehistoric hamlets and villages, it was without any preconceived plan. Crowded with tiny one-story mud-brick houses, its streets were narrow and winding. Only the wealthy lived in spacious two-story structures.

Central, often towering over the city, was the temple of the city god, occupying the largest and the holiest ground within its walls. Besides the temple of the chief deity, there were other religious shrines such as those of the chief god's wife and children. By the Early Dynastic period a recognized pantheon of deities had taken shape. Anu, god of the heavens, was a remote, supreme deity; Enlil, lord of the realm between heaven and earth, was more accessible to man and his temple at Nippur thereby assumed special importance. Nonetheless, each city continued to be the property of a particular deity: Enki of Eridu, Nanna of Ur, Nanshe of Nina, Ningirsu of Lagash, Shara of Umma, Ninhursag of Ubaid, and Enlil of Nippur. Each deity possessed its own temple.

The significance of the temple in the life of the city-states can be seen by its size, elaborate construction, and continuous use, repair, and additions. Enamzu, located in the city of Adab, was one of the most splendid temples of Early Dynastic Sumer. Dedicated to Nintu, the mother goddess and chief deity of the city, it had seven magnificent entrances with impressive names, such as

Illus. 2: *Restoration of a Ziggurat*

"Lofty Gate," "Door of Refreshing Shade," "Great Gate," "Gate of (divine) Decrees." Another magnificent temple of massive size was the Oval Temple at modern Khafaje (the ancient city of Tutub) in the Diyala district. Built on massive mud-brick foundations of the plano-convex type, the Oval Temple was enclosed by two formidable concentric walls and occupied an area of 74 by 54 meters. Not far from the Oval Temple was the Sin Temple which had been successively rebuilt on top of the earlier structures of the Jemdet Nasr period. Dedicated to the Moon god, the Sin Temple, a complex of courtyards and shrines, was expanded and remodeled over a period of a thousand years. At Tell Asmar (the ancient city of Eshnunna) the Abu Temple, dedicated to the god of vegetation, went through nine successive periods of remodeling and expansion.

In architectural form, Sumerian temples were rectangular or oval and were of two primary types: high temples constructed on artificially raised brick platforms, such as the ziggurat of the Oval Temple at modern Khafaje and those built on ground level, as was the Sin Temple at Khafaje. The latter type appears to have been more common during the Early Dynastic period. Buildings were usually constructed with plano-convex bricks, laid in a herring-bone pattern. Sumerian bricks were generally sun-dried, but in rare instances where extra strength or protection from water was needed, baked bricks were used. The mud-brick walls of the religious edifices were decorated with multicolored clay cones forming a variety of geometrical designs. The most important feature of the Sumerian temples was the central cellar, housing the chief deity's statue and his/her table of daily offerings of foods and drink.

In Sumer, the temple and its god came first; the belief that the Sumerian cities and their inhabitants existed for the benefit of their gods was an integral part of Sumerian consciousness. From their sacred myths Sumerians learned that man was created to serve his gods, to tend to their needs, and to labor on the gods' estates (i.e., the city-state). Consequently, art and architecture, as well as writing, which was invented to record goods brought to the temple, developed in service to the gods. In fact, economically, politically, socially, as well as religiously, the temples were the heart of the Sumerian city-states.

The next most prominent feature of Sumerian cities was the palace architecture. At least two examples of royal residences have been uncovered—those at Kish and Eridu. The Twin Palace at Kish, one of the finest Early Dynastic architectural complexes to be uncovered, consisted of numerous rooms, an imposing entrance flanked by fortified towers, and a thick outer enclosing wall, probably designed for defense. A massive building closely resembling the Twin Palace of Kish was uncovered at Eridu, consisting of large rooms serving as audience halls and double fortified walls with double gateways. These two palace complexes were just as impressive and elaborate as most of the temple complexes. Their appearance around the year 2,700 B.C. suggests that a secular power, independent of the temple, was emerging in Sumerian city-states.

Economic Foundations

By the Early Dynastic period the principal source of Sumerian wealth was a thriving agriculture, made the more productive by improvements in the intricate system of irrigation works. Barley was Sumer's main crop, supplemented by other grains such as emmer-wheat and millet. Vegetable and legume crops included lettuce, onions, garlic, leeks, mustard, chick-peas, cucumbers, and lentils. Dates were the most important cultivated fruit. While barley was the foremost dietary staple for the human populations, it was also used as cattle-fodder. Finally, this marvelous cereal was used in the extensive, and vitally important, beer brewing industry. The cattle, bred on the farms, were an indispensable part of Sumerian agriculture; they were used as draft animals for pulling ploughs and carts, and they also provided meat, milk, and hides. Sumerian farmers raised a variety of sheep and goats for meat and hides and especially for wool, making Sumer one of the greatest textile manufacturers in the ancient world.

Some of the arable land was held by the temples, some small plots were owned by families of free citizens, and by far the largest portion was owned by the ruling aristocracy. The free citizens worked their small garden plots as families. The aristocracy and especially the temple elite, however, employed a large number of nominally free tenants and slaves. In some respects the relationship between the owner and his tenants resembled that of the lord and vassal in European feudal states. For example, the temple allotted its land to its tenants according to their ranks; the tenants were allowed to keep an agreed portion of their produce for themselves or they might be paid in kind for their services with such staples as barley and wool. These tenants also constituted the temple's regular military force. In addition to its tenants, the temple had regular dependents who worked entirely in the service of the temples and their gods. Some of the dependents worked temple lands while others served within the temple complex as gardeners, cooks, carpenters, brewers, and servants. For their service, these dependents were paid in kind, mainly barley, and on special occasions they were given other goods such as meat, milk, fruit, and beer. A part of the temple work force consisted of slaves. While women slaves served in the temple's kitchens, flour-mills, and textile factories, male slaves repaired irrigation canals, and worked at other menial tasks. The work force of the nobility was patterned after the temple's work force, using tenants, dependents, and slaves.

Fisheries were an important part of the Sumerian economy. More than fifty varieties of salt water and fresh water fish were eaten in ancient Sumer. While many of the farmers exploited rivers, marshes, and canals to supplement their diet, the temples maintained certain control over the fisheries and received a regular provision of fish.

Agriculture was the foundation of the Sumerian economy, but by its very nature, a complex urban society requires craft specialization and economic diversity, including industry, commerce, and trade. And as in modern times, so too in ancient Sumer, agriculture, industry, commerce, and trade were closely intertwined so that they influenced each other. Surplus food fostered the emergence of professional craftsmen such as metal smiths, leather workers, carpenters, masons, scribes, artists, and potters. Skilled craftsmen, in turn, promoted commerce and trade. In Sumer there was a corps of merchants traveling from city to city, selling and exchanging goods produced in various cities. Economic records of Lagash indicate that thriving interstate commerce was carried out among the city-states of Nippur, Lagash, Uruk, Umma, Adab, and Der. Prosperous commerce among the city-states, in turn, encouraged further development of industry and technology. The interrelationship of these economic features was so close that a serious disruption in one economic activity would inevitably affect the other.

Development of trade was enhanced in Sumer by two natural factors: the presence of intricate waterways and limitations of raw materials. From the beginning of their history, the various states of Sumer were closely tied with one another by an efficient system of navigable rivers and canals which crisscrossed the entire land. The cities built along these waterways were within easy reach of one another. Under such circumstances it was easy for enterprising merchants to embark on trading activities. Equally important was the lack of some important raw materials, such as timber, stones, and precious metal— items essential to any sophisticated civilization. Ample evidence of Sumer's dependence on the outside world for its raw materials came from a chemical analysis of the items found in the "Royal Cemetery" of Ur which contained copper probably originating from Oman or Sinai; gold from Armenia or possibly Nubia (the major source of gold in the ancient world); lapis-lazuli from the area of Badkhshan; and carnelian from India.[16]

Sumerians exported grains, dates, and finished products in exchange for raw materials. Ur-Nanshe, a king of Lagash, used the "ships of Dilmun" to import timber logged from trees grown in the mountains beyond the Persian Gulf. From Dilmun also came copper. One Sumerian legend speaks of a trade relationship that once existed between Uruk and a distant city-state called Aratta which provided precious metals in exchange for Sumerian grains. The economic records of Lagash note the arrival of textiles from Ebla in Northern Syria, a significant entry because textiles were one of Lagash's main export items. It has been suggested that during the Early Dynastic period enterprising Sumerian merchants set up trading colonies as far away as at Kanesh in Cappadocia as well as in Syria.[17] Economic associations, such as merchant guilds, often become powerful political forces in complex societies. Whether such associations existed in the Sumerian city-states is uncertain although the *dam-gar* merchant class may have come closest to being such an association.

During the third millennium both the temple and the palace were involved in trade. Nippur's special deity, Enlil, and his wife were known as the "trader of the wide world" and the "merchant of the world," respectively. Enlil's status in the Sumerian pantheon may be additional explanation for these titles. At Lagash the Baba Temple boasted 125 sailors and pilots, who no doubt constituted the temple's merchant marine corps. During the Early Dynastic period the *dam-gar* merchant class acted on behalf of the palace. They carried out most of the intercity and interregional trade—evidence of the increasing role of the palace in secular matters. While acting as the king's agents, the *dam-gar* merchants may simultaneously have engaged in private entrepreneurship giving rise to the growth of private enterprise, a power base which would be eventually competing with both the temple and the palace.[18]

In the course of time foreign trade grew to be such an integral part of Sumerian economy that it became a cause of economic uncertainty. The interdependency and complexity of trade, economy, industry, as well as the underlying religious and political institutions, had become so intricate that Sumerian city-states could survive only as long as the intercity and interregional trade networks continued to function smoothly. Procurement of essential raw materials and exchange of goods depended on peace between the city-states and in the lands beyond the Sumerian border. Since military conflicts were intermittent, trade was precarious. Some historians speculate that neutral ports for traders may have come into being to aid the uninterrupted flow of vital intercity and long-distance commerce. Tepe Yahya in Iran and Bahrein, an island in the Persian Gulf, among others, may have served as neutral trading places for traders from various hostile and warring city-states.[19]

In each Sumerian city-state, revenues were expended, first and foremost, for the service of gods. This included not only daily provision of the gods' needs, such as food and clothing, but also for the ongoing operation of the temple, as well as for the building of new temples. Next came the upkeep of irrigation canals on which the state's existence was dependent. After that, the state's revenues went to the maintenance of the city-state's defenses and financing of wars.

Political Structure

The Sumerians did not have a sophisticated political philosophy as did the later Greeks; nor did they consciously seek to develop a specific political system. At the beginning of the Early Dynastic period, the Sumerian political structure seems to have been a form of democracy functioning through a bicameral assembly of elders and free citizens (*unkem;* later, *puhrum*). Thorkild Jacobsen in his study of the earliest political system of Mesopotamia concludes, "Our material seems to preserve indications that prehistoric Mesopotamia was organized politically along democratic lines . . . the indications which we have point to a form of government in which the normal run of public affairs was handled by a council of elders but ultimate sovereignty resided in a general assembly comprising all members—or perhaps better, all adult free men—of the community."[20] A democratic process among humans on earth was in perfect harmony with the Sumerian understanding of the world of celestial beings, who made all of their crucial decisions through a celestial assembly from decisions to create or to destroy, promote or demote.

The nature of Sumerian assemblies has been a subject of extensive discussion among scholars. Jacobsen has suggested that the upper assembly at Uruk was made up of elders. Called *abba uru,* or town fathers, the elders were none other than the heads of the large families which made up the town's population. In their relationship to the king of the city-state, the elders acted as counselors or advisors. In this sense the Sumerian upper assembly closely resembled "the Senate of regal Rome, whose members were likewise called 'Patres.'" The Sumerian elders were fundamentally representative of social position rather than of age—as were the aristocrats of early Greek and Roman times.[21]

The general assembly, on the other hand, consisted of ordinary adult freemen, probably above the age of 20 or 30. It cannot be determined whether all freemen of the state participated in the assembly or whether its membership was limited to residents of the city center. Even if the former is true, it is still likely that proximity tended to favor the regular participation of city dwellers rather than rural residents. The ultimate sovereignty belonged to the popular assembly. The general assembly had the power of decision in all major issues of state such as the making of war and peace. This is clearly evidenced in the story which tells how Gilgamesh, the king of Uruk, thwarted the opposition of the elders by persuading the general assembly to approve his proposal of war against Agga.

At the beginning of the Early Dynastic period, the council of elders elected an *ensi* to oversee the affairs of the city's temple, which, of course, included much of the city-state's affairs. Elected in the name of the city's tutelary god, the *ensi* understood himself to be the earthly representative of the divine ruler. As an elected official, the *ensi* exercised his political and social control with the consent of the assembly. Initially the *ensi*'s responsibilities included overseeing the temple's work forces and the administration of temple affairs, as well as such secular matters as the defense of the city and the upkeep of irrigation canals. In times of emergency, the council granted him special authority, which he would give up with the passing of the emergency.

By the middle of the Early Dynastic period, ca. 2,700 B.C., the *ensi* was emerging as the *de facto* ruler of the city-states. This transition of political power from the temple and the assembly to an individual was brought about by three exigencies: increasing intercity rivalry and warfare, the need for effective management of the vital irrigation system, and the protection of trade. Military conflicts between the city-states were often caused by disputes over water rights, and both the temple and the assembly appointed a warrior leader to settle the conflicts. With more efficient management of the city-state, the *ensi*'s prestige grew and along with it his power base, as in the case of Gilgamesh, the king of Uruk. The *ensi*'s power base was his army whose leadership he assumed during military conflicts. Originally the *ensi*'s army consisted of professional soldiers as well as the tenants living on the estates of the temple and the aristocracy. When military campaigns became frequent, a more permanent and stable professional armed force became necessary. The *ensi*'s supreme authority was based on his monopoly of military force, which was granted him by exigencies of the city-states. The emergence of secular political power is amply evidenced by the presence of great palaces at Kish and Eridu as well as by the splendor of the "Royal Cemeteries" of Ur.

With political power concentrated in the hands of the *ensi*, the palace exercised all governmental functions: legislative, judiciary, executive, and economic. In addition, the *ensi* oversaw the operation of the temple—one of the most powerful economic activities in Sumerian society. Through this process democracy slowly gave way to autocracy. Then during the Early Dynastic period, temporary kingship became a hereditary institution.

When an *ensi* conquered other city-states, he often assumed the title of *lugal* (literally, a big man). A good example of this is Lugalzaggesi, who began as the *ensi* of Umma and assumed the title of *lugal* after he successfully subdued the city-states of Uruk and Kish. In some cases a ruler would hold both titles simultaneously. Eannatum, the powerful king of Lagash, was addressed as "the *ensi* of Lagash as well as the *lugal* of Kish." An interesting feature was the special meaning attached to the *lugalship* of Kish. It was equivalent to the kingship of all Sumer, and only the more ambitious and more daring rulers would assume that title. Presumably, early domination by leaders of Kish underlies the significance of the title.

Exactly what role the popular assemblies played in political affairs under the autocracy is not clear. We know that the popular assembly was an important institution in the post-Sumerian period of old Babylonia. Generally, acting as a court of law, the old Babylonian assembly tried both civil and criminal cases. It could declare sentences including corporal and capital punishment and often the kings referred legal matters to the assembly. In view of the fact that the popular assembly survived into the imperial era, it may be safe to assume that the popular assemblies continued to play a significant role in Sumer as well.

Fundamental to our understanding of the role of the *ensi* is the Sumerian religious belief that the city-states were the private estates of the gods and whoever managed an estate was the personal representative of the deity. Jacobsen has compared the *ensi* to a manager of an estate who "is expected, first of all, to uphold and carry on the established order of that estate; secondly, he is to execute such commands as the owner may see fit to give with respect to changes, innovations, or ways to deal with unexpected situations. Quite similarly, the *ensi* was expected to uphold the established order of the god's temple and city in general, and he was expected to consult the god and carry out any specific orders which the god might wish to give."[22]

The *ensi*'s functions were all-inclusive. As the owners, the celestial beings had to be pleased, and what satisfied the celestial masters was the proper performance of the required rituals and ceremonies, including the daily offering of meat and vegetables and libations of water, beer, and wine. Despite their divinity, the gods of Sumer were considered humanlike in their basic needs: they had to be fed, clothed, and sheltered. Failure to satisfy the gods would incur divine wrath and bring calamity to the city-state.

Service to the gods was an enormous responsibility; it involved insuring the wellbeing of the temple itself and all that was related to it: administration of the temple precinct, repairing of old buildings, and the building of new temple structures. In actual practice, the *ensi* oversaw the temple with the assistance of an *en* and a *sanga*. While the *en* supervised cultic and spiritual matters, the *sanga* was in charge of temple administration, and the actual day-to-day activities of the temple communities were carried out by hundreds of temple personnel of different ranks under their leadership.

Building new temples and restoring old (or ruined) ones were events worthy of special commemoration: such deeds were not only pleasing to the city-state's gods, they enhanced the glory and pride of the city-state itself. The poet-historians of Sumer spared no efforts in extolling the *ensi* who raised great edifices for their divine protectors. An inscription commemorating the deeds of Lugalannemundu, the great king of Adab, ca. 2,600 B.C., devotes much space to the king's role as the builder of a magnificent temple called Enamzu, dedicated to Nintu, the mother goddess and the chief deity of the city. The temple was dedicated, the inscription indicates, with pomp and grandeur; representatives of many foreign lands and other city-states came to the dedication ceremony, bringing precious gifts. About a century and a half later, when Ur-Nanshe came to the throne at Lagash, he also erected temples for the gods of his city and his deeds have been eternally commemorated in inscriptions. One inscription states: "Ur-Nanshe, the king of Lagash . . . built the house of

Ningirsu; built the house of Nanshe; built the house of Gatumdug, built the harem; built the house of Ninmar."[23] And on one well-known votive plaque, Ur-Nanshe is pictured carrying a basket of earth on his head—a symbolic portrayal of the *ensi*'s active role in the building of temples.

Cultic rituals in the temple also served useful private religious purposes for the Sumerians. As a people whose basic cosmological orientation was naturalistic polytheism, the Sumerians were deeply concerned with achieving and maintaining a harmonious relationship with the supernatural beings in whose hands their destiny lay. For the fertility of the land, as well as the womb, the Sumerians turned to their gods: they worshipped them, praised them, and feared them. To procure health, wealth, and long life they offered sacrifices to the gods who had in their hands the power to give life and death. In times of personal or family misfortunes, they turned to priests for divine guidance.

Despite the temple's importance in their personal lives, it existed not so much for the benefit of individuals as for the sake of the gods and for the benefit of the city-state as a whole. Consequently, public or community rites were more important than private devotion. The New Year's Festival and its associated cult of *hieros gamos* were the most significant rituals in Sumerian religion. Rooted in their oral traditions of the dying and rising god of vegetation, the *hieros gamos* ceremony involved a symbolic "holy marriage" of a reigning monarch with Inanna, the goddess of love and fertility. On New Year's Day, the king, representing the resurrected god of vegetation, Dumuzi, would join Inanna in a ceremonial sexual union in order to activate the creative forces of spring for the coming year and thereby restore life and fertility to vegetation and to all living creatures in the lands.

Intimately related to his economic activities as administrator of the deity's estates was the *ensi*'s duty to defend the city-state (especially the city) from outside invaders. Frequent disputes over irrigation rights and territorial boundaries, as well as the schemes of the more ambitious *ensi*s and *lugal*s, forced all the Sumerian city-states to become proficient in the arts of warfare. The Sumerian city-state's military ethos was reinforced and perpetuated by persistent regionalism and its sense of local independence. It was the *ensi*'s task to organize, train, and maintain his city-state's armed forces as well as to lead them in times of war. As we have seen, the *ensi* functioned as a military leader from the very beginning. On some of the earliest cylinder seals of the Early Dynastic period, an *ensi* is depicted as a vanquisher of his enemies, and in Sumerian historical records, such as the "Stele of the Vultures," the *ensi* is described as the supreme military commander. The *ensi* went into battle in the name of his tutelary god and in gratitude for his military successes, he would bring his booty to his divine benefactor.

Perhaps the first such warrior-*ensi* was Etana of Kish, who is described in the King List as the one who "brought stability to all the lands." Another early warrior-*ensi* was Mekiaggasher, the founder of the city-state of Uruk. On the King List he is described as "one who entered the seas (and) ascended mountains"—a possible allusion to his military adventures. Both Etana and Mekiaggasher reigned during the first quarter of the third millennium B.C. It is not altogether idle to speculate that the origin of the *ensi* institution itself lay in the intracommunal warfare of prehistoric village days. At any rate, the rulers who succeeded Etana and Mekiaggasher, at Kish and Uruk respectively, all displayed military characteristics. Enmerkar of Uruk and his successor, Lugal-banda, carried on a protracted military campaign against the state of Aratta, whose identity is still obscure. Even Gilgamesh, the famous king of Uruk and a hero in the Flood Legend, was essentially a warrior-king who fought the kings of his rival cities, Kish and Ur. Another early Sumerian warrior-king was Lugalannemundu of Adab; historical documents describe him as "King of the four quarters (of the universe), a ruler who made all the foreign lands pay tribute to him, who brought peace to (literally, made lie in pastures) the peoples of the lands . . . who exercised kingship over the entire world."[24]

The military role of the *ensi* became even more conspicuous after 2,500 B.C. with the intensification of interstate rivalry for political supremacy over all Sumer. Particularly noteworthy in this regard was Eannatum, the king of Lagash. When he succeeded his father to the throne, Eannatum declared war on the city-state of Umma, which had long been engaged in border disputes with Lagash. After subduing the Ummaites, Eannatum led his troops against Elam, Uruk, and Ur, subjugating one after another. The documents of Lagash tell of his numerous battles with invading forces from Kish and Akshak, the city-states in northern Sumer.

By the second half of the Early Dynastic period the *ensi* began directing foreign relations with other city-states. In certain situations, a powerful *ensi* acted as an arbitrator between rival city-states. Mesilim, the ruler of Kish, intervened in a fierce border dispute between Lagash and Umma and designed a peace treaty acceptable to both parties. However, when the *ensi* of Umma came to consider the treaty unfair to his state, he had no hesitation in breaking the treaty and attacking Lagash territory.

Along with his roles as temple administrator, economic manager, supreme military leader, and executor of foreign affairs, the *ensi* was expected to be the giver of justice within his territory. The Sumerians saw their rulers as those selected and appointed by their gods to protect the poor and the needy, to curb abuses of the rich and powerful, and to establish order and justice in the land in accordance with divine laws. One of Sumer's ancient historians spoke of Urukagina, the just and righteous king of Lagash, ca. 2,350 B.C., as the representative of Ningirsu (the tutelary god of Lagash) handpicked for the specific task of restoring "decrees of former days," which had fallen by the wayside. Nothing stands as a greater testimony to the *ensi*'s role as the city's upholder of justice than the Reform Acts of Urukagina. By about 2,400 B.C., certain rulers and their close associates had secured enormous power in the socio-political chaos brought on by the never-ending warfare. In times of war, people are at the mercy of soldiers and Sumer was no exception. To support their wars rulers exacted varieties of taxes from the people—even taxes for a man's burial. The taxations were so oppressive that many of the poor threw their deceased relatives into the Euphrates river or simply left them unburied. The palace officials acquired the land and property of the smaller farmers at an unfair price or through outright expropriation. Even the temple was not exempt. "The oxen of the gods," we are told by an ancient Sumerian recorder, "plowed the *ensi*'s onion patches; the onion and cucumber patches of the *ensi* were located in the god's best fields."

It was in response to this crisis that Sumerian historians wrote that Ningirsu, the divine ruler of Lagash, "hand grasped" Urukagina out of a multitude of 36,000 men and told him to restore justice, to correct oppression, to defend the needy, and to curb the power of the rich and the mighty; Urukagina, we are told, "held close to the word which his king (Ningirsu) spoke to him. . . . He did away with [the necessity of] the artisans to beg for their bread. . . . He amnestied the citizens [literally, the sons] of Lagash who [were imprisoned because of the] debts (which they) had incurred. . . . [Finally] Urukagina made a covenant with Ningirsu that a man of power must not commit an [injustice] against an orphan or widow."[25]

Social Structure

In its basic character Sumerian society was hierarchic and patriarchal. At its top was the *ensi*. Below him were the high-ranking officials of the palace and the temple (i.e., important priests), who made up the majority of the nobility. These came from the powerful families and were also the owners of large estates. They constituted only a fraction of the total population. Below the nobility were the commoners or free citizens, who constituted more than half of the city-states' entire population and who owned their plots of land as families. Below the free citizens were the dependents of the nobility, the temple, and the palace. They owned no land, though some of them were granted temporary tenancy of land owned by the temple or the nobility. But generally the dependents were given such goods as grain and wool in payment for their services.

At the bottom of Sumerian social hierarchy were the slaves. Owned by the powerful families, the temple, and the palace, slaves were the major source of free, dependable labor and so were indispensable to the Sumerian economy. Generally slaves were acquired as prisoners of war, but the head of a family might sell his children or his entire family into slavery in times of need. As the property or chattel of their owners, slaves could be branded; they could be bought and sold, and they could be punished like animals when they displeased their master. Slaves were granted certain rights, however; they could borrow money and buy their freedom, and Sumerians who were forced to become the slaves of their fellow Sumerians were to be freed after three years of service. The distinction between slaves and dependents was not always sharp; slaves and clients worked side by side in farms and temple workshops and may have had similar standards of living.

Though Sumerian society was devoid of the rigidity of a caste system, the social structure, based upon the ownership of land, inevitably made birth the major determining factor in one's social status. Those born into families with large amounts of landed property would automatically belong to the nobility, and those born into families without land would automatically be dependents or slaves. People usually remained in the class of their birth. Even the exceptions to this general pattern were made possible by birth. For example, if a slave married a free woman, his children would be born free. And if a free man had children by a slave concubine, those children were free.

Despite the Sumerian emphasis on law and justice, the concept of the individual was alien to Sumerian thought. The individual per se had no value; he had meaning only as a part of the collective citizenry engaged in a common task. This was, like so many other Sumerian cultural elements, an inevitable outcome of religious beliefs—the gods were supreme and men were mere tools, created to serve them. In a world dominated by such religious and philosophical attitudes, the value of an individual and his human self-expression were meaningless. Nowhere is this fact more clearly evident than in the Sumerian concept of history and civilization. History, to the Sumerians, was a record of the work of the gods. Man had nothing to do with the flow of historical events. Events, institutions, and cultural achievements, such as the writing system, wheels, and religious edifices, were believed to have been brought down from heaven. Even cities, towns, agriculture, and the irrigation canals were considered to have been there from the beginning of time, prepared and given by the gods. Man's free will and his active role in the making of civilization were totally alien notions to the Sumerians. Humans were expected to live by the plans already decreed by the gods.[26] This view of man's role is clearly manifested in Sumerian art and literature, which is characterized by "collective impersonality and anonymity." Moscati observed that Sumerian art was essentially "a public art, concerned with the official celebration of religious beliefs and political power; subjects drawn from private life are of little or no interest. The style is official, too, and so it is impersonal, collective. There is no place for attempts to express individuality, and the artist is no more concerned than the writer with recording his name. In art, as in the literature, the producer is more craftsman or artisan than artist in our modern sense."[27]

Interstate Relations

A theocratic state demands the loyalty of its citizens to its god and his temple, which in turn generates and intensifies regionalism and local patriotism. The Sumerian city-states, though unified by language and culture, were destined for incessant interstate rivalry and warfare. Rivalry between the various city-states was often motivated by a desire for supremacy, the acquisition of more territory, or the control or protection of irrigation rights; but underlying such political and economic motives was the Sumerian world-view and the Sumerian sense of raison d'etre deeply rooted in their religious convictions. Living under the grace and beneficent protection of their tutelary deity, the inhabitants of each city-state had a sense of identity and belonging. They knew that it was their duty to bring honor and glory to the god who gave them life and light, and to put aside all private and personal interests. Nowhere is this more clearly illustrated than in the story of Gudea's reconstruction of the temple of Ningirsu at Lagash where it is written that when Gudea "gave direction to his city as to a single man, Lagash followed him unanimously like the children of one mother."[28]

From the beginning of this historical period the Sumerian city-states' internecine quarrels were interrupted only by occasional foreign invasions. According to inferences drawn from the Sumerian King List, Kish was the first city to acquire political supremacy over the others. After the death of Etana, its able leader, Kish was challenged by the city-state of Uruk. Then in the course of time, during the reign of Gilgamesh, Uruk's most celebrated king, warfare raged between the three cities of Kish, Uruk, and Ur, each vying for supremacy over the others.

Weakened by long interstate rivalry Sumer became an easy prey to invasions from abroad, and for nearly a century all the Sumerian city-states became enslaved to the Elamites who overran Sumer from the southwestern part of today's Iran. The Elamites were overthrown by Lugalannemundu, an able leader of the city-state of Adab. With his military might Lugalannemundu succeeded in unifying all Sumer under his hegemony; but as soon as he died, rivalry flared up again between the city-states and lasted nearly 200 years. In the course of the long protracted civil war, the city of Lagash gradually emerged as the dominant power. However, Lagash was not left unchallenged very long, for Umma, its mortal enemy, attacked and razed it to the ground under the leadership of Lugalzaggesi. Following his victory over Lagash, Lugalzaggesi succeeded in establishing his lordship over other Sumerian city-states. He even moved his palace from Umma to Uruk, one of the greatest fortified cities of the Early Dynastic period. Still, like all other victorious conquerors before his time, Lugalzaggesi could not long remain supreme. By this time, all Sumer was exhausted by centuries-old feuding and by the lessening of the land's productivity and it once again became an easy prey to foreign invaders. Around 2,350 B.C., Sargon the Great, a powerful Semitic ruler from the north, conquered Sumer and created the first empire, encompassing much of Mesopotamia—the Empire of Akkad. With it came the end of the independent Sumerian city-states. Once they were absorbed into the imperial administrative complex, the city-states became provinces, responsible to an imperial court, losing both their political and economic independence. Their dependent relationship to the imperial regime was symbolized by regular payment of tribute.

In retrospect, perpetual warfare among Sumerian city-states was the consequence of what Woolley has called the clash of two motives: the desire for centralization and the desire for disruption. Local patriotism generated by special loyalty to the local deities acted as a perpetual counterforce against the desire for political unification. Regional loyalty encouraged efforts to strengthen regional economy and to secure territorial boundaries and irrigation rights vital to regional welfare. However, Sumerian cultural unity was a reality—in language, in writing, in law, in customs, and in religion. In a region where all spoke the same language, observed the same laws and customs, and worshipped the same pantheon of deities, it was tempting for an ambitious ruler to bring about political unification and centralization. Kings who successfully unified Sumer by conquest, though only temporarily, proudly claimed the support of Enlil who was regarded as the chief deity of the Sumerian pantheon. Following his brilliant victories, Lugalzaggesi wrote this votive inscription:

> When Enlil, the king of all the lands, had given the kingship of the Land to Lugalzaggesi . . . Lugalzaggesi, the king of Erech, the king of the Land, dedicated, for his life various vases to Enlil, his beloved king; in these he brought large food offerings to Enlil, his king, in Nippur, [and] out of these he poured libations of sweet water—with (this) inscription, "May Enlil, the king of the lands, plead for me before An, his beloved father; may he add "life to my life"; under my rule [literally, under me] may the lands lie peacefully in the meadows; may all mankind thrive like plants and herbs; may the sheepfolds of An increase; may [the people of] the Land look upon a "fair earth"; the good fortune which [the gods] have decreed for me, may they never falter.[29]

Such a divine mandate sanctioned even the most extreme means to effect unity. On the other hand, it also provided a sense of Sumerian unity which transcended the boundaries of individual city-states. It is on this basis that certain kings could act as final arbiters between independent city-states over boundary disputes. When the city-states of Lagash and Umma had been engaged in a long, bitter feud, their cause was taken up to Enlil and Mesilim, who was the king of Kish and was considered a suzerain by both parties. And in the Entemena Inscription we are told that "Enlil, the king of all the lands, the father of all the gods, marked off the boundary for Ningirsu [patron god of Lagash] [and] Shara [patron god of Umma] by his steadfast word, [and] Mesilim, the king of Kish, measured it off . . . [and] erected a stele there."[30] In like manner, Uthegal, the king of Uruk and the most powerful ruler in Sumer in his day, helped settle boundary disputes between Ur and Lagash on behalf of Enlil.

This perennial opposition between a tendency to regionalize and a tendency to unite was fundamental to Sumerian civilization. When relatively free from external invasions, the Sumerians fought with each other for supremacy; but when subjugated by foreign conquerors such as the Elamites, the Akkadians, and the Gutians, a sense of shared interests was intensified. For example, when Sargon, the king of Akkad, invaded Sumer and destroyed the city of Uruk (which by then had become a sort of national capital under Lugalzaggesi's influence) fifty Sumerian *ensis* responded to a call for Sumer's struggle against the Akkadians.[31] This same spirit supported the rise of the Sumerian empire under the Third Dynasty of Ur.

What became of the city-states when one of them succeeded in establishing hegemony over the others? What kind of relationship existed between the conquering *lugal* and the local *ensi* in times of political unity? Throughout the Early Dyanstic period, the chief concern of the *lugal* was that his subject states formally acknowledge his supremacy and that they pay him appropriate tribute as a symbolic gesture. In local affairs, however, the *lugal*, it seems, limited his personal interference. No efforts were made to tamper with the hereditary position of the local *ensis*. At the most, the *lugal* would intervene when local city-states were deadlocked in territorial disputes, somewhat in a capacity of an arbitrator, as Mesilim did in the Lagash-Umma controversy.

During imperial rule of the Third Dynasty of Ur, however, the situation was far less amicable. Occupying a more formidable position than the earlier *lugals*, the kings of the Neo-Sumerian period patterned their actions on the Semitic rulers of the Sargonic empire, treating the city-states as mere provinces under the central government at Ur. They had no hesitation in removing local *ensis* whose loyalty they suspected. The appointment of all the important offices including that of the *ensi* was now in the hands of the king and his central government. By this act, the *lugal* was actually placing himself in the position of the local tutelary deity. Some powerful *lugals*, such as Shulgi, even deified themselves and had their images set up in each provincial capital in place of the city's tutelary god. So the city-states became the personal estates of a reigning monarch, the *lugal*, and the *lugal* symbolically resided in his estates through his statues. His estates were managed by his hand-picked stewards, in the pattern that had been used in earlier times when the temples were supreme. The *ensi*'s chief function under the *lugal* was to raise taxes on behalf of his king and for the sake of the central government.

However, the old local loyalty to the earlier city-states persisted to the very end of Sumer's history. If the Third Dynasty of Ur managed to hold its imperial sway over all Sumer, it was certainly not because of genuine loyalty on the part of local cities. Rather it was due to the *lugal*'s skill in ruling and administering. As soon as the power of the central government at Ur waned, local provinces returned to the defense of their own local interests. It was therefore not an historical accident that the breakup of the Third Dynasty of Ur was followed by another period of independence for the city-states of Sumer, such as Isin, Ur, and Larsa, before Hammurabi finally closed the Sumerian chapter of Mesopotamian history in the eighteenth century B.C.

Decline of the Sumerian City-States

The success and prosperity of the Sumerian city-states depended on a number of factors: an efficient irrigation system, a sufficient amount of cultivable lands, unhindered trade, effective organization, and wise *ensis*. Without efficient irrigation canals Sumerian farmlands would quickly revert to desert sand dunes. An insufficient amount of cultivable lands would bring on food shortages. Deprived of intercity and interregional trade, Sumerian artisans would be cut off from the sources of essential raw materials and the Sumerian merchants would be excluded from their markets. Without efficient organization both agriculture and commerce would suffer. A wise and just *ensi* was needed to prevent exploitation of the population of the city-state by powerful, greedy individuals.

Unfortunately for Sumer, the city-states carried with them the seeds of their own destruction: regionalism, interstate rivalry, and military conflicts. Warfare between the city-states acted against their well-being in at least three crucial ways. First, warfare reduced the amount of cultivable lands. Protracted military conflicts required continual conscription of adults, which gradually deprived the countryside of manpower essential to farming. Without men to work the lands, much of the Sumerian farmland was left uncultivated. Secondly, warfare disturbed trade networks and impeded intercity, interregional, and long-distance trade. Thirdly, warfare caused an excessive drain in the city-states' agricultural surplus so vital to economic development: feeding an army diverted human and other resources that, under conditions of peace, would have stimulated the internal growth of the city-state's economy. These self-defeating effects of interstate rivalry and military conflicts characterized much of the Early Dynastic period, and they continually weakened Sumer's city-states. By the end of the Early Dynastic period, ca. 2,350 B.C., they were worn out and too exhausted to defend themselves against the invaders from surrounding regions. The internal weakness brought on by the long intermittent conflicts was further aggravated by social corruption within Sumerian societies. Oppression and exploitation of the masses—the farmers, the herdsmen, the fishermen, and the merchants—by the rich and the powerful widened the gap between classes, fomenting rebellion within the walls of the city-states themselves.

Decreases in the cultivable lands and in their productivity was further aggravated by the increasing salinization of Sumerian farm lands. The process of salinization gave Sumer the death blow, as Adams and Jacobsen have observed so perceptively. It began early in the Dynastic Period and was intensified as time went on by excessive irrigation, frequent flooding, and occasional marine transgression of the alluvial plains. One clear piece of evidence pointing to the intensification of salinization is the gradual dominance of the more salt-resistant barley over wheat as Sumer's staple crop. Around 3,500 B.C., wheat and barley were cultivated in equal proportions; by 2,500 B.C., wheat constituted only one sixth of the total crop; by 2,100 B.C., wheat was grown even less; and by 1,700 B.C., wheat cultivation was completely discarded in Sumer.[32] Salinization affected fertility of the soil, seriously reducing the productive capacity of Sumerian agriculture: around 2,400 B.C., each hectare produced 2,437 liters of grain; by 2,100 B.C., 1,400 liters; and by 1,700 B.C., no more than 898 liters of barley were being produced.[33] Such a drastic decrease in agricultural productivity was devastating to the city-states' economy. The strength of the Sumerian city-states had depended on agricultural surplus, and without it, demise of the states was predictable. It is not a mere accident that the movement of the Mesopotamian political centers northward and the increasing salinization of the alluvial plains of Sumer in the south coincided during the early part of the second millennium B.C.

The formal end of Sumerian city-states was brought about by the Akkadian invaders under Sargon. Having unified the Semitic inhabitants of northern Mesopotamia around 2,370 B.C., Sargon turned to Sumer in the south and conquered the Sumerian city-states, one by one, starting with the city of Uruk. And with Sargon's successful subjugation of all Sumer, the Sumerian city-states were absorbed into an empire under a single, powerful administration that effectively suppressed any local claim for political independence. Politically, administratively, as well as economically, all the former city-states were now responsible to the central imperial court. The local power bases were weakened in all respects. Under the imperial administration the city-states could no longer expend their surplus wealth for their own local projects, nor could they employ their armed forces for self-aggrandizement. Much of the local economy went into payment of taxes and tribute required by the imperial regime; local armed forces were either disbanded or placed under the imperial army's control; and local administrative heads were appointed by the imperial court. In effect, the Sumerian city-states had been successfully transformed into the provinces of an empire.

Notes

1. Charles L. Redman, *The Rise of Civilization* (San Francisco: W. H. Freeman, 1978), 105–116.

2. *Ibid.*, 151, 166–168, 183, 196.

3. *Ibid.*, 182.

4. Prominent among scholars who have advanced single-cause (prime mover) theories of the origins of urban development in the Mesopotamian world are: Karl Wittfogel, *Oriental Despotism: A Comparative Study of Total Power* (New Haven: Yale University Press, 1957); Julian Steward, "Cultural causality and law: a trial formulation of the development of early civilization," *American Anthropologist* 51 (1949, p. 1–27): V. Gordon Childe, "The urban revolution," *Town Planning Review* 21 (1950): 3–17; Robert Carneiro, "A theory of the origin of the state," *Science* 169 (1970): 733–738; Igor M. Diakonoff, "The rise of the despotic state in ancient Mesopotamia," *Ancient Mesopotamia: A Socio-Economic History,* ed. Igor M. Diakonoff (Moscow: Nauka Publishing House, 1969); Henry Wright, "A consideration of the interregional exchange in greater Mesopotamia: 4000–3000 B.C.," *Social Change and Interaction,* ed. E. L. Wilman, no. 46 (Ann Arbor: University of Michigan Museum of Anthropology Papers, 1972); Kent V. Flannery, "The Olmec and the Valley of Oaxaca," *Dumbarton Oaks Conference of the Olmec* (Washington, D.C., 1969), 79–110; Robert McC. Adams, *The Evolution of Urban Society* (Chicago: Aldine, 1966); and Flannery, "The cultural evolution of civilizations," *Annual Review of Ecology and Systematics* 3 (1972): 399–426.

5. Redman, *The Rise of Civilization*, 229.

6. *Ibid.*, 229.

7. *Ibid.*, 247, 255, 264.

8. Brian J. L. Berry, *Geography of Market Centers and Retail Distribution* (Englewood Cliffs: Prentice-Hall, 1967); and Redman, *The Rise of Civilization*, 265–266.

9. Robert McC. Adams and Hans J. Nissen, *The Uruk Countryside: The Natural Setting of Urban Society* (Chicago: University of Chicago Press, 1972).

10. Adams, *The Evolution of Urban Society*; I. J. Gelb, "The Ancient Mesopotamian ration system," *Journal of Near Eastern Studies* 24 (1965): 230–243; Karl Polayni, C. M. Arensberg, H. W. Pearson, *Trade and Markets in the Early Empires: Economies in History and Theory* (Glencoe, Ill.: Free Press, 1957).

11. For a general overview, see Tom B. Jones, ed., *The Sumerian Problem* (New York: Wiley, 1969). Charles Burney, *The Ancient Near East* (Ithaca, N.Y.: Cornell University Press, 1977), 53–55, Redman, *The Rise of Civilization*, 251, 254, are advocates of the first thesis while Samuel Noah Kramer, *The Sumerians* (Chicago: University of Chicago Press, 1963), 39–41, presents the second.

12. Kramer, *The Sumerians*, 76.

13. Adam Falkenstein, *The Sumerian Temple City*, trans. Maria deJ. Ellis (Los Angeles: Undena, 1974), 7.

14. Kramer, *The Sumerians*, 76.

15. Redman, *The Rise of Civilization*, 264, 293; Paul Lampl, *Cities and Planning in the Ancient Near East* (New York: Braziller, 1968), 15.

16. C. J. Gadd, "The cities of Babylonia," *The Cambridge Ancient History*, 3rd ed., vol. 1, pt. 2 (Cambridge: Cambridge University Press, 1965), 132.

17. C. Leonard Woolley, *The Sumerians* (New York: W. W. Norton, 1965), 132.

18. Falkenstein, *The Sumerian Temple City*, 9; Gary A. Wright, *Archeology and Trade*, Addison-Wesley Module in Anthropology, no. 49 (Reading, Mass.: Addison-Wesley, 1974); Robert McC. Adams, "Anthropological perspectives on ancient trade," *Current Anthropology* 15, no. 3 (1974): 239–258.

19. Polayni, Arensberg, Pearson, *Trade and Market in the Early Empires: Economies in History and Theory*.

20. Thorkild Jacobsen, "Primitive democracy in ancient Mesopotamia," *Journal of Near Eastern Studies* 2, no. 3 (1943): 159–172.

21. Geoffrey Evans, "Ancient Mesopotamian assemblies," *Journal of the American Oriental Societies* 78 (1958): 1–11.

22. Thorkild Jacobsen, "The function of the state," *The Intellectual Adventures of Ancient Man*, ed. H. and H. A. Frankfort, J. A. Wilson, Th. Jacobsen, W. A. Irwin (Chicago: University of Chicago Press, 1946), 188.

23. Kramer, *The Sumerians*, 308.

24. *Ibid.*, 5.

25. *Ibid.*, 319.

26. Samuel Noah Kramer, "Sumerian historiography," *Israel Exploration Journal* 3, no. 4 (1953), 217.

27. Sabatino Moscati, *The Face of the Ancient Orient* (Garden City, N.Y.: Anchor Books, 1962), 49.

28. Falkenstein, *The Sumerian Temple City*, 8.

29. Kramer, *The Sumerians*, 323–324.

30. *Ibid.*, 313.

31. C. Leonard Woolley, *The Sumerians*, 72–73; Kramer, *The Sumerians*, 60.

32. Thorkild Jacobsen and Robert McC. Adams, "Salt and silt in ancient Mesopotamian agriculture," *Science* 128, no. 3334 (1958): 1251–1258.

33. *Ibid.*

Chapter Two

THE GREEK POLIS

Carol G. Thomas

The Greek *polis* has generated as much discussion as any other single topic of Classical Greek history. Its only rivals are Homer and Alexander the Great and in significant respects they too entail consideration of the polis since its origins can be seen in the Homeric *Iliad* and *Odyssey* while Alexander was closely associated with the decline of the independent city-states of Greek history. *Polis* is indeed one of the most important single words for understanding Classical Greek history and culture. It is not easy, however, to reach an agreement on its definition, origin or decline. In a spirit of partial jest but some sincerity its very existence has been credited to the gods. Certainly the pantheon of great gods does deserve much of the credit for the health of the *polis* since it was a religious entity quite as much as a political or economic unit. But divine inspiration and direction are not the total answer and in a very real sense there can be no single answer since the Classical Greek world included some 1500 independent states. While they possessed enough common characteristics to be described by one and the same term, the history of their rise, growth and decline was markedly individual.

One of the most satisfactory definitions of the Greek *polis* is that of Victor Ehrenberg who has studied the question carefully and at length: for him the *polis* is a "community, self-absorbed, closely united in its narrow space and permeated by a strong political and spiritual intensity that led to a kind of special culture of every Polis."[1] The Greek polity was, above all else, a unified body of individuals among whom a larger, common concern had superseded purely individual interests. However, a community of interest is movable; it is not necessarily tied to a specific location and, in listing the essential bases for the construction of an ideal state, Aristotle named two: a citizen body and a territory.[2] For Aristotle, at any rate, the *polis* was also a community of place, the area in which people with common interests resided. The characteristics of community of place and community of people were so inextricably fused that it may be without profit to debate the priority of one or the other factor. Still in

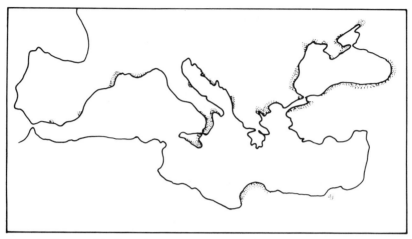

Map 2: *Geographic Distribution of the* Polis

origin and decline, one characteristic developed or disintegrated before the second.

Archeological discoveries of the last century have added yet another dimension to discussions of the *polis*. Regionalism was a distinguishing characteristic of the Bronze Age civilization of Greece as it would remain in the Dark Age and Classical period. Moreover, the disasters at the end of the Bronze Age did not produce total discontinuity in the Greek world; there was a definite decline in the cultural level, in the size of the population and in the number of settlements from 1200 to 1100 B.C., but there was a direct link between the periods. Consequently, it is possible that the roots of the city-state, or some of them at least, extend back into the Bronze Age. If this is the case, the Greek *polis* may be a distant relative of the ancient Near Eastern city-states.

Historical Framework

Since the time of Heinrich Schliemann it is improper to begin Greek history with 776 B.C. and the first Olympic games; instead, the end of the third millennium marks the entrance of an Indo-European people who settled, intermarried and adapted themselves to the culture and to the people they found in Greece. Out of the merger there resulted the civilization of the late Bronze Age (1600–1200 B.C.) which is named after the important site of Mycenae. The Mycenaean civilization kept written records whose language has been deciphered as an early form of Greek; the Mycenaean culture, then, was the first Greek culture.[3] Do the roots of the *polis* extend back to the second millennium?

From 1600 B.C., the mainland of Greece and parts of the Aegean Islands were partitioned into a number of fairly extensive subdivisions; each region was controlled from a central fortress-citadel like that at Mycenae. It appears that each area was a separate and independent realm ruled by an individual king. While there may have been loose confederations of rulers for purposes of warfare, the evidence strongly suggests that such unions were only temporary. Unlike most of the eastern Mediterranean, Greece did not undergo political consolidation under a single power. The individual citadel centers cannot properly be termed cities since only the chief figures of the political and economic system lived within the strongholds. Most of the population of the territory continued to live in small villages throughout the region as it had from the Neolithic period. Although they did not house a mixture of the population, the citadels did serve as the focus of life within the region: political, economic and military affairs were regulated from them; they served religious purposes; and a high degree of cultural uniformity was spread from these centers.

The political structure of the Mycenaean states rested on three bases: the Indo-European background of the Greeks, the earlier "Anatolian" culture of the inhabitants of the mainland and the Minoan culture of Crete. Indo-Europeans entered the mainland in tribal bands whose cohesion was based upon the ties of kinship. Personal ability with the additional base of religion determined the nature of leadership. With settlement and control of increasingly larger segments of the Anatolian population there occurred cultural fusion along with political consolidation and the resultant need for an organized system of administration was met by the implementation of a structure modeled, in large part, on the palace-centered, administrative structure of Minoan Crete which was similar to the palace centers of the contemporary ancient Near East.

The result of these developments was a political structure centered on kingship: each state was governed by a sole king, termed *Wanax*. Kingship in its established form had several foundations: the original base was personal leadership in war, a feature which persisted although it was tempered by control of a subject population and over a specific territory. As individual Mycenaean kingdoms were consolidated, central control regulating the use of the land, of natural resources and of labor produced a hierarchy of officials extending from key state officials through lesser functionaries who exercised a limited, local authority in the small villages. Especially important for later developments were village officials known as *pa₂-si-re-u*, a word that would become the normal title—as *Basileus*—for kings in the Dark Age and beyond. In the Mycenaean era these officials were concerned with the allocation of bronze or were listed among people contributing gold or were recorded as holders of a certain type of land, in all instances of minor importance to the system.

The administrative systems of the kingdoms do not appear to have included a regular judicial structure. It may well be that the kings of Mycenaean Greece, as in most monarchical societies, were responsible for the adjudication of law: law was customary and there were no formalized procedures or written codes; the king was judge as well as leader in war. Religion was closely associated with the citadel centers and it is virtually certain that the king exercised certain cult functions even though there is no reason to describe Mycenaean kingship as divine or sacral. Nor was the Mycenaean kingly rule absolute; the most significant check on royal power was effected by aristocrats who exercised control over large quantities of land and its produce and who held important official positions. They may well have constituted a council of advisors. On the other hand, there is no certain evidence for the existence of an assembly of the people and surely the degree of control held by the king and other central officials over agricultural and crafts production argues against the view that the people exercised significant political power during the late Bronze Age.

Centralization over a fairly extensive region achieved through military means and a sophisticated administrative structure were essential features of the mature Mycenaean kingdoms. It is these very features that reveal the difference between the Mycenaean polity and the Classical *polis,* inasmuch as military control and an official hierarchy were replaced by the concept of citizenship and the citizens' assumption of the direction of communal affairs. However, it is essential to understand that all states of the Classical Greek world witnessed gradual growth and alteration and that they incorporated and adapted features over a long period of consolidation. Some of these features reveal an ultimate Mycenaean origin; the legacy is shown clearly in the terminology of kingship, which had a continuous history from the end of the Mycenaean era through the Dark Age and into the Classical Age of the *polis.* The Mycenaean term for king was *Wanax* while the later kingly title, *Basileus,* described a lesser village magistrate in the official hierarchy. This second word underwent a change in meaning during the Dark Age as political realities changed; still the word itself and the original function derive from the preceding period. Nor is this term the only instance; other terms with Mycenaean roots continued in use.

Not only official titles but the social stratification of the early Greek polity reflects elements of the Bronze Age: Mycenaean records refer to the *da-mo* (*damos* or *demos* in Classical Greek), a term which describes the people collectively in the Classical period; during the Bronze Age it may have had the administrative purpose of denoting the people of a particular district. The later regional divisions of *demes,* for instance, may well have a link with the Mycenaean *da-mo.* Indeed, the very terms for the Greek polity and the lower city—*polis* and *asty*—were part of the Mycenaean vocabulary.

The most visible similarity between the states of the two periods was territorial configuration due to geographical conditions that served to divide the country into relatively small, compact regions. In the Bronze Age, these territorial regions appear to have been politically independent and this condition is nothing but more pronounced during the Classical era of the city-states. Equally significant is the division within regions, a reciprocity between country and capital. Officials at Pylos controlled the inhabitants of two provinces and of at least sixteen towns or villages just as Athens would enjoy a similar commanding position for all of Attica or Sparta for Laconia in the Classical period.

Centers in both ages expressed the religious role of the state as well as its political order. In neither case is it proper to speak of a theocratic organization although key officials had the responsibility for cult practices and the health of the state could not be separated from the instrumentality of the gods. The Mycenaean citadels had a religious purpose, among others, and it was this purpose that came to predominate on the acropoleis of the Classical Age.

It is wise—more than that, it is essential—to follow the roots of the *polis* back into the Mycenaean civilization of the second millennium B.C. for, as summarized above, there are points of similarity between the Classical *polis* and the Mycenaean polity of both a general nature and a more specific character. But just as similar bulbs produce distinctly different flowers, so did the political roots of Greece yield various plants. The Mycenaean state was not a *polis*; developments of the closing decades of the Bronze Age and the whole of the Dark Age from 1150 to 750 B.C. altered the Mycenaean inheritance producing a product of accretion—the *polis*—which assumed its first clear outlines toward the end of the eighth century B.C.

The administrative structure of the Mycenaean kingdoms was broken by the difficulties at the end of the Bronze Age, even in places like Athens which had no break in habitation. Scholars still debate the causes of these difficulties but major climatic change may have precipitated agrarian distress, disruption of trade, movement of people and political upheaval. Local village communities were thrown back on their own resources—both natural and human—and lesser leaders than the *Wanax* assumed responsibilities of direction. The size and number of settlements shrank, population declined dramatically and most individual sites were effectively isolated from one another as well as from larger Mediterranean and European areas.[4] The Aegean world of the early Dark Age was extremely unstable: there was movement on the mainland itself and away from the mainland to the Aegean Islands, Asia Minor and toward the west, into the Ionian Islands. Small settlements were located in areas that provided good natural defense. Regions formerly unified were broken into autonomous village units, each attempting to survive in a hostile environment. Circumstances such as these demanded not a formal state structure so much as direct, personal leadership.

Descendants of the village officials of the Mycenaean state endeavored to provide security for their kin and followers: the pa_2-si-re-u emerged as the most effective leaders in the disunity and confusion of the twelfth and eleventh centuries; the word itself came to be the designation for kings for the remainder of Classical antiquity. The first description of the Dark Age leaders is preserved in the *Iliad* and *Odyssey,* products of the continuous oral tradition of the Dark Age which were fixed in written form when the Greeks became literate again in the second half of the eighth century B.C. In the epic tales of Agamemnon, Achilles, Odysseus and other leaders of men, the reader—or auditor—learns that leadership was based almost exclusively on personal ability: the epics are insistent that the two qualities required of a leader are excellence in physical

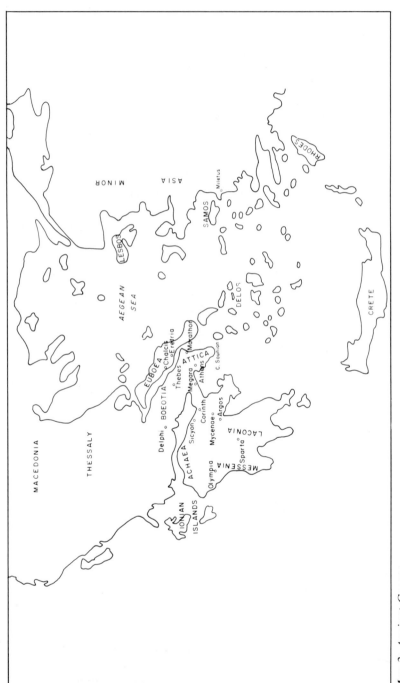

Map 3: *Ancient Greece*

combat and wisdom in deliberation. It is also clear that the formal state structure of the Mycenaean Age has disappeared. People live in small groups and must rely on one another, especially on their strongest members, for security. The collapse of the Bronze Age kingdoms was absolutely essential to the development of the *polis*, albeit in a negative rather than a positive fashion: Greek communities were reduced to self-sufficient entities in which decision-making was carried out in a direct, personal manner. There was little, if any, formal state structure in the first centuries of the Dark Age, but when it did reemerge, it arose from the "village raised to a new level of self-consciousness."[5]

The late tenth century witnessed the return of more peaceful conditions and, concomitantly, of more enduring political orders. Control of a certain amount of land came to be the measure of an individual's status and, further, became the focus of increasing communal concern. Economic life was simple, based primarily on agriculture; trade assumed renewed importance only toward the end of the Dark Age and, even then, only in certain communities. The social structure of the small Dark Age communities was uncomplicated by standards of the Mycenaean era and society was relatively fluid so long as there was unoccupied land suitable for agriculture or herding. Fate and personal abilities determined whether a person's lot would be that of a slave or a man of account in battle and counsel. Only as the empty spaces disappeared did more rigid lines of demarcation between social orders form and then harden.

Leadership in the later Dark Age continued to rest upon personal ability: a man had to be able to assert control over his own property for sheer survival as well as for retention of his position in the community; the extent of his property, in turn, indicated ability and merit relative to other men's rank. Additionally, with the reestablishment of ordered communal life, leadership assumed other dimensions which initially led to an increase in the power of the Dark Age kings. It was in the exercise of war that kings most readily strengthened their positions: the reunification of Attica, for instance, appears to have been the work of the kings of Athens; Spartan kings, even of the Classical period, revealed their importance in warfare; the early Ionian League, headed by a king, had warfare as its primary activity. Moreover, their wisdom, strength and wealth marked kings as natural adjudicators in the community and their obvious favor by the gods made them the communal priests. A successful leader won the allegiance of others by his status and proven ability and thereby enlarged his renown within and beyond the immediate community. While it was not automatically the case that a son would possess the same qualities that enabled his father to gain or retain power, still the sons of kings were regarded in a special light; they were likely to inherit their fathers' considerable personal possessions and they could be brought into public notice through opportunities which were denied to other young men. Furthermore, a king would naturally attempt to secure the succession in his own family and if several generations of one line had provided competent leadership, it was thought likely that the present generation could carry on competently.

At the same time that kingly power increased, kingly responsibilities expanded, producing conditions that ultimately led to the limitation of the rule of one leader. The acquisition of additional territory as well as of more followers led to greater demands upon the king. Simultaneously, others came to rival the king in high status inasmuch as possessions and birth were matters of degree that could be met by more than one man. Quietly and gradually, monarchy based upon personal leadership gave way to aristocratic control by men who shared the powers of the king among themselves. The change can be seen in the slow emergence of two organs of state, namely, the council and the assembly. The epic poems attest the existence of both a group of advisors to the king and assemblies whose primary purpose was the consideration of something of common concern. Archeological evidence has revealed places of assembly dating to the late eighth century.

In other words, rudimentary forms of the three organs of *polis* government had evolved by the end of the Dark Age. Personal leadership was giving way to limitations effected by near peers of the kings, on the one hand, and it was yielding to the necessity of dividing responsibilities among a number of officials, on the other. The advisory council may have had a history leading back to the Bronze Age Mycenaean states, but its membership was now fixed by standard requirements, primarily the amount of property and birth. The assembly of people had begun the ascent that would make it supreme, in theory if not always in practice, in the fully-formed *polis*. Consequently, the importance of the Dark Age in the formation of the Greek city-state cannot be overemphasized. It is true that many modern scholars argue that the fully-fledged polity that is properly called the *polis* cannot be seen until the middle of the fifth century. Yet a contemporary of that time, the historian Thucydides was describing the decline of the *polis* in his account of the Peloponnesian War. Remembering that there were as many variations in the form of the *polis* as there were *poleis* is essential to a proper estimate of the city-state's origin and subsequent history. A view of general developments reveals that the three constituent organs of the *polis* emerged in the course of the Dark Age when the inheritance from the Mycenaean civilization was simplified and transformed. During those four centuries a sense of community was deepening and creating the exclusive bond between a few people living in a limited territory. Further developments in the nature of the *polis* occurred during the Archaic period of the seventh and sixth centuries and since the *polis* was never a static entity, changes continued throughout the whole of the Classical period. These later developments can be summarized as democratization and greater differentiation of the functions and responsibilities of the state and its officials.

Ancient political theorists were wont to argue that constitutional change was cyclical among six forms of state government: monarchy, aristocracy and democracy alternated with their corrupt counterparts, tyranny, oligarchy and ochlocracy. Historical observation reinforced the theory for the Greeks since it is true that more and more individuals were included in political decisions through the course of the Classical period: limited aristocracy had replaced monarchy by the start of the Archaic period in approximately 700 B.C., but it was, in turn, enlarged.[6] In many states it was individuals, known as tyrants, who placed themselves in a position above the laws and broke the bases of aristocratic control. The success of the tyrants in individual states was itself due to another significant change, the military innovation that replaced individual combat with mass formation. Soldiers were equipped in new fashion with greaves, corslet, helmet and a convex round shield and carrying a long stabbing spear and a short stabbing sword. Known as *hoplites*, they provided supports for champions who could and did effect economic improvements for the lower orders of society: land was often redistributed; new crops were encouraged; building programs were fostered. By supporting public cults at the expense of regional cults where aristocratic priesthoods predominated, the tyrants weakened another source of aristocratic strength and, in the sphere of justice, the tyrants frequently inaugurated a state administration of overseeing the laws: traveling judges heard disputes and rendered judgments; no longer was a local lord the only recourse for settling a dispute between neighbors. The first generation tyrant in a state was both successful and welcomed; second generations had major problems in maintaining control simply because the task had been accomplished so effectively and rapidly. When tyrants were replaced, it was not the old aristocratic lords who returned, as a general rule, but rather elements of the community previously excluded: oligarchies of individuals whose wealth came from new economic pursuits or limited democracies were the products of democratization by the end of the sixth century.

A second development of the Archaic period was an increase in complexity within the state as military, economic, political, religious responsibilities all necessitated more officials and boards to carry out the business of state. For example, military power in Athens passed from the sole control of a Dark Age *Basileus* to one aristocratic official, the *Polemarch*, who in turn was superseded by a board of ten generals or *Strategoi*. To continue with Athenian developments, a second aristocratic magistracy, the *Archon eponymous*, assumed the kingly judicial concerns of the state but, already by the early seventh century, the *Archon* was aided by a board of six other judicial magistrates. And by the early sixth century an elaborate structure of law courts was the business of all citizens serving in their dual role as jurors and judges. A like process of parceling of duties occurred in all the *poleis* of Classical Greece, a subject to which we shall return.

Since the *polis* resembles the chameleon in its ability to change outward appearance without altering its generic nature, it is as difficult to date the decline of the *polis* as it is to specify an exact point of origin. The Greek city-state continued to be the basis of organization under Roman rule in the eastern Mediterranean, both during the Republic and during the Empire. The physical form of these later Greek cities approximated that of the Classical *polis*; Greeks under Roman rule, like the writer Plutarch, held positions corresponding to those of their ancestors six and seven centuries earlier. To appreciate the nature of decline, one must emphasize the function of the *polis*: each autonomous unit claimed to be sufficient to fulfill the needs of its acknowledged citizen body. While it is true that no *polis* could be truly and completely autonomous, still the claim is a useful measure of the health of the city-state system. It was when all pretense of autonomy and independence was abandoned that the *polis* became a city retaining only its vestigial form and not its substance. This principle is not highly debatable, but it is far more difficult to fix a specific date for the abandonment of a claim to autonomy since Greeks themselves refused to acknowledge its loss. A logical beginning date appears to be either 338 B.C., the battle of Chaeronea, or 323 B.C., the death of Alexander the Great and the start of the Hellenistic Age. The end of the process may be as early as the conclusion of the Chremonidean War in 262 when Athens relinquished hope of independence or as late as the initial successes of Rome in the East in the first half of the second century.[7]

For the modern historian the defeat of the Greeks at Chaeronea by Philip II of Macedon clearly concludes the era of unfettered city-state sovereignty: not only were the *hoplite* forces of the *poleis* shown to be inferior to the professional Macedonian army but also the states were joined into a League—the League of Corinth—through the will of a king of a foreign territorial state. The alliance creating the League was both offensive and defensive and military campaigns were led thereafter by Philip. It was further dictated that no citizen of a member state could serve with a foreign power against Philip or the League. To ensure loyalty, garrisons were established in key Greek states such as Corinth and Thebes. Philip's action did not differ markedly from that taken by Greek states prior to 338. He arranged individual treaties with the members of the League of Corinth as Sparta had forged in developing the Peloponnesian League in the sixth century; the resultant association in both instances was a union of separate states who retained their independence. There was even less control exercised from Pella in matters of internal political organization and economic activity than the subjects of Athens had felt in the fifth century B.C. Philip's principal aim was to settle affairs in Greece to the extent that he would be free to embark on a larger campaign in the east; that is, he attempted to secure Macedon from attack from any direction while he was away in Asia Minor. Still, the Greek states were no longer completely independent—foreign policy was decided jointly and executed by other than *polis* officials. Philip was the most dominant individual in the Greek world after 338—and even before that date his influence was decisive—and it is significant that he and his Macedonians were not regarded as true Hellenes. Moreover, Philip had demonstrated that he could and would intervene in the internal politics of a *polis*.

Alexander was less preoccupied with affairs in Greece, in part because he benefited from his father's accomplishments, in part because of his own ambitions. Thebes was sacked, to be sure, but during the years 334 to 323 continual and effective reform was carried out in Athens. It was possible for Sparta under her King Agis III to mount a serious threat to Macedon under the rule of the regent Antipater. The Greek states recovered a fair measure of their spirit of independence in both internal and foreign affairs, and the sense of hostility toward foreign meddling is demonstrated by the Greeks' reception of Alexander's two edicts delivered from Babylon in 324: while they were willing to offer Alexander due honors as a self-proclaimed deity, they were enraged by his order that exiles must be received back into their respective states.

However, Greece could not drive out foreign arms and money and the position of the *poleis* declined in relative strength during the fifty years following the death of Alexander when his successors fought—with arms and diplomacy—to divide the empire. The battleground was much enlarged over that of the Classical period or even most of the fourth century when the Aegean was still the focus of major developments. But the Greek *poleis* were, to their ill-fortune, not excluded from the contest and they became prizes, at first, and later pawns in the wars between rival contenders for power. Greece was still a world of individual political entities; not until well into the third century, after the division of Alexander's empire had been accomplished, did unification of separate states into larger leagues gain momentum and even then much of the unification was effected by compulsion. During the years of the struggles of the Diadochi from 323 to 275, the Greek *poleis* retained their accustomed machinery even while they were garrisoned or controlled by tyrants imposed upon them. Members of these *poleis* retained the belief that the state could and should take action for itself in foreign affairs as well as in internal matters. From 294 to 288 Athens negotiated with Ptolemy in Egypt, Lysimachus in Thrace and Seleucus in the Near East to find succor against the domination by yet another threatening Macedonian, Demetrius Poliorcetes. Spartan kings like Cleomenes III and Agis IV were able to make remarkable—even feared—attempts to reassert Spartan military hegemony in the second half of the third century. All such endeavors were fruitless, put down by more powerful outside states. The stature of the city-states had declined; they had not recognized that development.

The final Spartan attempt to recapture her old position serves to mark the last breath of life not only of Sparta but of the independent *polis* in Greece. The Spartan venture was smashed by two larger forces—the territorial kingdom of Macedon and the federal association of the Achaean League. After her defeat, Sparta had her ancestral constitution restored by the Macedonian king Antigonus Doson. She was enrolled in the Hellenic League of Doson modeled on Philip's League of Corinth in which Sparta had refused to participate and, moreover, a Macedonian governor was installed. Even earlier, Athens had witnessed many of the same developments: at the conclusion of the Chremonidean War (ca. 262) Athenian magistrates were controlled by Macedon and the assembly ceased to meet on a regular basis. A vital symbol of political and economic independence disappeared at the same time: Athens ceased to issue her own coins. It is true that autonomy was restored to Athens in 229 B.C., but as a gift from the Macedonian kings. During the remainder of the Hellenistic Age, certain privileged cities would be autonomous but only by special grant from a king; clearly the notion of autonomy and special grant of autonomy by a stronger power are antithetical. Both internal affairs and foreign relations were ultimately controlled by an outsider and for Athens as well as for the *poleis* under the sway of other Hellenistic monarchs, the second half of the third century witnessed the end of citizenship in the Classical sense of the word. In the Hellenistic states the king was the state and it has been said that there were no citizens but only subjects.

The Romans were the beneficiaries of the altered political atmosphere of Greece when they became involved on the Greek mainland and later in Asia Minor in the second century. The Romans established their influence in the Greek world at a time when they had already come to prize the value of Roman citizenship and were increasingly selfish about grants of either public or private rights. In creating a larger empire, therefore, areas were treated as friends and allies, client states and subject provinces. In all three categories, foreign affairs were under the close scrutiny of Rome; in none of the instances were inhabitants of the foreign states initially accorded citizenship as Romans. Thus, the Romans simply perpetuated a condition in Greece that had been accelerating for the fifty or sixty years prior to their success at Cynocephalae in 197 B.C. Even more so than the Hellenistic kings, the Romans utilized the form of the *polis* while divesting it of its political autonomy.

If one looks at ancient Greek civilization in the context of the larger Mediterranean and Near Eastern worlds, the *polis* system is shown to be an anomaly. The pattern of the ancient Near East tended to larger and more populous territorial kingdoms with the passage of time and both the Macedonians and Romans continued that pattern. Endeavors toward empire are a recurring theme even in Classical Greek history—Athens, Sparta, Thebes in turn all understood imperialistic ambition and sought to realize it. For several centuries, however, that ambition was channeled through a number of independent polities of comparable strength; there was no large territorial state capable and simultaneously desirous of dominating Greece by force of arms. One might well conclude that the Greek *poleis'* existence was dependent on the weakness or sufferance of contemporary states. As long as the most serious opponents of a particular *polis* were other similar states, the system continued. When the *poleis* were compelled to compete with much stronger, larger states, they had to play subordinate roles. The strength of the system is revealed by the stubborn attempt to retain independence in the face of the Macedonians and later the Romans. Greeks of the third century—perhaps those living in the second as well—would not have recognized that the *polis* structure was no longer operable; from their perspective, they continued to live in city-states. In retrospect, however, we can see that the second half of the third century effectively marks the end of the Greek *polis* as an autonomous political unit: its foreign affairs

were controlled from elsewhere—Pella or Rome—and even internal administration came to be closely supervised by outsiders. Citizenship had another
meaning in the later Hellenistic and Roman periods of antiquity than it possessed during the Classical phase of Greek history.

Physical Appearance

The ambiguities of the translation city-state from *polis* are especially pronounced when physical appearance is considered for while the functions and
forms of modern states and cities were combined in the Greek polity, still an
ancient Greek *polis* was not necessarily recognized by its degree of urbanization
or its size. Thucydides remarked, for instance, that the power of Sparta could
not be guessed by posterity through its surviving temples and the foundations of
its public buildings, while the ruins of Athens would make it appear to have
been twice as great as it was (1.10). A more satisfactory definition of the *polis* is
perhaps a community of people and of place. It was a unified body of individuals among whom purely individual interests or family matters had been
superseded by a larger, common concern. The Greek *polis* was also and equally
the area where people with common interests resided for it was the particular
features of the territory that influenced and directed the nature of the
politically-organized body of people and served to perpetuate the intense
exclusiveness of the independent states.

The territory of the *polis* was small and restricted: Attica, one of the largest
territories unified into a single polity, was some forty miles long by twenty-five
miles in width. Corinth, one of the most important states during the whole of the
Classical period, had some 340 square miles. The island of Lesbos originally
was divided among six independent states. In consequence, the population was
necessarily small: perhaps only a dozen city-states ever had more than 10,000
citizens, a figure which suggests a free population of approximately 40,000.
Limited population was deemed both necessary and good: Aristotle maintained
that the city-state must have a population "self sufficient for the purpose of
living the good life after the manner of a political community," although he
insisted that "in order to decide questions of justice and in order to distribute the
offices according to merit it is necessary for the citizens to know each other's
personal characters" (Rackham, Aristotle *Pol.* VII 4).[8]

The Classical *polis* was absorbed with its own concerns, claiming to be independent and autonomous and exerting most of its efforts in maintaining that
autonomy: the military history of Greece is a story of the expansion of individual states in order to further their own interests but, in the process, infringing on
the territory and the rights of other states which, by definition, were compelled
to take up arms to ensure their own independence. The struggle was intense, as
devotion to the *polis* form of life was similarly intense. Socrates's refusal to
consider leaving Athens after he had been tried and found guilty is perhaps the
best-known illustration of this devotion. The words of the Spartan mother to her
son reveal the same attachment: "Come back with your shield or on it."

There was an overwhelming sense of attachment to the territory which helps to explain the particularism of ancient Greece. Dislocation and movement were results of the collapse of Bronze Age civilization and life was unsettled throughout much of the Greek world for at least a century (from ca. 1150 to 1050 B.C.). When permanent resettlement on any scale occurred, it was in a land that was fragmented by nature: mountains, non-navigable rivers, irregular coastline and offshore islands divide Greece into relatively self-contained compartments and, as more recent history has demonstrated, it has been difficult in all periods to tie those compartments into a unified political entity. Initial occupation of territory was dependent upon the leadership of a strong individual who was able to prevent the dislodging of his immediate family or clan from their lands. Certain leaders were successful in maintaining possession and, in some cases, even won control over neighboring areas. However, on reaching the limits of the natural territorial unit, expansion was difficult if not impossible. The Athenians attempted to build an empire by land during the fifth century, expanding into Euboea and Boeotia; it was an immediate failure. Even her maritime empire proved impossible to retain. In crossing Mount Taygetus, the Spartans conquered Messenia and held it for some four centuries. It was a remarkable feat—Messenia was in a state of potential, if not actual, revolt the entire time—and the conquest caused the Spartans to reshape their whole way of life. When institutional change accelerated in the later Dark Age, it was within the context of fragmentation: the territory was recognized as the sphere of one leader—it was a political entity; the adult males could adequately defend the area—it was a military unit. Moreover the gods and heroes of the land assumed special aspects associated particularly with the region. And growing specialization and incipient trade were adopted to the economic base of the area.

Identification with a certain amount of territory was felt and hence demonstrated in a variety of ways. The land itself possessed features which were described as wondrous: near Aegiae in Laconia "there is a lake called Poseidon's lake, with a shrine and statue of the god beside the water. The people are frightened to take fish from here, because they say any fisherman who disturbs these fish turns into a frogfish" (Pausanias III.21.5).[9] There were, further, witnesses of the gods' and past heroes' presence throughout the land: temples and statues commemorated the spots where deities had performed marvelous acts or where the bones of a hero had been laid to rest. Individuals honored could be as remote as the Age of Heroes or as recent as the previous generation. A place in Sparta called Hellenion is an excellent witness to the fusion of past and present. One story is that "when Xerxes crossed into Europe and they were getting ready to fight for Greece, this was where they planned their method of defense. The other story is that the men who fought the Trojan War for Menelaos made their plan here to sail to Troy and punish Paris for the rape of Helen" (Paus. III.16.8). "The leftover bit of the reality of a long past event" is Helmut von Moltke's definition of locale, a view that is in full accord with Hellenic thought.[10] The memorials served as more than passive testimonials; annual festivals and celebrations demanded active participation on the part of men, women, adolescent boys and girls. In these celebrations inhabitants of a state gave annual renewals of their bond to the gods of that state.

The land itself—its geographical configuration and its testimonials both natural and man-made—imparted a sense of identity and, with it, a sense of community. It also was deemed capable of providing self-sufficiency for its members. Of course the goal could not be accomplished at any period after the introduction of metallurgy since Greece possessed only limited mineral resources. But still each small territory might hope to produce the bare necessities of life for its population: all states provided cereals, vegetables, animal products, oil and wine and there was no need to trade internally for these essentials so long as the population was neither excessively large or small. Aristotle defined the proper size of population for a *polis* as "the greatest surveyable number required for achieving a life of self-sufficiency" (*Pol.* 1326 b22-24).

A sense of unity for a small territorial area is only one side of the coin; the other side is the particularism fostered by the sense of identity between a community of people and a community of place. The land of each *polis* had unique features; gods and heroes had chanced upon particular experiences in various parts of Greece and had given differing forms of aid or revenge in certain regions. The territory of each city-state was gradually marked by testimonials to the particular figures and events of its past were remembered in specific ceremonials; the result pointed to the differences among Greeks from the heroic past to the present. Classical Greeks, like Herodotus, could write of the bonds that united all Greeks: "There is the Greek nation—the common blood, the common languages; the temples and religious ritual; the whole way of life we understand and share together . . ." (VIII.144).[11] Still there was as much variety as there was uniformity in each of these categories: Pericles could speak of the alien mode of Spartan life and the Lycurgan laws of Sparta excluded "foreigners" from other Greek states because of their power to corrupt the Spartan way of life. Surely this diversity fostered as well as derived from the regionalism of the *polis* and made unification impossible on cultural grounds quite as much as political terms.

In spite of the variety, however, the separate *poleis* shared basic characteristics even in physical form. Activity of the *polis* came to be concentrated at one point—Athens for Attica, Sparta for Laconia—and especially at this center there were public buildings that expressed the corporate nature of the state. According to Pausanias, Panopeus could not be called a *polis* because it had "no government offices or gymnasium, no theatre or agora or water flowing down to a fountain" (X.iv.1). For a true *polis* there would be a vital hub, the agora, around which were located structures in which political, economic and cultural life was planned and, in large measure, acted out. A second feature of the center was the acropolis which assumed a special character and function as the *polis* matured: from being a palace and administrative center in the Bronze

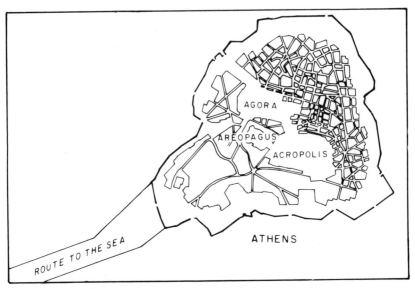

Illus. 3: *Plan of Athens*

Age and a place of defense during the Dark Age, it became the home of the *polis* gods. Even the Spartan acropolis which was "not so high as to be a landmark" (Paus. III.17.1) was covered with temples, sanctuaries and statues of the gods. The third standard feature of the *polis* center from the late sixth century on was a wall of circuit: the vital hub had to be defended and, hence, as the center included more than the acropolis, the wall extended to take in the whole settlement fanning out from the base of the acropolis. In some states the wall could be a gift of nature: Sparta had no wall but she did have Mount Taygetus which attains its greatest elevation directly above Sparta, 7900 feet above sea level.

The entire population of the state did not live in its center even though people were not far distant since most states had territory of four hundred square miles or less. Sparta grew to an enormous size—by Greek standards—of 3300 square miles but even for such a large state it was entirely possible to know at first hand all parts of a region extending fifty miles north and south of one's home and some fifteen miles to each side. In this compact area there were a number of settlements: citizens lived throughout the entire territory of the state in separate villages, not in suburbs of an urban mass. The agrarian basis of the ancient Greek economy dictated the importance of the countryside and attachment to the land was strengthened for these reasons. Even in Periclean Athens which had become a flourishing urban center, half of the population continued to live in the Attic country. No matter where one lived, however, there was only one citizenship—that of Sparta, not Laconia; Athens, not Attica. Citizens whose homes were in Marathon on the east coast of Attica, for instance, belonged to the city-state of "the Athenians" quite as much as did citizens from Sounion or from Athens itself.

Citizenship

In spite of the importance of its territorial base, the ancient Greek community could not be equated simply with the residents of a certain territory; membership included, but was more than, residence. For Athens just before the start of the Peloponnesian War it has been estimated that 43,000 individuals held citizen rights out of a population of 317,000. Sparta had four to five thousand full citizens out of a total population of 190,000–270,000 during the first half of the fifth century.[12] The most generous estimate in each case would give a figure of 2.63 percent citizenship for Sparta and 13.6 percent for Athens. Surely the *polis* was an exclusive entity. The dual implications of citizenship, or *politeia*, reflect this exclusiveness for while all residents were governed by the existing constitution, only certain residents were included within the community of citizens empowered to manage the constitution.

The one essential requirement of citizenship was descent: proper birth right accompanied by acceptance into the societal units of family, clan, phratry (brotherhood founded originally on ties of blood, later developing into hereditary membership) and tribe. As the exposure of unfit infants shows plainly, birth and social acceptance were not inseparably connected. In most periods and in most states of ancient Greece, both parents must be full members of the community in order for a child to be accepted as a fully enfranchised citizen. As we shall see, the exclusiveness of the *polis* extended to Greeks of other city-states quite as much as to true foreigners. Under the requirement of descent are subsumed all of the other specifications of citizenship. If both parents were full members of the *polis*, they would be, by definition, free rather than non-free and certainly citizenship was grounded on the requirement of freedom. The notions of free man and citizen were as inextricably connected with one another as they were firmly separated from the concept of the slave. Equally firm was the line of demarcation between male and female: only males could be fully enfranchised citizens. The original equation of citizen-soldier does much to explain the limitation and in places like Sparta where women's role in defending the *polis* was more visible, their rights were correspondingly higher. Nevertheless, even the standard view of procreation attributed the life force solely to the father; women were thought to be inferior to men in most respects.

Still, the blood of both parents came to be an essential requirement demonstrating that they belonged to the civil communities of the *polis* in which they fulfilled their associated obligations. The test of officials at Athens, the *dokimasia*, sought to determine, first, a citizen's legal birth and, second, whether he provided for his parents, paid taxes and participated in military campaigns. Such responsibilities of citizenship were logical extensions of obligations to kin.

Proper descent further carried a tie with the territory of the city-state; ownership or use of land was closely connected with citizenship. An agrarian economy had been the basis of the emerging *polis* and agriculture remained central to Greece throughout antiquity. It is not surprising to find a direct association between ownership of landed property and citizenship. Thebes showed this connection in a law that barred from full citizenship anyone who had traded in the *agora* in the previous ten years. In Athens where such a severe restriction did not obtain, the class comprising individuals most active in trade and commerce remained resident aliens. Atypical in extending the franchise to residents lacking landed property by the mid-fifth century, even Athens linked projected reforms of citizenship to property qualifications. Ownership, or use of the land as in Sparta where ownership belonged to the *polis*, was a *de facto* qualification for full rights inasmuch as ownership of land was an exclusive right of the citizen population. *Polis* citizenship, in sum, required proof that an individual belonged to both a community of people and a community of place: the first proof was offered through descent and the second was attested by means of ownership of property.

Social Structure

The citizenry was not, however, an undifferentiated whole in any *polis*, even in Sparta where citizens were, theoretically but not practically, equals or *homoioi*. In all *poleis* there were categories of social division that can be defined as classes and that, in many instances, gave rise to specific orders, that is juridically defined groups within the population. The *polis* arose in comparatively simple circumstances in which men were divided into the *agathoi*, or nobles in every sense of that term, and the *kakoi*, or the non-nobles (the adjective has the general meaning of evil or bad). Men belonged to one or the other category because of the full complement of their position: birth, property, prowess, wisdom all were determinative. *Agathoi* were able to benefit their society; *kakoi* could not. Hence the classes differed not only in possessions and capabilities but also in obligations. Responsibilities that might be defined collectively as political belonged to an aristocracy and with responsibilities were associated rights.

A break in this clear division came with the increase in trade, manufacture and commerce from the close of the Dark Age into the early Classical period. Although the *polis* claimed to be self-sufficient, that goal was unattainable. Moreover, a rise in population in the eighth and seventh centuries forced individual states to find additional land which only rarely was at hand in neighboring regions. Sparta was almost unique in expanding into Messenia; most states exported their surplus population by colonization abroad. As a result of the colonization of the regions of the central and western Mediterranean and of the Black Sea, new impetus was given to non-agrarian economic activities; the success of members of a community in the developing trade and commerce created a new class in the previously two-fold system. Certain *kakoi* could rival the *agathoi* in almost every respect save one—acknowledged rank in the community. The difficulty of accommodating these individuals in the long-established scheme is reflected strongly in the poetry of the Archaic period: from Hesiod in ca. 700 B.C. to Solon in the early years of the sixth century there is a call for *eunomia* or a state that is well-ordered and where all people keep to their proper status. Solonian Athens found a solution that was adopted by many other states in timocracy where grades of political rights corresponded to grades of wealth. Aristocracy, in other words, gave way to oligarchy throughout most of the Greek world.

Only in very few instances did the process continue of incorporating more of the population into the full citizen body. Greece experienced "democratization," not the widespread growth of "democracy." Far-flung grants of citizenship betoken, in fact, a decline of the value of citizenship and, simultaneously, a decrease in the strength of the *polis*. Even in Athens of the fifth and fourth centuries, officials continued to derive from the upper classes although the entire citizen population determined communal policy through their participation in the assembly and the council of 500. Although it is impossible to give percentages, it is indisputable that throughout antiquity most people made their livelihood from the land. To be sure, many lower class citizens were potters or stonemasons or leatherworkers but such craftsmen were never so numerous or urbanized as to become a proletariat. Individuals who, by their occupation, would have been categorized as urban poor in other societies were often employed in areas of their expertise on a temporary, seasonal basis.

In most states, as we have seen, the majority of the population consisted of individuals without citizen rights. Excluded from citizenship automatically were the non-free elements of the population as well as resident aliens who were granted certain legal rights but were seldom accorded citizenship. There were further orders intermediate between slaves and full participants in the composition of the states.

Slaves were numerous; in fact, it is a truism that the ancient world was based on slave labor and Greece is no exception to this general rule. Chattel slavery was of underlying significance for the established *polis*. The definition of a slave as a thing not a person may be even more in keeping with the Greek world than it was for Rome where slaves could and did become citizens upon manumission. In Greek city-states, manumitted slaves became resident aliens, not citizens. Estimates of numbers of slaves for classical Athens range from 20,000 to 400,000 and even the low figure gives a ratio of one to one for slaves and citizens. The most depressed occupation reserved for slave labor was mining but, other than that, slave and free labor were employed in the full range of normal occupations; slaves and free men worked at the same crafts and also in the same professions. Slaves seem to have been especially numerous and prominent in the Greek equivalent of banking.

The Greek states followed the unspoken rule that only outsiders could be enslaved. Since all other *poleis* were regarded as foreign states, however, Greeks were regularly enslaved by other Greeks. In the fourth century, Plato argued that this situation should be altered, a fact notable not for any real effect but for the proof it offers regarding the origins of slaves. The practice of enslaving only outsiders supports the view that debt-bondage was not a regular practice of the Greek *polis,* at least after the Archaic period. In Athens where the evidence is fullest, Solon dealt with the results of enslavement for reasons of debt in the first decade of the sixth century; both here and elsewhere the practice of debt-bondage of members of the community was replaced by chattel slavery of outsiders.

Nonetheless, various forms of dependency remained. The state of *helotage* in Sparta, Crete and Thessaly was not chattel slavery; although *helots* were not free, they could not be bought and sold by individuals. They were owned by the state and attached to portions of land to work it for the full citizens. Their lives, though carefully controlled for economic, military and political reasons, involved all normal human institutions except those demanding a free status.

There were other marginal orders within each *polis* especially the resident aliens who were technically free but without either rights or obligations of the full citizens: they could not participate in the decisions of state governance, could not own property and were liable to special taxes for the privilege of residing in their adoptive state. In Athens they were required to register and to find a citizen to serve as a sponsor (*prostates*); the penalty for neglect of either requirement was sale into slavery. Resident aliens often performed extraordinary services for their adoptive homes and occasionally, but only very occasionally, were given the honor of citizen rights in gratitude for such services. Not only foreigners but natives as well could belong to marginal orders of the *polis*; Sparta had its inferiors, *hypomeiones,* and new citizens, *neodamodeis,* and there were similar rankings especially in states with limited oligarchic governments.

The Individual and the State

All the orders of the population of a given *polis* greatly outnumbered the citizen population: a ratio of ten to one is by no means implausible. Bonds to the city-state varied considerably among the orders of society in accord with political rights, but perhaps a generalization is not out of order: the *polis* was both a community of people and community of territory and all orders were part of the *polis* in its latter sense while only a privileged few were incorporated into it in its former sense. Resident aliens were closely tied to the state for economic reasons—why otherwise would citizens of one state move to another where they would possess no citizen rights? Since resident aliens were necessary to the well-being of the state, they were accorded certain protections by the state. Those slaves who belonged to households were bound to the family and, hence, to the territory. The *Perioecci*, or dwellers-round about, carried on for centuries an independent life in their Laconian villages lacking only such rights as the privilege of office and deliberation in larger state policy in matters of war and foreign relations.

However, the *polis* was above all else a community of people and the closest possible association between an individual and his state could only exist among members of that community. Slaves employed in the mines in Attica used the incursions of the Peloponnesians to flee the mines and the territory; *helots* were in a constant, if only potential, state of revolt from the Spartans. For the health of the *polis* it was necessary that the individual subordinate himself to the interests of the state. This is not to say that individuals did not emerge as powerful forces in the history of their city-states during the Archaic and Classical periods: we need think merely of the tyrants of the seventh and sixth centuries, Athenians of the mold of Themistocles, dynamic Spartan kings and generals such as the first Cleomenes and Brasidas. If the *polis* were to prosper, however—indeed if it were to continue—individuals must willingly conform to the will of the community or, alternatively, there must be means of controlling over-ambitious citizens. Perhaps the wonder of the Greek *polis* is that these means or voluntary submission of self-interest developed and persisted as long as they did.

We possess a striking description of the identification of the individual with his *polis* ascribed to Socrates by Plato in his *Crito*: in answering his friends who would have him flee Athens after he had been found guilty, Socrates counters with the argument the Laws of Athens would give. They would say:

> Socrates, we have substantial evidence that you are satisfied with us and with the State. You would not have been so exceptionally reluctant to cross the borders of your country if you had not been exceptionally attached to it . . . you have been content with us and with our city. You have definitely chosen us, and undertaken to observe us in all your activities as a citizen; and as the crowning proof that you are satisfied with our city, you have begotten children in it. Furthermore, even at the time of your trial you could have proposed the penalty of banishment, if you had chosen to do so.

Earlier the Laws had asked:

> Are you so wise as to have forgotten that compared with your mother and father and all the rest of your ancestors your country is something far more precious, more venerable, more sacred, and held in greater honor both among gods and among all reasonable men?[13]

Certainly the portrait and the words are idealized; although Socrates did serve his state by holding public office and on the battlefield during the Peloponnesian War, he believed that he might better serve the state in ways peculiar to his own talents.

So instead of taking a course which would have done no good either to you or to me, I set myself to do you individually in private what I hold to be the greatest possible service: I tried to persuade each one of you not to think more of practical advantages than of his mental and moral well-being, or in general to think more of advantage than of well-being in the case of the state or anything else.[14]

Socrates, a gad-fly, attempted to sting others into rigorous examination of life and its value. In this he shows the dissolution of the bond of the *polis* which emphasized the collective whole rather than the individual. Yet an attachment such as that described by Plato surely reflects the intensity of the sacrifice of individualism for the good of the community. The *polis* was founded on the premise that there was no life, at least no proper or good life, apart from the state. Hence there was an attempt to equate the state with society. The difficulty of such an identification is all the more pronounced inasmuch as society included far more than the citizens of any state and, consequently, it was inherently impossible to make the equation. The bond between that privileged segment of the society comprising the citizen population and the *polis* had, therefore, to be even more intense to counter the far weaker links between the state and the marginal orders of society. The words ascribed to Socrates—indeed the very events of Socrates' life and death—bespeak the effectiveness of that tie for much of Classical antiquity.

Functions

The bond between the individual and the city-state was forged through the execution of functions that the state gradually assumed. Passing from a personal political order to a territorial state, the established *polis* took to itself certain functions that earlier had been in the hands of individual heads of clans: law, warfare, relations with the gods and economic well-being were entrusted to the collective whole—the *polis*. The transition was gradual and the tempo varied from one area of Greece to another. There were some inheritances from the Bronze Age which were stronger in particular areas; new conceptions and institutions grew out of conditions of the Dark Age when the small communities were isolated from one another and, hence, developing at differing paces; and the declared function of economic self-sufficiency could not be realized in practice by any *polis*. In all cases, however, initiative passed from the individual to the collective entity of the state in an attempt to execute these functions.

The *polis* came to embody and safeguard justice for its members, and to serve this end specific organs evolved. To understand the emergence of a communal concern for justice, one must turn to the Homeric poems where the most common means of obtaining redress—self-help, action by peaceful means or reprisals, the evidentiary oath—are quite informal. Indeed the bard knows of people where "each man is lawgiver to his children and his wives, and nobody cares a jot for his neighbors"[15] (*Od.* IX.114–115). Yet the beginnings of public worry over justice are discernible: a system of challenge and wager

(*Il.* XVIII.497) to induce a reluctant opponent to submit to arbitration has been developed. When the son of the still absent Odysseus appeals to the assembly asking for aid, he recognizes the possibility of persuading the *demos* out of its normal position of neutrality into action on his behalf. There are two cases in the *Odyssey* where the people meet in the absence of the king and after deliberation reach a decision against him (XVI.420, XXIV.426). In the Greek camp at Troy there was a place in or near the *agora* for the administration of justice with seats for the judges (*Il.* XI.807, XVIII.497 and 504). The trial scene on the shield of Achilles, depicted as a typical incident of public life, indicates that the community realized that arbitration was in the public interest as an aid in reducing possible sources of danger to itself. Odysseus knows that a man can spend a whole day in the *agora* judging disputes, a situation which implies more or less regular litigation (XII.439). The *Oresteia* trilogy of Aeschylus, some two hundred years later, traces the supplanting of the individual exercise of justice: Orestes, hounded by personal Furies, finally is brought to trial in Athens where he receives a collective decision overseen by the goddess Athena. That trilogy may be viewed as a full statement of the principle only just beginning in the epics. From that beginning, the equation between *polis* and law, *nomos,* grew and became firmly rooted as shown in the lines from the *Crito* quoted above. Aristotle argued that "Where no Nomoi rule, there is no Politeia" (*Pol* 1292 a32).

Decisions affecting peace and war and the execution of warfare were another responsibility of the established *polis* and it may well be that this function emerged later than a communal concern for justice. The *Iliad* reveals throughout a pre-*polis* conception of warfare in which Nestor can reminisce over "that time, when a quarrel was made between us and the Eleians over a driving of cattle, when I myself killed Itymoneus . . . as I was driving cattle in reprisal" (*Il.*XI.669).[16] For the Trojan expedition itself, a force was raised through contingents supplied by individual leaders from various regions of Greece. There was no communal levy of troops in the bard's description; rather personal loyalty and obligation formed the bond of the force. Men of each local contingent were bound to the king of their region; the local kings, in turn, were bound by oaths of loyalty to the leader of the avenging or defending force. The earliest indications of warfare as a conscious state policy are found in the quarrel of Corinth and Megara under the Megarian leader Orsippus, who was an Olympic victor in 720 B.C., and the Lelantine War between Chalcis and Eretria at the start of the seventh century.

When warfare became a collective enterprise, decisions determining war and peace were placed in the power of the largest body of the *polis,* i.e., the assembly which, after all, had developed from the united men under arms. In some city-states, the final decision may have followed directly on policy formulated earlier by officials of the state or by the members of a smaller council. In Sparta, for instance, the assembly could only affirm or deny a measure put to it by the five ephors and if the *demos* decided "crookedly," its judgment could be set aside. Still it was necessary to ask for formal ratification and, moreover, the Spartan assembly from the time of Cleomenes I at the end of the sixth century determined which of its two kings should lead the expedition.

A third function of the *polis* was the assumption of direction in matters of communal religion. As public cults grew along with the consolidation of the city-state, the *polis* was increasingly drawn into providing means of celebration and officials to direct activities. From the time of the emergence of the *polis*, religion could serve as a cement to bind the inhabitants of a certain region into a larger entity: the inhabitants near Delphi, for instance, knew Apollo in a guise different from his appearance to the Amyclaeans of Laconia. And, too, the residents of Delphi knew lesser divinities peculiar to the slopes of the Phaedriades or the waters of the Pleistus. On the other hand, the differentiation of divine power was so splintered that individual villages worshipped Artemis or Poseidon in a guise other than that of neighbors who were members of the same *polis*. Religious belief, consequently, was a centrifugal force within states quite as much as between them. It was essential to the stability of the city-states that religious identity be used as a centripetal agent and this was the goal of *polis* leaders in fostering cults whose appeal would be to inhabitants of the entire state.

During the eighth century local sanctuaries, like those of Samos and Eretria, began to show planning by the state for the purpose of honoring major patron deities. In the seventh and sixth centuries, deliberate efforts of the early tyrants began to displace private, aristocratic cults by the promotion of more inclusive cults. Early efforts, like those of Cleisthenes of Sicyon in attempting to supplant the cult of Adrastus by that of Melanippus, point to end results such as the Great Panathenaea in Athens or the Hyacinthia of the Spartans which was of sufficient force to prevent Spartan participation at Marathon. The absolute need of concluding the celebration of the festival need not be understood as an excuse for avoiding battle; *polis* religion was a true binding agent of state cohesion.

Finally, the *polis* undertook to make its territory and its citizens autonomous and self-sufficient: *autarkeia* was a declared fourth function of the state. It is true that, given the limitation of resources in Greece, this aim could not be realized and it was necessary to go beyond the boundaries of the state for necessary goods and services. Even basic foodstuffs came from outside the state: in order to support her large population of the fifth and fourth centuries, Athens was compelled to import 800,000 *medimnoi* of grain annually, or approximately 1,200,000 bushels. As trade increased throughout the Archaic period, so too was there a rise in manufacture and industry within the *poleis*. Accompanying the expanded activities and the resultant specialization of labor, new organs of regulation and control emerged. Coined money, harbors with their tolls to be levied and collected, management of city markets, control of special resources such as the mines of Laurion in Attica—all these activities required control and overseers who would be responsible to the city-state. It was not until the fifth century that a degree of sophistication developed;

nonetheless, a steady growth in communal control is visible from the eighth century when the first colonies were sent out as deliberate state enterprises.

The *polis,* then, possessed political organs to safeguard justice for its members, regulated war as a conscious state policy, assumed control over certain religious activities and developed organs to guide the management over the resources of its territory.

Organization

It is misleading to argue that the state exercised a religious function for it was, by nature, a religious entity. Victor Ehrenberg has said, "There was no real community among the Greeks that was not also a religious community."[17] The Greek view of the gods and their sense of the constant interaction between the divine and human spheres imparted cohesion among certain groups of people while, at the same time, the Greek beliefs promoted a particularism that could not be bridged during the Classical period of Hellenic history. Natural features themselves testified to the activity of the gods as, for instance, among the people of Brasiae of Laconia who could "show you the Grotto where Ino brought up Dionysos, and the level ground there is called Dionysos' garden" (Pausanias 111.24.3). Laconians may have possessed a grotto named after Dionysos, but Thebans or Athenians could counter with descriptions of groves or grottos with special characteristics in their city-states. Corinthians, Milesians and residents of all other city-states had equally precious souvenirs of the gods. All Hellenes accepted a pantheon of deities yet these divinities had enjoyed different experiences in various states and, accordingly, they received differing honors.

The identification of gods and *polis* occurred in two ways: specific cults were fostered—financially as well as ideologically—and religious responsibilities were given over to officials of the state. One of the best examples of a fostered cult is the Panathenaea of the Athenians, the chief *polis* festival for which outlying towns of Attica and colonies sent cattle and the allies provided both cattle and panoplies in honor of the goddess. Sacrificial victims were provided by the city-state for other festivals and tracts of land were designated as cult property, whose revenues furnished the costs of the sacrifices. Proper management of cults was essential to the well-being of the *polis* and, consequently, religious responsibilities were placed in the hands of regular officials. For Athens, where our information is fullest, all three major *Archons* had duties associated with cult practice. The *Archon Eponymous,* in addition to appointing the *Choregi*—virtually financial sponsors—for the dramatic performances, also organized processions: "The one celebrated in honor of Asclepius when the initiated keep watch in the temple, and the one at the great Dionysia. The latter he organizes together with ten Supervisors . . . and they receive one hundred *minae* from the public funds for the expenses. He [the *Archon*] also arranges the procession of the Thargelia and the one in honor of Zeus the Savior. He also presides over the contests at the Dionysia and the Thargelia" (*Ath. Pol.*

56.3,4,5).[18] The *Archon Basileus* had care of the mysteries, organized the Lenaean Dionysia and all torch-race contests, and, "generally speaking, he administers all the ancestral sacrifices. Indictments for religious offenses are brought before him; likewise, disputes concerning hereditary priesthoods. He gives the decisions in regard to all conflicting claims concerning religious privileges which arise between families and between priests. All actions for homicide are brought before him, and he is the one who proclaims that a person is excluded from all customary religious rites" (*Ath. Pol.* 57.1–2). Even the *Polemarch* officiated at certain sacrifices—those to Artemis the Huntress and to Enyalius—and he arranged the funeral games for those killed in war (*Ath. Pol.* 58.1). Lesser officials too had specific duties for festival celebrations: there were ten *Hieropoioi* for expiatory sacrifices "who make the sacrifices prescribed by oracle and who, when it is necessary to obtain favorable omens from sacrifices for an enterprise, make these sacrifices with the collaboration of soothsayers." There were ten annual *Hieropoioi* as well who "make certain sacrifices and make the arrangements for all those religious festivals which are celebrated every fifth year, except the Panathenaean festival" (*Ath. Pol.* 54.6–7).

The minute attention paid to religious celebration is well demonstrated by the care given to the collection of olive oil given to contestants in the Panathenaea. "This olive oil is collected from the sacred olives. The *Archon* levies it from the owners of the farms on which the olive trees grow, three-quarters of a pint from each plant. In former times the state used to sell the fruit; if anyone dug up or cut down a sacred olive tree, he was taken before the *Areopagus*; and if the *Areopagus* found him guilty, the penalty was death. Ever since the owner of the farm has been paying the olive oil as a tax, the law has nominally remained in force, but the trial has gone out of use. The oil is now a state charge on the property and is not taken from the individual trees. After the *Archon* has collected the oil that is due in his year, he hands it over to the Treasurers at the Acropolis; and the *Archon* is not allowed to go up to the *Areopagus* before he has handed over the full amount to the Treasurers. The Treasurers keep the oil in the Acropolis for the rest of the time" (*Ath. Pol.* 60.2–3).

Religion was perhaps the most powerful bond between individuals and the *polis*: an association of gods and men with a certain territory was, in large measure, responsible for the growth of the *polis* during the Dark Age and a belief in this special association explains much of the perpetuation of the particularism of the Greek states during the Classical period. As a city-state grew to its natural geographical limits, the gods of newly-incorporated regions were joined to the *polis*: a cult might be moved to the ruling city, a branch of that cult could be established in the center if it was unthinkable to move the cult entirely, or, by means of processions, a god might become a regular visitor to the successful city. The *polis* showed the deep roots of its religious foundation by assuming care for its deities through the maintenance and proper performance of cults, games and festivals.

Illus. 4: *Restoration of the Acropolis of Athens*

The *polis* was a military as well as a religious entity and therefore defense became the business of the city-state. Members of the emerging *polis* of the Dark Age were the people in arms and full citizenship continued to possess military service as an essential requirement. From the Dark Age into the Archaic period there were developments that permitted more inhabitants to take a significant role in the defense of their city-state as *hoplite* armor and tactics replaced individual combat. Indeed, once any *polis* won a temporary advantage through the new tactics it was incumbent upon other city-states—especially those in close proximity—to follow suit. Nonetheless, privilege tended, in most states, to remain with those classes who were "best able to serve the state in person and property" and even *hoplite* armor and weapons were within the means of only a minority of the citizenry.[19] Solon's ranking of the Athenian citizenry by classes stems from differences in both wealth and military qualifications. That ranking was revealed in the offices that were open to the four classes: only members of the two upper classes could hold the highest offices so that *Archons* and treasurers were selected solely from the most elevated order. It was not until 457/456 that the third order was included among those eligible to hold the archonship. There remains some question concerning the eligibility of the lowest class; even in democratic Athens, these *thetes*—or landless citizens—may not have been granted the right to hold the highest magistracies.

Protection of the *polis* was such vital business that its supervision was entrusted to the highest authorities. In the *Laws* (626 b7–c5) Plato has the Athenian ask: "As to the definition of a well-constructed city, it seems to me that you are saying that it must be so ordered that it will prevail over other cities in warfare. Am I right?" And to the Cretan's assent, "Clearly so, and I think our friend will agree," the Spartan replies, "Why, my brother, how else could I answer, the Lacedaemonians being the sort of men they are?"[20] It is instructive to recall that warfare, which in the Dark Age was the business of kings, continued to be the sphere of activity of the Spartan kings throughout the Classical period. Consequently, it would seem, the kings retained a higher level of importance within the Spartan constitution than they did in other *poleis*. Even in Athens where responsibilities were distributed among various magistrates, the *Polemarch* and later the ten *Strategoi* were entrusted with the military direction of the *polis* and, although selection of officials by lot came to prevail in Athens in the late fifth century, her generals continued to be elected. The citizen body voted on questions of war and peace in the assembly; these same citizens were liable for military service for some forty years from ages 18 or 20 to 60; they were led by the highest officials of state.

The administration of justice came to be the responsibility of the city-state, representing the collective citizenry. As in the case of military necessities, questions of justice moved from the sole concern of the head of a household or clan to the review of an outside adjudicator and finally to the sphere of official magistrates or bodies. It has been argued, quite plausibly, that the *Oresteia* trilogy of Aeschylus represents the transition from familial responsibility in the punishment of injustice to the communal assumption of jurisdiction: the Furies who have pursued Orestes for his murder of his mother are settled in Athens by Athena and their role of avengers is given over to the Council of the Areopagus.

The communal concern for jurisdiction was promoted by the codification of laws beginning at the start of the Archaic period when the art of writing reappeared in the Greek world. As the skill of writing replaced the elaborate system of the oral tradition of the Dark Age, that tradition quickly weakened since the techniques employed by a literate society differ radically from those of an oral culture. Once the oral tradition did weaken, it was incumbent upon society to preserve its most essential and treasured rules, laws and songs in another form, by fixing them in writing. Surely customary laws were preserved immediately as knowledge of them was imperiled; consequently, it is not surprising that law codes date from the early seventh century B.C.

It is unlikely that the codification sprang from demands for reform made upon the aristocratic governments of the early states by non-aristocratic elements. Although written codes were a precondition for the eventual perception of inequities, such a perception was surely the result, not the cause, of the codification. When the laws can be read and reflected upon, there will develop feelings of dissatisfaction if those laws rest upon different standards for the various orders of society. A development of this sort can be suggested for the later Archaic and Classical periods but not before. Any demands for change were met, generally, in an attempt to make the rendering of justice more impartial by involving more and more of the full citizen population in the legal process. Even in oligarchic city-states where political privilege was concentrated in the hands of few individuals, appeal to the assembly was often possible in matters of justice. Private cases, even in democratic city-states like Athens, were decided by single magistrates, but public cases which affected the whole *polis* were decided by a body which represented the entire community of citizens. In Athens this body was simply the assembly sitting in another capacity and in another part of the city; for Sparta the council of the *gerousia* held jurisdiction in criminal cases. In other words, the sovereign body of the *polis* enforced the law of the *polis*: in democratic city-states, the body was a fairly large assembly; for oligarchies, it was a council composed of a comparatively small number of men.

Citizens were both judges and jurors; ancient Greece did not know the specialized profession of attorneys. Only as late as the fourth century in certain city-states did semiprofessional speech writers make their appearance in the sphere of court cases but even then they merely wrote the speeches and took no active role in the cases themselves. Decisions were reached rapidly; even when a verdict of guilty would involve the death penalty, the Athenians rendered their decision in a day's time. Plato wished to revise both procedures for his *Republic*: three days would be allotted to capital cases and those individuals rendering decisions would be more specifically educated for the purpose.

A greater degree of expertise was called for in the establishment or revision of law codes than in their application. Greek tradition ascribed the early codes to individuals and later revisions were the work of small commissions. There is no good reason for doubting those traditions that settle responsibility for codification on figures such as Draco and Solon of Athens, Lycurgus of Sparta or Thaletas of Crete. When the Athenian code was revised at the close of the Peloponnesian War, 500 *Nomothetae*—or law-setters—were elected for the purpose; much of the actual work was carried out by expert registrars, especially a certain Nicomachus for whom the new code has been named. In vital spheres the Greeks recognized the need for expertise—and, it might be added, impartiality—that selection by lot or assignment to the competency of a council or assembly would not furnish.

The city-state placed less emphasis on its fourth function, superintendence over the economy and the finance of the *polis*. Moreover, the *polis* was not successful in developing an efficient, ongoing means of control in these matters. Its failure was largely due to the fact that it had set itself an impossible goal: in theory the *polis* was intended to provide *autarkeia,* or self-sufficiency—a virtual impossibility for any Greek state of antiquity. Since the purported goal and actual means were incompatible, the development of a state mechanism to accomplish economic aims effectively did not materialize. It is interesting to note that the difficulties of the fourth century that speeded the decline of the *polis* provoked attempts to order the regulation of resources and finances of the city-state while the earlier history of the flourishing *polis* did not occasion any such measures.

This is not to say that there was no control over finances and no officials whose responsibilities were confined to this sphere. Aristotle in the *Constitution of the Athenians* includes among the public officials chosen by lot the following: 10 treasurers of Athena; 10 *Poletai* or sellers of the property of condemned people and controllers of state contracts; 10 receivers of public debts and fines; 10 auditors and 10 assistants to the auditors; 10 *Astynomoi* who see to such matters as the hiring of flute girls, harp girls and lyre girls at proper wages; 10 *Agoranomoi* or market officials; 10 *Metronomoi* or controllers of weights and measures; 35 *Sitophylakes* or controllers of grains who regulated both the price and quality of grain; 10 inspectors of cargoes; 5 commissioners of roads. The list is impressive in its numbers and in its variety of responsibilities, but it may not be typical of most states, nor is it illustrative of sophisticated controls.

There were concerns involving the acquisition or distribution of resources held to be communal rather than individual just as the collective citizen body possessed wealth above and beyond that of any one citizen. Still, even as late as the decade of the 480s, the proceeds from a new vein of silver discovered in the Attic mines at Laurion were destined initially to be distributed among the citizens. It required the persuasion of Themistocles to convince the assembly to use the total sum collectively for the purpose of constructing a fleet of ships. The city-state funds that did exist were entrusted to the care of the gods, that is, to temples or treasuries within temple precincts. Even though bankers had separate places of business shortly after the Persian Wars if not earlier, their business was with individuals rather than states except in cases of unusual urgency when a state was forced to borrow from a wealthy banker. In addition to state funds, the treasuries had their own sacred funds which could and did serve as sources from which states borrowed.

Wealth was drawn from both citizens and non-citizens. The former were not subject to direct taxes, except in dire circumstances, paying only certain indirect taxes as, for example, market dues. The wealthiest citizens were expected to perform liturgies which entailed duties as diverse as equipping a ship or sponsoring a dramatic festival; in the best days of the city-state, liturgies were voluntary services occasioning the erection of commemorative monuments. It was non-citizens who paid direct taxes: resident aliens and foreigners paid for the privilege of residing or carrying on business in the *polis* where they had chosen to live. These individuals were often attracted to a region other than their place of birth for reasons of trade and commerce and, indeed, customs duties yielded the largest share of resources for most city-states during the Classical period. Collection of customs dues as well as taxes on individuals and city-state monopolies was done by private individuals who had contracted by lease with the *polis* to do so.

Individual enterprise characterized much of the economic organization of the Greek *polis*. Small workshops remained the rule throughout the Greek world and, even in so important a manufacture as that of pottery, it has been estimated that no more than 150 workers were employed at any one time in the production of fifth-century Athenian ware. Nor were craftsmen united by a common bond in guilds of potters, bakers and the like during the centuries of the *polis*. It is mistaken to speak of a "working class" united in any sense—socially, economically or politically. Guild-like associations did become prominent in the Hellenistic Age but only after the decline of the independent city-states. Individuals engaging in trade and commerce were similarly not associated with one another. For the vital importing of grain, for instance, only three individual figures were involved: someone who financed the venture, the dealer who often traveled with the cargo and a ship-owner who leased his vessel for a particular venture. Bankers also operated privately: most large banking concerns were known by the single name of the person who owned and managed them, aided by slaves who served in the menial tasks of weighing and storing or had more technical knowledge that enabled them to act as cashiers and bookkeepers. Even city-states that possessed unusual, highly valuable resources—such as Athens did in her silver mines—arranged to have them worked by private leasees. Officials of the *polis* were responsible for granting the leases and for receiving the rents and taxes, but the *polis* was not directly engaged in business and finance. Only in the fourth century did Xenophon write a tract proposing that Athenians develop working of the mines into a profitable, city-state enterprise.

There were *polis* expenditures: for cult and festival purposes; to provide and maintain buildings and roads; to support the military forces and operations; and, in democratic city-states, as a minimal wage in return for official public service. While many of the expenditures were annual and, consequently, could be reckoned in advance, the Classical *polis* seems to have been unaware of budgeting. Individual chests were designated for specific purposes but the *polis* lived largely from hand to mouth in meeting its needs. Extraordinary developments could mean either unusual surpluses of state funds or, quite the opposite, state deficits. The growth of the Delian League in the fifth century provided the treasures of Athena at Athens with a huge surplus—enough to provide for the Periclean building program on the Acropolis through a tithe of the sum. Shortly thereafter, the expenses of the Peloponnesian War depleted the treasury so completely that the Athenians were forced to borrow from almost any available source, including the Persians.

Foreign Affairs

The development of a multi-state division within the limited territory of the Greek world forced the *poleis* to assume another function, an equivalent of the modern art of diplomacy. City-states had to deal with one another for a variety of reasons and those dealings gradually fell under the purview of the *polis* although a systematic means of regulating foreign affairs did not emerge until the Hellenistic era. The earliest mechanisms by which the rights of "foreigners" were protected—the term included Greeks from other city-states, of course—were entrusted to the gods or were assumed by individuals. The Olympians and especially Zeus protected strangers through a code of hospitality that survives into modern times in Greece. The Homeric epics describe numerous instances where a stranger is received, bathed and fed before his hosts think of inquiring his name or his business. In addition to the unwritten code of behavior the gods provided asylum at their temples and sanctuaries; *asylia* became a means of interstate relations quite as much as it was a way of dealing with residents.

While it was the gods whose protection shielded strangers, the protection had to be provided by humans and, from an early time, individuals established ties with inhabitants of other states. Trade and simple happenstance were the most frequent causes of ties; alliances of marriage described for the "age of heroes" continued to operate during the Archaic period for the seventh and sixth centuries but disappeared during the Classical Age as citizenship depended upon birth from both mother and father who were recognized members of the *polis*. An early instance of the operation of such a tie influenced events on the plain at Troy when the Greek Diomedes and the Trojan supporter Glaukos found that they had inherited ties of "guest friendship" and, hence, they exchanged armor and agreed to refrain from combat with one another (*Il.* 6.215–236). It was this guest friendship that developed into a form of unofficial ambassadorship, or *proxenia*, where an individual by his ties with specific individuals or families of another state would represent the interests of all residents of that state when they chanced to be present or when a decision affecting that state was public business.

Undoubtedly it was traders who had most contact with other states and whose business concerns required regulation. Legal rights of the trader were recognized and agreements on the nature of legal aid furnished to "foreigners," especially those engaged in commercial activity, took shape as *symbola*. Cases involving citizens and non-citizens in conflict were treated within the legal system: the established Athenian constitution, for instance, assigned private suits involving *metics* (resident-aliens) to the jurisdiction of the *Polemarch* while the actions concerning commerce were heard in the popular courts.

The activity which occasioned the most frequent negotiation between states, as distinct from relations with individual foreigners, was warfare. Oaths were sworn and treaties were made to end warfare between states and to bring about a condition of peace. More than treaties, however, common military concerns were strong enough to bring about alliances having both defensive and offensive purposes: the Greek word is descriptive of their nature in its very simplicity—*symmachy* or joint struggle. The need of common alliance was great enough to produce associations of some size and durability—the Peloponnesian League is perhaps the best instance—yet the *symmachy* never overcame the limits of *polis* particularism by the creation of a federal citizenship. In essence, the *symmachy* revealed the power of certain states—Sparta was the *hegemon* of the Peloponnesian League—and it was this power that occasioned the formation of the association and perpetuated its existence. The *hegemon* made individual treaties with all states that became part of the *symmachy*; there were no federal officials, no federal army beyond that provided on specific occasions by the individual members. Only in the late fourth century and more noticeably in the third was *polis* mentality replaced by an acceptance of federalism; it was a tacit acceptance that the *polis* could no longer hope to fulfill all of its functions adequately. The military strength of large states such as Macedon was the most impelling reason for *poleis* to combine their armies and, eventually, their institutions.

Particularism meant that rather than attempting to preserve peace "Every state is in a natural state of war with every other, not indeed proclaimed by heralds, but everlasting" (Plato, *Laws* 1 626a). Consequently, certain forms of intelligence and counterintelligence were commonly practiced. Formal means, such as sending embassies when required, and informal means, the use of merchants, actors or outright spies, were equally familiar in the world of the *polis*. Fugitives and traitors were all too often helpful in betraying the plans of their abandoned homes, as Alcibiades and Cleomenes I demonstrate at the highest levels of Athenian and Spartan leadership.

Political Form

The specific means by which a city-state fulfilled its functions described its constitution, or *politeia*, a term that indicates both constitution and the citizenry of a city-state. The two meanings are intrinsically connected inasmuch as the composition of the citizenry did define the nature of the constitution. If only one member of the community enjoyed full powers of decision-making, the constitution was either monarchical or tyrannical depending upon the regard in which the laws were held. If a few residents were privileged above the rest, the constitutional form was regarded as aristocratic or oligarchic, a distinction being made on the sources of wealth (was it solely expressed in land or was it more broadly defined?). Where the many rather than the few prevailed in decisions, the constitution was democratic or, as charged by oligarchic opponents of democracy, ochlocratic (mob-rule).

Classical Greek historians and philosophers tended to view their constitutional history as a development from more limited constitutional forms to those based on a broader sharing of power, a gradual process of democratization. There is some validity in this view inasmuch as kingship appears to have been the normal means for the exercise of power in the Dark Age giving way to aristocracies which were dominant during the Archaic period and leading to democracies which flourished in a number of city-states in the fifth and fourth centuries. On the other hand, the scheme is artificial: kingship never disappeared from the ancient Greek world—we need think only of the Spartan kings; some oligarchies became more rather than less exclusive; democratic constitutions were not a normal development in Greece—their spread in the fifth century was largely due to Athenian imposition.

The offices and bodies of the 1500 *poleis* were not significantly different from one another even where constitutional form was not the same. In all cases there were executive officials, that is, magistrates who performed the functions once in the hands of the king—war, relations with the gods, justice. As the *polis* increased in complexity and size, its needs grew to the point that they could not be managed satisfactorily by one individual. Hence, the end of the Dark Age witnessed a multiplication of official positions and a division of responsibility. In Athens, for instance, the sole *Basileus* was replaced by an *Archon Eponymous* whose sphere was primarily judicial; a *Polemarch*, or chief leader in war; and an *Archon Basileus*, whose role was essentially concerned with religious matters. These three magistracies were soon increased to nine and eventually entire boards were created for the execution of affairs of state: for instance, the board of 10 *Strategoi*, or generals, essentially replaced the *Polemarch* in all but traditional ceremonial duties concerned with warfare. In Sparta where the two kings continued to be the major military officials of state, a board of five *Ephors* gradually assumed more judicial responsibilities, took over the presidency of the assembly, presided over Spartan discipline, received foreign embassies, controlled the mobilization of the army. In Sparta the council had jurisdiction in criminal cases. A division and multiplication similar to Athenian and Spartan developments occurred in all Greek city-states, although nothing remotely resembling a bureaucratic structure emerged.

Under all the city-state constitutions, the usual means of determining officials was by election; lot was employed extensively only in democracies and even in Athens certain official positions were filled by election. Only rarely were offices inherited as in the case of the Spartan kings, whose position was abnormal in several other respects. More of the citizenry was eligible for magistracies in democratic city-states than in oligarchies, which often set requirements such as age or wealth for the exercise of high office. At Chalcis one had to be at least 50 to serve as a magistrate and the lowest of the wealth classes of Athenian citizens probably was not made eligible for the archonships until the very end of the Classical period. Both requirements helped to distinguish those individuals who could best serve their *polis*: a wealthy, older man had the means and the leisure to devote himself to political responsibilities, while a poor, younger man would not have either means or the luxury of time. It was the introduction of pay for state service that permitted men of the lowest property classes in Athens to participate actively and regularly in the exercise of political office. This was a democratic institution, however, not to be found in the oligarchies.

In all the constitutions save those of monarchies and tyrannies, offices were annual. Democracies tended to extend this principle to all organs of government—deliberative and judicial in addition to magisterial—while oligarchies often had annual magistracies but councils appointed for life. This distinction points to the source of most effective power within the *polis*: the council was the most important element in oligarchies while the assembly played that role in democratic city-states. The oligarchic council was composed of those citizens who met the highest standards of birth and wealth and, consequently, were comparatively few in number. Since, according to oligarchic principle, these same men were best qualified to manage the business of city-state, they continued in official capacity as councillors for life. As an ongoing body, the council could effect permanent policy and generally did so, controlling both the annually-appointed magistrates who came from its ranks and the assembly of all citizens summoned to assent to decisions already formulated. Sparta is an excellent instance of the power of the council; although the assembly of all Spartans known as equals was early made sovereign in *polis* decisions, the assembly could be set aside if its decisions were judged to be "crooked" by the elders of the council who served for life.

Democracies regularly had councils, but councillors were less important to the final decisions of *polis* due to a limited duration of office and to various checks on the power of the council. The Athenian council of 500 established by Cleisthenes at the end of the sixth century changed annually, had members chosen by lot from the entire citizenry and submitted all preliminary decisions to the assembly on a regular basis for ratification or rejection or amendment. It is quite true that the business of Classical Athens would not have been accomplished without the Council of 500; it is equally true that final jurisdiction rested with the whole people and the organ that represented the *demos*—the assembly. If one met the general requirements for citizenship—as distinct from special qualifications for the holding of office—one attended and voted at meetings of the assembly. In the established constitution of the Athenians there were forty regular meetings a year with special meetings called by the generals or the supervisory committee of the Council. A catalogue of business of the assembly by Aristotle includes matters of every category from confirming magistrates in office to dealing with defense of the country, the food supply to impeachments and sacred matters. Similar matters would be brought to assemblies in oligarchic city-states, but the power of decision would be weakened by procedural policy—the Spartan Equals could only vote "yea" or "nay"; no amendments were permitted.

Parties/Factions

As an official, a member of the Council or a participant in the Assembly, one made decisions on the basis of certain interests, but those interests did not produce an ancient equivalent of political parties. Citizens of the higher property classes did form associations known as *hetaireiai* whose activities could carry over into the sphere of political behavior. Essentially, however, these groups were informal, social clubs of men possessing like interests: they were propertied, did not have to work at a craft, probably liked to drink and hunt, were concerned with helping their friends. There were a number of ways in which aid could be furnished; political cooperation was only one area of concern. Consequently we find friends helping one another into positions of honor; the basis of that aid is quite simply friendship, not a similar political philosophy. It was expected that one would attempt to hurt one's enemies: the find of numerous potsherds inscribed with the name of Themistocles and written by few hands is a good instance of a combined endeavor to exile an enemy since it is likely that they were prepared in advance by a small group of people. Still, even in such cases, it was more likely to have been personal enmity than political philosophy that produced the hatred.

There is one further element within the *polis* that might fall under the heading of "parties"; advocates of certain forms of city-state constitutions—especially oligarchs and democrats—were definitely to be distinguished from one another, by the fifth century at any rate. A tract decrying the unwarranted equality among the population of Athens during the fifth century goes under the name of "The Old Oligarch," and Thucydides recounts the attraction of the oligarchic elements of city-states to the Spartan cause in the Peloponnesian War while the democratic elements supported the Athenians. Such constitutional preferences could lead to revolutions within a *polis,* but they did not promote the rise of definite party platforms and principles.

Individuals could and did fall out of favor, not with members of a political party, but with the entire active citizen population. The size of the active citizenry varied between the extremes of an oligarchy and a democratic *polis,* but in both cases something deemed to be an injury to the city-state was judged by a body representing the community as a whole. Since the Greek *polis* involved a bond between men and gods as well as between men, an injury to the city-state could take any number of forms. Impiety to the state's gods was as injurious to the welfare of the community as was the betrayal of plans or a failure of leadership. The Spartan king Pleistoanax was condemned for failing to accomplish anything of significance in 446 when he led the Spartan army into Attica. Alcibiades, not many years later, was called to account after the stone busts of Hermes were found mutilated on the eve of the Athenian expedition to Syracuse. Both deeds were of equal concern to the city-state. Offenders were tried by the council or the assembly, generally, and, if found guilty, were exiled or given a death sentence. It may have been difficult to apprehend someone found deserving of the death penalty (the ease with which Socrates could have escaped the confinement of prison attests to this); at any rate, much of the history of the Greek *poleis* is a history of exiles—Athenian tyrants, Spartan kings, generals, historians, poets, sculptors. The Athenians developed an almost unique way of devising an honorable exile: according to the reforms attributed to Cleisthenes, the Athenians voted annually whether they wished to banish anyone from the *polis* for a period of ten years. If an affirmative vote for ostracism occurred, another session of the assembly was given over to the selection of an individual to be so banished. After the duration of the ten year period, the individual could return to citizenship, family and property left in abeyance. The formal procedure was not typical of most city-states but the tendency of permitting—or at least not preventing—convicted persons to leave the state may be described as normal.

Success/Failure

We cultivate good taste with simplicity and combine culture with manliness; and we employ our wealth rather as a means for action than as a subject for boasting. Poverty is nothing shameful for a man to confess, but not to escape it by effort is more shameful. In attending to our private affairs we do not neglect the state, and others who are engaged in business can still form a sufficient judgment on political matters. For we are the only people who regard the man who takes no part in these things not as unofficious but as useless (Thucydides II.39).[21]

The above is an excerpt from the familiar Periclean oration at the close of the first year of the Peloponnesian War. The speech glorifies Athens and the Athenians, demonstrating the superiority of this *polis* to all others. Yet the words quoted here are applicable to all city-states of the ancient Greek world and provide an excellent basis for assessing the value of the *polis* to its citizens. Above all else the city-state demanded and received direct participation; the principle of representation was increasingly employed only after the fourth century. The *polis* had assumed certain responsibilities for the welfare of its members; but, lacking an elaborate administrative structure, it demanded the time and expertise of its citizens to execute those responsibilities. For the Classical period, the identification of individual and city-state interests made possible this devotion. One should read the epitaph of the Spartans who fell at Thermopylae with a glad, not sad, voice:

Go tell the Lacedaemonians, thou who passeth by,
That here, obedient to their laws, we lie.

Not only human energies but material resources were given over to the well-being of the city-state and, consequently, the "good taste" and "culture" described by Pericles are witnesses of the success of the *polis*. It was not a surplus of resources that produced the Parthenon or the *Oedipus Rex*; rather it was an allocation of scarce resources for the needs of the communal whole. Such a remarkable display of human expression is rarely to be duplicated in the history of mankind and stands, surely, as a testament to the power of the *polis*.

The very same words of Pericles (or Thucydides) express the insurmountable difficulties of the Greek city-state. Pericles was describing the superiority of the Athenians: "Alone of the states we know, Athens, when brought to the test, turns out superior to what was imagined of her . . . ." Intensity of devotion to one *polis* had as its counterpart friction with all other states, friction that led to active hostilities throughout the whole of the Classical period in all parts of the Greek world. From the Lelantine War through the Peloponnesian and Corinthian Wars, Greek city-states fought one another. By no means was the period of the Persian War an exception to the general rule. Argos, for instance, remained neutral rather than fight alongside the Spartans.

A form of friction, *stasis,* was also endemic with each *polis*: the city-state never succeeded in incorporating the entire society within itself and only a portion of the citizens were entitled to full, active participation in all the affairs and every office of state. As a result:

> The leaders in the cities, each provided with the fairest professions, on the one side with the cry of political equality of the people, on the other of a moderate aristocracy, sought prizes for themselves in those public interests which they pretended to cherish, and, recoiling from no means in their struggles for ascendancy, engaged in the direct excesses; in their acts of vengeance they went to even greater lengths, not stopping at what justice or the good of the state demanded, but making the party caprice of the moment their only standard, and invoking with equal readiness the condemnation of an unjust verdict or the authority of the strong arm to glut the animosities of the hour (Thucydides III.82).

These too are the words of Thucydides describing the *polis* of the fifth century.

The city-state attempted to care for all the needs of its members; the claim could not be met. In economic terms, the *polis* was bound to fail since no territory of Greece could be self-sufficient. In all other respects, the *polis* could hope to suffice so long as the citizen population met its military needs, and it remained truly devoted to the peculiar manifestations of the gods associated with the territory of the city-state and recognized the equation of state and law. The demands on the members of the *polis* were immense. It is no wonder that the *polis* system was eventually incorporated and submerged within larger impersonal, territorial orders. The wonder is that its life was so long.

Notes

1. Victor Ehrenberg, *The Greek State* (London: Basil Blackwell, 1960), 94.

2. Aristotle, *Politics* 1325 b 40. See Rackham translation for Loeb ed. (London: W. Heinemann, 1932).

3. On the Mycenaean civilization see the two recent studies of J. Chadwick, *The Mycenaean World* (Cambridge: Cambridge University Press, 1976) and J. T. Hooker, *Mycenaean Greece* (London: Routledge and Kegan Paul, 1976).

4. Thorough treatments of the Dark Age—its evidence and developments—are V. R. d'A. Desborough, *The Greek Dark Ages* (London: Benn, 1972) and A. M. Snodgrass, *The Dark Age of Greece* (Edinburgh: Edinburgh University Press, 1971).

5. The description is that of L. Mumford, *The City in History* (Harmondsworth: Pelican, 1966), 147.

6. L. Jeffery, *Archaic Greece: The City-States ca. 700–500 B.C.* (London: Benn, 1976) is a recent, thorough discussion of the first two centuries of the Classical phase of Greek civilization.

7. One of the most sensible arguments concerning the decline of the *polis* is that of A. W. Gomme, "The End of the City-State," *Essays in Greek History and Literature* (Oxford: Basil Blackwell, 1937), 204–248. While I agree with the central premise that no single date such as 336 B.C. can be used to date the end of the Classical city-state, I believe that effective decline was perceptible earlier than Gomme grants.

8. Aristotle, *Politics* 1326 7 and 14 (Rackham's translation).

9. The translations of Pausanias's *Guide to Greece* are from the edition of Peter Levi (Harmondsworth: Penguin, 1971) in two volumes. Subsequent references will be noted in the text.

10. Quoted in H. Bengtson, *Introduction to Ancient History* (translated from the sixth edition by R. I. Frank and F. D. Gilliard for University of California Press, 1970), 36.

11. Herodotus, *The Histories,* trans. A. de Selincourt (Harmondsworth: Penguin, 1954; repr. 1971) Book VIII.144.

12. The figures for Athens are those of A. W. Gomme, *The Population of Athens in the Fifth and Fourth Centuries* B.C. (Oxford: Basil Blackwell, 1933), 26; for Sparta they are those of Ehrenberg, *Greek State,* 33.

13. Plato, *Crito* 52 b–c; 51 a–b (Tredennick translation).

14. *Apology* 36 c (Tredennick translation).

15. Homer, *Odyssey,* trans. V. Rieu (Harmondsworth: Penguin, 1946; repr. 1969).

16. Homer, *Iliad,* trans. R. Lattimore (Chicago: University of Chicago Press, 1951).

17. Ehrenberg, *Greek State,* 16.

18. Aristotle, *Athenaion Politeia,* in *Aristotle's Constitution of Athens and Related Texts,* trans. K. von Fritz and E. Kapp (New York and London: Hafner, 1950). Subsequent quotations are from the same edition.

19. Thucydides VIII.65. 3.

20. Plato, *Laws* (Barker translation).

21. Thucydides II.39 and, later, II.42 (MacL. Currie translation).

22. Thucydides III.82 (Crawley translation).

Chapter Three

THE ITALIAN CITY-STATE

Gordon Griffiths

The Political Setting
(Fourth to Ninth Centuries)

In central and northern Italy between the eleventh and sixteenth centuries towns acquired such power and independence as to call to mind the city-states of the ancient world. In law the independence of the Italian town was never absolute, and we should not, strictly speaking, use the term *city-state* of towns that continued to recognize, if only in theory, the ultimate sovereignty of an emperor or pope. The use of the term may nevertheless be justified, if only because it forces us to consider what circumstances could account for the phenomenon and because it encourages a comparative study of Italian and other city-states.

To explain the development of the city-state in Italy, it is necessary to take both economic geography and political history into account. Access to the Mediterranean may explain why Italian towns prospered, but it does not explain why, after the eleventh century, they developed into city-states in the north and center but not in the south. An explanation requires attention to the political history that permitted the development of a territorial monarchy in the south but prevented any national monarchy from appearing until the nineteenth century.

Italy had been the site of city-states in ancient times—Greek, Etruscan, and Latin—but these had all been subjected by the most powerful among them: the city of Rome. The administration of an empire, however, proved too difficult for the institutions of a city-state, and the Empire was created. This continued to be referred to officially as Roman even after Constantine transferred his capital to Constantinople; in Italy the emperor remained the supreme political authority. That authority was weakened but not destroyed by the Visigoths and the Ostrogoths. In the sixth century the Emperor Justinian reestablished imperial authority in fact as well as in theory throughout the Mediterranean, but only for a time. He had exhausted imperial resources to the point that it was impossible to resist the new Germanic invasion of the Lombards.

Map 4: *Italy in the Second Half of the Fifteenth Century*

The Lombards created a kingdom in northern Italy and established themselves along the ridge of the Appenines, which stretch the whole length of the
Italian peninsula, but were unable to take Rome or the coastal cities. These
retained their ties to the imperial capital in Constantinople. But the emperor
could no longer guarantee the security of Rome, much less provide the forces
necessary to drive the Lombards back. In this situation, the bishop of Rome

began to exercise an increasingly important political role. To counter the Lombards he called upon the Franks, who defeated the Lombards and made the Lombard or "Italic" kingdom part of the larger empire whose center was north of the Alps. As for the lands which the pope had undertaken to administer and to defend, these were not returned to the possession of the eastern emperor, but became the "States of the Church," stretching from sea to sea across the middle of the Italian peninsula and separating north from south. Upon the king of the Franks the pope conferred the crown of a new Roman Empire of the West, but the rulers of this "Holy Roman Empire" were not Romans but Germans and they were never able to obtain control of the whole peninsula.

The Maritime Cities
(Seventh to Twelfth Centuries)

Meanwhile the shores of the Mediterranean, which Rome had once controlled, were falling into the hands of the Arabs: Syria and Egypt in the seventh century, the whole north African coast by the beginning of the eighth, and Spain by the year 711. The subsequent conquest of Corsica, Sardinia, Sicily, and the Balearics put the western basin of the Mediterranean under Arab control. Coastal areas exposed to Arab raids were abandoned, and the population found refuge in hilltop towns or in fortifiable ports like Gaeta and Amalfi.

Amalfi was one of several southern Italian maritime towns that prospered during the centuries of Arab predominance. Like Naples and Gaeta, Amalfi was nominally subject to imperial authority. But Constantinople (Byzantium) was far away and protection from the Arabs depended much more on the strength of Amalfi's own navy. To survive Amalfi depended on her own resources and on a policy determined exclusively by self-interest. This meant trade with the Arabs as well as with the Byzantines, and on occasion, alliance with the Arabs to sack Lombard or papal territory.

After being conquered by the Lombards in 785, Amalfi rebelled in 839 and proclaimed her independence. At first she was governed by annually elected magistrates called *comites,* but then for a century (859–958) by *prefecturii* who aspired to princely power. This was attained by Sergio I in 958 when he proclaimed himself duke.

The example of Amalfi shows that the phenomenon of the city-state could make its appearance in southern Italy in the early Middle Ages when the right conditions were present. The necessary conditions were access to the Mediterranean and its commerce and the opportunity to play the greater powers off against one another: Byzantium against Rome and the Arabs against the Lombards. Events of the eleventh century were, however, to bring an end to these conditions and to the existence of independent city-states in the south, while at the same time creating the conditions for the development of city-states in the north during the later Middle Ages and the Renaissance.

What transformed the situation in the south was the decline of Arab power, beginning in the tenth century, and the Norman Conquest in the latter part of the eleventh. The Byzantines, the Lombards, and the Arabs, who had so long been occupying parts of Sicily and the south, were defeated one by one. Palermo, the splendid Moslem capital of Sicily, was captured in 1063 with the aid of the Pisan and Genoese navies. It was the scene in 1130 of the proclamation of a new state, the Kingdom of Apulia and Sicily. The island of Sicily was lost in 1282 to the Aragonese, but the mainland, known commonly as the Kingdom of Naples, survived, with various changes of dynasty, until the unification of Italy in 1861. The cities of the south were allowed to have their municipal constitutions and to be represented in the parliaments of Sicily and Naples respectively, but there was no further possibility of independent city-states.

Amalfi fell into the hands of the Normans in 1073; after unsuccessful efforts to regain her independence she was permanently subjected to the Kingdom of Sicily in 1131. Six years later, her fleet was destroyed by the Pisans.

The success of Norman knights on land depended on their alliance with the navies of Pisa and Genoa. These maritime cities had defeated the Arabs off the coast of Sardinia as early as 1015, and in the following year the Pisans had occupied parts of the island. The great event, however, was the conquest of the Sicilian capital in 1063. The gold and silver of Palermo went to the building of Pisa's cathedral, begun in the same year. It stands as the symbol of the Christian counteroffensive against Islam. In 1091 Corsica was captured, and in the first part of the twelfth century, the Arabs were driven out of the Balearics. The western basin of the Mediterranean, which had been a Moslem lake since the ninth century, was now in Christian hands.

The rise of Venice can also be better understood against the background of events in the south, although the sphere of Venetian influence would naturally be in the eastern basin of the Mediterranean. Venice long remained a dependency of Byzantium. Her commerce with the imperial capital began to expand in the ninth century, and by the eleventh it surpassed that of Amalfi. Command of the Adriatic meant a secure trade route to Byzantium and opened the way for the later establishment of an overseas empire in the eastern Mediterranean. At the same time, the development of trade routes up the valley of the Po and across the Alps to Germany gave Venice a geographical advantage for commerce with northern Europe over the southern Italian towns.

Venice did not, however, like Genoa and Pisa, collaborate with the Normans in the conquest of the south. While they were driving the Byzantines out of southern Italy, Venice seized the opportunity to gain a privileged position in the other parts of the Byzantine empire. The emperor was persuaded to extend to the Venetians privileges previously held by the southern Italian towns, nominally dependencies of Byzantium, but now overrun by the Normans. This explains the treaty of alliance which the Byzantine emperor signed with the Venetians in 1081. This treaty, in which the imperial overlord was obliged to treat the nominally subject city in terms of equality, is the diplomatic recognition of the power that Venice had attained in the course of the eleventh century.

It was also the basis for the further strengthening of the Venetian position in relation to that of her rivals in the south.

The treaty of 1081 granted the Venetians trading privileges, free of certain customs, throughout the empire. In the capital itself, they were permitted to establish a colony (*fondaco*) with the privilege of being judged by their own magistrates and under their own laws. Similar Venetian colonies were soon established in other Byzantine ports. On the other hand, a tax was imposed on the Amalfiot colony. "From the end of the eleventh century," according to Pirenne, Venice "may be said to have held a practical monopoly of the overseas trade in all the provinces of Europe and Asia still possessed by the rulers of Constantinople."[1]

The gains recorded by the Pisans, the Genoese, and the Venetians in the eleventh century were dramatically extended by the Crusades (first proclaimed by the pope in 1095). The crusading knights depended upon the Italian merchant seaman for transport and logistical support. The first Crusade was undertaken in 1096; the next year the Genoese sent reinforcements to Antioch, and in the following year they were granted the right of establishing a colony there with commercial privileges throughout Palestine. In 1104 they created a colony at St. John of Acre. King Baldwin ceded them a third of the town, a seaside quay, and part of the customs. Acre may serve as an example of the colonial system which was built up as a result of the Crusades, not only by Genoa, but by Pisa and Venice as well. Every center of economic potential (Antioch, Beirut, Tripoli, Laodicea, Jaffa, Jerusalem, Cyprus, Damascus, Caesarea, Aleppo, etc.) was forced to accommodate an Italian colony. Each was a replica of the metropolis, governed by its laws and by its own magistrates (*consuls*). The merchants there were exempt from local taxes and could attend their own church, dedicated generally to the patron saint of their mother-city.

The Christian provinces of the Byzantine empire were, as we have seen, obliged to accommodate similar Italian colonies and permit similar economic penetration. The empire fell rapidly under the influence of the Italian maritime towns, which now monopolized its import and export trade. In this perspective, the conquest of Constantinople in 1204, during the fourth Crusade, was the climax of a process that had been maturing for a century. By the treaty of 1081, the Venetians had gained commercial privileges in the Byzantine empire. Little more than a century later, they felt themselves strong enough, with the help of the Crusaders, to overthrow the political structure of the empire itself and to substitute for it the so-called Latin empire (1204–1261). Since this was really a Venetian enterprise, it provoked the opposition of the Genoese, who were largely responsible for restoring a Greek dynasty in 1261.

> The one lasting and essential result of the Crusades was to give the Italian towns, and in a lesser degree, those of Provence and Catalonia, the mastery of the Mediterranean. Though they did not succeed in wresting the holy places from Islam, and though only a few places on the coast of Asia Minor and in the islands

remained of their early conquests, at least they enabled Western Europe not only to monopolize all the trade from the Bosphorus and Syria to the Straits of Gibraltar, but to develop there an economic and strictly capitalistic activity which was gradually to communicate itself to all the lands north of the Alps.[2]

The legal relationship of the maritime towns to their respective overlords varied from the proud imperial loyalty of Pisa to the outright independence of Venice. A more compelling reason for designating them city-states is their behavior in practice. A town which maintained a navy, which established overseas colonies, and which pursued an independent foreign policy was acting as an independent state. But while colonies and a navy make it easy to recognize a coastal town like Amalfi, Pisa, Genoa, or Venice as a "city-state," other attributes must be looked for when it comes to inland towns.

The Cities of the Interior under Episcopal Leadership (Ninth to Eleventh Centuries)

Among the thousands of centers of population in Italy, some hundreds were designated as cities (*città*), and of these, some eventually acquired the independence to deserve to be called city-states. Before tackling that later development, we must first come to terms with the meaning and the role of the city in its Italian context. The jurist Bartolus of Sassoferrato (1313–1357) offers an illuminating definition:

> Towns (*villas*) are what we call those agglomerations of buildings that lack walls or moats; but such towns, or villages (*vici*) possess no jurisdiction under the common law, but are subject to some city (*civitas*).[3]

A wall, then, was a necessary but not sufficient condition, according to Bartolus, to qualify as a "city." He goes on to explain that a fortress (*castrum*), though provided with walls or a moat, usually lacked common law jurisdiction and so was like a village; although it might possess magistrates, they were placed there by the city to which it was subject.

After telling us the shortcomings of towns, villages, and fortresses with respect to walls, moats, or jurisdiction, Bartolus should next, one might think, say that a city was distinguished precisely by the possession of these characteristics. Instead, he says that "a city, in our usage of the term, is a place which has a bishop." He adds that the place had been a city, however, before it acquired its bishop. Only then does he say that

> to a city belongs the power to elect the defenders of its common law (*de jure communi defensores*), who shall have jurisdiction, though not full jurisdiction in either criminal or civil matters (*merum imperium, vel mixtum*) . . . And even a place without a bishop may be called a city, if it has the aforesaid officials, and jurisdiction.

Despite the difficulties of this passage, it seems clear that the distinguishing mark of a city is the possession of jurisdiction, and jurisdiction not only over those within its walls, but over subject towns, villages, and fortresses.

Bishops intruded into the discussion either because the Roman Church limited the use of the term *city* to those places that were the seats of bishops, or because Bartolus recognized that the city magistrates of his day were the heirs of a jurisdiction that had once belonged to bishops. Bishops originally established their headquarters in the cities (*civitates*) of the Roman Empire. When civil government broke down during the Lombard or Frankish period, bishops undertook its responsibilities, often receiving or assuming the authority of a secular count. This meant that spiritual administration of the diocese was combined with secular administration of the county (*contado*). The boundaries of the two jurisdictions tended to coincide, and both were administered from the city which was the capital of both. In the eleventh century, however, this dual administration came to an end. The bishop was deprived of his secular administration, his place was taken by the *commune*, under magistrates called *consuls*. These new officials did not confine their activity to business within the city walls but assumed jurisdiction over the *contado* as well.

Creation of the Commune

The overthrow of episcopal government took place within the context of the Gregorian reform of the eleventh century and may be illustrated by the story of Florence. At issue was the involvement of bishops in secular affairs, their resort to simony to obtain office, and their concubinage. The movement is identified particularly with Hildebrand, who took the name Gregory VII when he was elected pope in 1073. However, the story in Florence begins earlier, with another Hildebrand, who became bishop in 1008 and exemplified both the positive and the negative aspects of secular episcopal government. It was under Bishop Hildebrand and his successors in the eleventh century that the Baptistery was given its splendid marble façade in green and white geometrical design, an indication of the splendor and the wealth of the city in the early eleventh century.

The initiative in the building activity was taken by Bishop Hildebrand, who founded the monastery of San Miniato on the hill overlooking Florence from the left bank of the Arno. This monastery produced the rebel who was to lead the movement for reform in central Italy, Giovan Gualberto, who gave up a soldier's career in the time of Bishop Hildebrand to become a monk at San Miniato. The young monk did not venture to attack his patron, even though Hildebrand had obtained his bishopric by simony and was anything but celibate, but Giovan Gualberto did attack Hildebrand's successor, Atto, who also obtained his office for a price. Giovan Gualberto one day mounted a sales counter in the Florentine market place to denounce the bishop, but the crowd pursued the reformer instead, and he was barely able to escape. The people of

Florence were not yet ready to listen to the message of the reformers; they still looked upon their bishop as the personification of the city's power and glory.

Giovan Gualberto found refuge in the mountains above Florence at Vallombrosa. There he gathered followers and founded the famous monastery. He espoused the movement which had begun at Cluny and obtained the support of that other Hildebrand who became Gregory VII. He also gained support of St. Peter Damiani and of the chief monasteries of Tuscany. With such backing he was prepared to renew the contest with the bishop of Florence.

Against a new bishop of Florence, Pietro Mezzabarba, Giovan Gualberto delivered the familiar accusation of simony. This time there was sufficient popular support to force a trial. It took place at the abbey of Settimo on 13 February 1068. One of Giovan Gualberto's brothers from Vallombrosa was chosen to endure the trial by fire, and he passed through untouched. The cry went up that there had been a miraculous divine judgment. The bishop was deposed. The humble monk became a cardinal and eventually St. Peter of the Fire. In the story of this miracle, however, we may recognize the first of the revolutions that were to mark the political history of Florence. A man who had been the secular leader of the community had been deposed by a popular movement supported by Rome.

Eight years later the new movement in Florence became associated with a political struggle on a much larger scale. When the Countess Matilda inherited Tuscany in 1076, she became caught in the great battle between Gregory VII and the Emperor Henry IV. When she elected to resist the emperor, she found the people of Florence ready to stand with her and with the papal cause. They closed their gates against Henry IV. The alignment of forces against the emperor was a foreshadowing of what was to become the traditional alignment of Florence with the papacy against the empire. By this strategy of playing off the two supreme authorities against one another, Florence and other cities managed to become more and more independent.

During this same period, which also witnessed the investiture conflict between pope and emperor, a new form of government made its appearance in the cities of northern and central Italy. The bishop had sought the advice of *boni homines,* but when the bishop was relieved of his responsibility for temporal rule, a permanent executive body of elected laymen took his place. They were called *consuls;* the first surviving record of the use of the term is for Pisa in 1085, but in the subsequent four decades it crops up in many cities.[4]

The consulate was the executive, administrative, and judicial organ of the commune. Later, those who wished to emphasize their Roman heritage would use instead the term *respublica,* but it is important to remember that the medieval commune or republic was neither a democratic nor, in the first years, a sovereign institution. The *consuls* were drawn from the noble families prominent in the city's affairs: the commune was not the invention of merchants or guildsmen. All citizens, it is true, had the right to participate in the *parlamento* (or *arengo*), but this institution is not evidence of a direct democracy. It was summoned only in emergencies and to approve proposals drawn up by a more select body. Citizenship, moreover, was limited to property owners.

Nevertheless, the creation of the commune was a new departure, and the oaths taken by the *consuls* upon entering office, detailing their various obligations, may be regarded as the original nuclei of subsequent constitutions.[5]

Despite the innovative character of the consular form of government, it was in some respects a continuation of the tendencies of the previous episcopal leadership. This is particularly evident in external affairs. The bishop had sought, with the support of the citizens, to obtain respect for his claim to temporal authority over the *contado*, to match his spiritual authority over the diocese. The *consuls* inherited the temporal part of this policy. This involved the subjection of feudal lordships and rural communes. A lesser lord might be required to establish residence in the city and to swear the oath of citizenship; a greater lord might be required to sign a formal treaty of alliance. The submission of the rural commune was not necessarily an unwilling one, for the great city offered to protect the rural commune against its enemies, including its former lord.

The tendency of the Italian city to extend its authority to the borders of its *contado* has been seen as a typically Italian phenomenon to be contrasted with the government of the countryside in Europe north of the Alps.[6] There, despite the developing power of the towns, control of the countryside generally remained in the hands of a rural and feudal nobility or fell under the control of a territorial prince or national monarch. The same might be said of the duchy of Savoy or of the kingdom of Naples. But where, as in northern and central Italy, the claims of a higher authority were eventually reduced to a nullity by the contention between empire and papacy, the city gained sovereignty over the countryside. It was a situation to evoke expressions of astonishment from a perceptive observer, acquainted by experience and family connections with the workings of imperial and princely rule in Germany. Here is Otto of Freising's description of Italy:

> The entire land is divided among the cities; scarcely any noble or great man can be found in all the surrounding territory who does not acknowledge the authority of his city . . . They are aided . . . by the absence of their princes, who are accustomed to remain on the far side of the Alps.[7]

Relations with the Hohenstaufen
(Twelfth to Thirteenth Centuries)

Frederick Barbarossa (1152–1190) tried to restore imperial power, but his plan of imposing taxes and an imperial governor (*podestà*) on each city provoked the revolt of Lombard towns, led by Milan (1160–62). Milan was razed to the ground, but by 1167 a Lombard League, including a reconstructed Milan, had been formed with the support of Pope Alexander III. The Milanese and their allies defeated Frederick at Legnano in 1176 and forced him to sign a truce, which became definitive in the Peace of Constance (25 June 1183).

The Peace of Constance gave communes the right to nominate their own magistrates, to raise taxes, to make their own laws, and to try their subjects under their own laws but with the right of appeal to an imperial tribunal. In return, citizens were to swear loyalty to the emperor, and consular magistrates were to receive their investiture from him or from his representative. By this peace, Italian communes, which had been growing for a century in their *de facto* political power, acquired *de jure* recognition. The requirement that *consuls* be invested by imperial authority soon fell into disuse.

Frederick had friends as well as enemies among the Italian cities. Cremona and others that had been oppressed by Milan welcomed the emperor's intervention and participated in the destruction of Milan in 1162. In return, Cremona and other Lombard cities had received imperial privileges. In 1162 Genoa was granted exemption from imperial taxation and her right to self-government was recognized. In Tuscany Pisa was made the base of imperial authority, and the city was given the government of the whole coastal area from Portovenere to Civitavecchia.

On the other hand, Frederick sought to counter Florentine claims to jurisdiction over the countryside by encouraging the resistance of feudal nobles like the Alberti. Frederick's son, Henry VI, did recognize Florentine jurisdiction, in a diploma that gave imperial sanction to Florentine jurisdiction a few miles beyond the city walls, perhaps hoping that this definition of its jurisdiction would check its further expansion. At Henry's death in 1197, the Florentines organized a league of Tuscan cities, under the protection of the pope, to protect themselves against a reassertion of imperial power. The league was based on the recognition of each city's jurisdiction over its own *contado*. It is significant that Pisa, which had received from the emperor jurisdictions extending far beyond its *contado,* refused to join.

The climax in the effort of the Hohenstaufen to achieve imperial sovereignty came in the latter part of the reign of Frederick II. His lieutenant, Frederick of Antioch, came to establish imperial authority over Florence in 1246. Within the city partisans of the pope "Guelfs" were replaced by partisans of the emperor "Ghibellines"; beyond the walls, Florence was deprived of jurisdiction over her *contado.* This was, however, the last effective attempt to establish imperial sovereignty over the cities of central and northern Italy. Frederick II died in 1250, too early to realize his ambition, and the efforts of would-be successors were doomed to failure. It is not even clear that the future would have been very different if Frederick had lived, for the city of Florence revolted against his regime and established a new government in October 1250, three months before his death.

Before examining the revolutionary developments of the second half of the thirteenth century, we should consider the weaknesses that had become apparent since the eleventh century in the consular form of government. This was, as we have seen, representative of the town's noble families. These were extended families, or *consortia,* formed essentially to retain the collective patrimony within the family. The wealth and prestige of such a family would be exhibited in its *loggia* on festal occasions: baptisms, weddings, funerals, etc., when all its members and hangers-on would be gathered together and would be on public display, for the *loggia* was a ground-floor area whose arcades were open to the street. The power of the family was demonstrated also by its tower-house; indeed, another name for the *consortium* was *societas turris*. A tower-house was built, like the rural castle, to withstand sieges, whether mounted by a rival family or by the commune itself. The tower, around which the family's houses were clustered, might be no more than twelve feet square, but it rose to tremendous heights. In a town like San Gimignano, the tourist may still get a sense of what it was like to live in a town dominated by the fortified towers of the noble families. Neighboring towers could be joined together by bridges at the upper stories, thus enabling the families of a common faction to withstand their rivals or the communal government. Another indication of the importance of the *consortium* may be found in the criminal law: when a crime such as murder was committed, the family, and not just the individual suspected of committing it, was held responsible.

The difficulty of maintaining order in a society where families and factions were so powerful suggested the need of concentrating the executive power (*potestas, podestà*) in the hands of one man. In the course of the twelfth century, the office of *podestà* came to be generally adopted. It might seem to indicate the abandonment of the principle of communal government in favor of dictatorship and an early example of the despotism that was to be so characteristic of Italian politics in the fourteenth and fifteenth centuries. The twelfth-century *podestà*, however, did not possess absolute power, even though he combined military, executive, and judicial responsibilities. He was not supposed to initiate but to execute policy determined as in the past by the representatives of the chief families in their councils. These were especially careful to keep matters of finance in their own hands. Even in what was perhaps his most important activity, that of chief judicial officer, the *podestà* was not expected to be arbitrary but to rule in accordance with the Roman or customary law, including that enacted by the councils. He should therefore be regarded as the agent of essentially the same noble and mercantile families as had been directing the commune in the past.

The conception of the *podestà* as agent of the established noble families is confirmed by the manner in which he gained his office. It was not an illegal, violent seizure of power, like that employed by the later despots. The *podestà* was invited by the persons who sat in the constitutionally established councils of the commune. At first he was a fellow citizen, but soon it became the practice to elect a "foreigner," which meant someone from another city.

The *podestà* was an effective solution to the problem of the local vendetta, but not adequate when this was enmeshed in the wider contention between Guelf and Ghibelline. These were the names given to the supporters of pope and emperor respectively, and when all Italy was drawn into the struggle between

Frederick II and the Church, it became impossible to defend the autonomy of the city without creating a broader base of support in the people.

The Government of the People
(Thirteenth Century)

The second half of the thirteenth century was marked by the widespread adoption of regimes that professed to be based on the people (*popolo*). One factor behind this development was the death of Frederick II and the failure of his would-be successors to reestablish his power. Another was the determination of the papacy to invite the French, in the person of Charles of Anjou, brother of Louis IX, to establish a dynasty in Naples as a permanent means of preventing the restoration of German power in the south. A third was the ambition of Guelf nobles to avenge themselves upon the Ghibellines who had enjoyed the favor of Frederick. Thus the events of this half century are often seen in terms of a struggle between empire and papacy, between rival French and German dynasties, and between their Guelf and Ghibelline supporters. Such an interpretation, however, overlooks the fact that the new popular governments rested essentially upon the internal resources of the cities. Florence will again serve as our illustration.

The first popular government in Florence was actually established in October 1250, three months before the death of Frederick II. While the city was still in Ghibelline hands, the "good citizens" took up arms, elected a Captain of the People, provided him with a popular militia of twenty companies, and established a council of twelve aldermen (*anziani*), two to represent each of the city's six sections. The Guelfs had nothing to do with the creation of these institutions; they may even have been promoted by the Ghibellines in the hope of building last minute support for their regime.

"Popular" government did not imply democratic government. *Popolano* was the term used to describe the status of everyone who was not a noble, and those who held office in the new councils of the people were generally wealthy merchants or lawyers, not plebeians. When Italian chroniclers refer to the *popolo* of a particular city, they mean merely that it has a republican as opposed to a tyrannical form of government. The word *popolo* thus has something of the flavor of the French term *bourgeois*.

The creation of popular government did not mean the abolition of the institutions of the old communal government. The old communal councils, in which the nobility predominated, remained, as did the *podestà*. What happened was that "popular" institutions were now established parallel to the older and more aristocratic ones: the Captain of the People opposite the *podestà*, each flanked and advised by his respective council. The council of aldermen (*anziani*) played the leading role in determining policy under the first popular government in Florence (1250–1260). The exile of the Ghibellines did not mean the establishment of a Guelf government; the term *popular* indicates rather that the base of participation and of support has been broadened.

Nevertheless, though not a Guelf creation, the first popular government in Florence soon became affiliated with the wider cause of the Guelfs. It showed signs of moving in this direction when it exiled Ghibellines associated with the previous regime. It switched the colors on the flag. The old flag, associated with the Ghibellines, had a white lily on a red field; the new, a red lily on a white field, and this, the flag of the commune and People of Florence, just because it was the opposite of the Ghibelline, proclaimed Florentine adherence to the Guelf party.

More significant is the way in which the first popular government expanded Florentine power over much of Tuscany during its decade of rule (1250–1260). The imposition of Ghibelline and imperial rule had involved a contraction of Florentine jurisdiction in the years 1246–1250. It was natural that the new government should attempt to recover the lost ground, and by associating itself with the Guelf cause, it was able to do so. It was inevitable that the victims would be those who had espoused the Ghibelline side. Siena, Pisa, and Pistoia had to accept heavy terms. San Gimignano, Poggibonsi, and Volterra—all strategic points in the contest with Siena—were occupied. Arezzo was compelled to accept alliance. By taking advantage of the weak position of the Ghibellines, the Florentine popular government was able to attain hegemony over Tuscany as never before. In later Florentine tradition, to be a Guelf was to be for a free, independent, and powerful Florence, while to be a Ghibelline was to be unpatriotic and subversive.

Alignment with the Guelf party, rather than the popular form of government, was indeed what made Florentine expansion possible during these years. Pisa, too, had adopted a popular government, but she had been too committed to the imperial and Ghibelline cause to be able to take advantage of the opportunities opened up by the death of Frederick II.

The situation was transformed, however, when Manfred, the illegitimate son of Frederick II, reestablished his father's power over the kingdom of Sicily and Naples. Everywhere the hopes of the Ghibellines were raised. Siena saw the opportunity to avenge herself upon the Florentines and obtained the assistance of troops supplied by Manfred. At Montaperti on 4 September 1260 the Florentines were so badly defeated that the Guelfs retired to exile in Lucca, while within Florence the institutions of the popular government were abolished. Manfred restored imperial authority by installing the Ghibelline Count Guido Novello as *podestà* of Florence, and later as vicar general of Tuscany. Florence was deprived of some of the strongpoints, like Poggibonsi, from which she had been able to dominate her Sienese rival. The setback to Florentine hegemony, however, proved to be only a temporary one.

To counter Manfred, whose position in Naples and Tuscany encircled the papal states, the pope invited Charles of Anjou, brother of Louis IX of France, to take the Neapolitan throne. After being crowned in Rome on 6 January 1266, Charles pressed his army southward and defeated Manfred at Benevento on 26 February. Manfred died on the field of battle. A final threat from the house of

Hohenstaufen was presented by Frederick's grandson, Conradin. He was defeated by Charles at Tagliacozzo in 1268, taken prisoner, tried for treason, and executed. The papacy was free of the Hohenstaufen, but at the cost of establishing a French dynasty to the south.

The Angevin victory of course restored the fortunes—both political and economic—of those throughout Italy who had espoused the Franco-papal cause against the partisans of the Hohenstaufen.[8] In addition to a military success, the Angevin conquest was also a commercial revolution. Under the Hohenstaufen, commerce had been monopolized by the crown, or conceded to Pisan, Genoese, or Venetian merchants. Now the Guelfs, and particularly the Florentine Guelfs, were drawn fully into the business activity of the southern kingdom. Furthermore, the Guelf nobility was strengthened by new blood. Many merchants had buckled on armor to fight alongside their noble compatriots in Charles's cause. Many were now rewarded with knighthoods. The Angevin conquest was in this way a social as well as a commercial and political revolution.

After the expulsion of the Ghibellines in 1267, the Guelf party in Florence became an institution. Confiscated Ghibelline property was distributed, one-third for public needs, one-third as reparation to those Guelfs who had suffered at the hands of the Ghibellines, and one-third to "the Captains." The term does not refer to the captains of the popular militia. They and their chief, the Captain of the People, had been important elements in the first popular government and had been briefly restored in 1266 but were now suppressed. The Captains now designated as beneficiaries of the distribution of confiscated Ghibelline property are officers, not of the commune but of the Guelf party. The Guelf party also developed executive and legislative councils, parallel to those of the city. To house these bodies and its staff, the party constructed a palace, the Palazzo della Parte Guelfa, and as another symbol of its prestige, there was the Guelf flag, originally presented by the pope to the Florentines who had fought at Benevento. In Florence, as in other Guelf cities, the party was a state within the state.

The establishment of centers of Guelf power in Florence and other cities in northern as well as in central Italy offered to Charles of Anjou the prospect of extending his influence beyond the bounds of the kingdom of Sicily and Naples. But Charles was no more successful than the Hohenstaufen in translating nominal into actual rule. His lieutenants, at first French but later Italian, did occupy the office of *podestà*, but as we have seen, the *podestà* ruled only with the consent of the governed.

On the other hand, attempts like that of Nicholas III (1277–1280), who belonged to the Roman family of Orsini, to make central Italy independent of the Angevin were unsuccessful.

In the last decade of the thirteenth century, it was clear that the papacy would no longer serve as a restraining power against the royal ambition of Charles. This fact led the Florentines to return to the institutions of popular government.

New officers were created in 1282 called the Priors of the Guilds. They were drawn from among guildsmen and came to be elected by the captains of the twelve major guilds, but a Prior did not represent a particular guild; he represented a section of the city.

The Priorate almost immediately became the executive branch of the commune and remained so to the end of the republic in the sixteenth century. Fear of concentrating too much power in an executive may be noted, however, in the fact that the executive was a collective one (with six, later eight, members) and that the term of office was limited to two months (the whole body of the Priors who took office on 1 January was replaced on 1 March, etc.).

The Florentine Priors proceeded to promote legislation of a far-reaching character. This included a direct tax on income from real and personal property; the noble *consortia* were made collectively responsible for payment. They were also required to furnish caution money as security for the pledge not to resort to vendetta. Nobles were not to bear arms without authorization. In 1289 serfdom was abolished. This legislation has led some historians to assume that it was aimed at destroying the nobility, but the aim was probably to civilize rather than to destroy it.

The institutions of popular government were formalized in the Florentine Ordinances of Justice.[9] They are specific and technical, like the provisions of similar medieval documents, for example, the Magna Carta. They are not expressed in general principles derived from natural law in the manner of eighteenth-century constitutions. Nevertheless, since they provided the framework of the political system in Florence for the next two centuries, a framework to which Florentines would always refer when complaining against some departure from these first principles (just as Americans refer back to their constitution), the Ordinances of Justice may properly be thought of as a constitution.

The first of the Ordinances (rubric No. 1) shows that the constitution of the city rests (at least henceforth) upon the guilds (to be described later). The twenty-one guilds, "whose support is the guarantee of the defense of the city and commune of Florence," were each to name a *syndic*, and the *syndics*, in the name of their respective guilds, were to swear to uphold the Priors, the city, the *contado*, and all the Florentine people in peace and tranquillity. Another rubric set forth the method of election of the Priors of the Guilds.

Serious complaint had been voiced against the Priors for their failure to enforce the reforms they had proclaimed during the first decade of their existence. Accordingly, the Ordinances provided for a new executive officer. Just as it had been found necessary a century earlier to add a *podestà* to the *consuls*, now it was felt desirable to put the enforcement of the enactments of the Priors into the hands of a single individual. He was called the Standard-Bearer of Justice (*Gonfaloniere di Giustizia*); he was to be elected, like the Priors, for a term of only two months; he was to be chosen from the six sections of the city in turn; and he must not be of noble status. His function was to see to it that the *podestà* and Captain rendered justice to all and did their jobs of punishing crimes and preventing disorder. To enable the Standard-Bearer to carry out his function, he was supplied with a banner (a red cross on white field), a special guard, and a force of a thousand foot soldiers, to be drawn from among the *popolani* and guildsmen each February. The foot soldiers were to bear shields painted with the same device of the red cross and were to stand ready to respond immediately to the orders of the Priors and of the Standard-Bearer.

The creation of the Standard-Bearer of Justice did not, however, mean that the Florentines were resorting to the rule of one man. The Standard-Bearer sat with the Priors in their meetings over which he presided but which he did not dominate.

On the positive side, then, the Ordinances gave statutory authority to the guilds and gave them the dominant position in the government of the commune. On the negative side, the Ordinances attached corresponding disabilities to the nobility.

To enforce legislation against the nobility, and in particular to prevent their continuing to occupy the chief offices in government, it was obviously necessary to supply a definition of nobility that would stand up in court. Accordingly, in a text of 1289, we find the question squarely put: "Who should be called nobles and magnates?" And the answer:

> Those houses and persons are magnate, in which there is a knight, or has been during the past twenty years, or who are by common opinion referred to and commonly held to be *potentes, nobiles* or magnates.[10]

In the Ordinances, it is the third of these terms that is used, but as they are apparently synonyms, we shall use the more familiar English word *noble*. To remove all possibility of doubt, the Florentines drew up and published a list of the names of all the families that should be regarded as noble. It numbered some thirty-eight families (it should be noted that the names of some nobles, favorable to the popular regime, were omitted from the list, in order that they might not be disqualified for office).

Thirteen of the original twenty-two rubrics of the Ordinances had to do with the nobility. Two of them imposed special penalties on a noble who injured the person or the property of a *popolano*. Another denied nobles the right of appeal. Two other rubrics restricted a noble from acquiring the real property of a *popolano*. Equality before the law was not the spirit behind these Ordinances; the authors were reacting against an inequal system which had worked to the disadvantage of the *popolani,* and their solution to the problem was to create a new system of inequality. The clearest expression of this is the provision that nobles guilty of injuring *popolani* should be liable to double and in some cases sextuple the sanctions of the common law. Furthermore, the Standard-Bearer was instructed to proceed immediately with his forces on the mere report of such an offense to destroy the house and to confiscate the property of the accused noble. A system like this was an invitation to abuse, but it had an equalizing effect upon the social and even upon the physical structure of Florence.

The social value of destroying houses becomes intelligible when we reflect that the nobility had been able to overawe the community from their tower-houses. The populace took such good advantage of the license to tear them down that most of them were leveled in the course of the next few decades with the result that Florence no longer looks, as once it did, like San Gimignano. That city, subjected by the Florentines at the end of the thirteenth century, had its development arrested while still in the noble stage of urban history. In Florence since the fourteenth century there has been only one tower to dominate the city: the tower of the city hall, the palace whose construction was begun in the same decade of the 1290s that saw the publication of the Ordinances of Justice and whose function was the same: to strengthen the authority of the Priors of the Guilds and to enhance their prestige. Soon they came to be referred to as *Signori* and their palace as the *palazzo della Signoria* (what has been known since the sixteenth century as the *palazzo vecchio*) in recognition of their collective lordship over the city. Their tower symbolizes the victory of the public law of the city over the private law of the nobility.

Public, but not equal. The full exercise of the rights of citizenship under this government "of the people" came to be restricted to those who were members of a guild. Soon it was made illegal for a noble to serve as Prior. At the other end of the social scale, inhabitants who were not guild members had no political rights.

Population and Walls

The growth of the Florentine population in the thirteenth century is shown by the fact that the walls begun in 1172 enclosed approximately 80 hectares (197 acres) but were already inadequate a century later. The new walls, projected in 1284 and completed about fifty years later, enclosed 620 hectares (1556 acres).[11] Large sections of these walls may still be seen today. The way such walls separated city from country is best illustrated in the fresco on the wall of the city hall in Siena. The fresco, painted by Ambrogio Lorenzetti between 1330 and 1340, portrayed the effects of good and bad government on city and country.

The purpose of the walls was not only to afford protection against external enemies but to make it possible to provide internal security at night. The gates were locked and a curfew imposed. Only the few could obtain permission or afford the necessary armed escort to go about the streets at night.[12]

After the Black Death in 1348 there was no further need to expand the walls. As a result of this and subsequent visitations of the plague and of famine, the population of Florence dropped from an estimated high of 120,000 in 1338 to below 40,000 in 1427.[13] Other cities suffered comparable losses and did not regain their pre-Black Death populations until the nineteenth century.

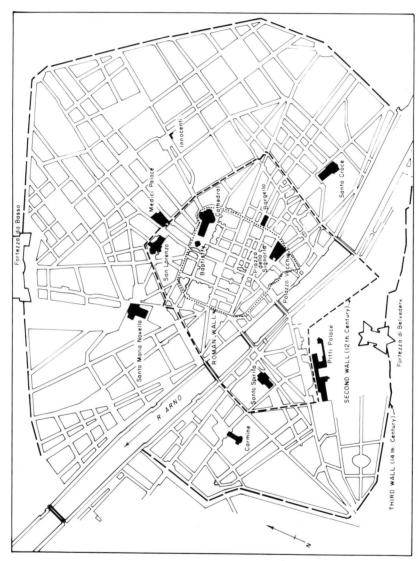

Illus. 5: *The Three Walls of Florence*

Illus. 6: "The Effects of Good Government," Siena

The Guilds

Though the Ordinances of Justice were based on the idea of a guild community, they recognized that distinctions must be made between the twelve major guilds, whose captains were to elect the Priors, and the nine minor guilds, whose members were in theory eligible, but who did not take part in the process of election until later in the fourteenth century. The guilds were then grouped in three categories: seven major, five middling, and nine minor. The major guilds were devoted to the four branches of the textile industry and to the professions of banking, law, and medicine. The five guilds of middling rank were made up of the butchers, the shoemakers, the smiths, the stone- and wood-cutters, and the second-hand clothes dealers. The nine minor guilds included the wine retailers, the innkeepers, the olive oil merchants, the tanners, the armor and sword makers, the locksmiths and forgers, the girdle makers, the joiners, and the bakers.

The reason why a particular trade was put into the minor or middling group may be obscure, but it is clear that the major seven belonged to a class apart. They included not only the members of the learned professions but all the enterprises engaged in international commerce. The middling and minor guilds, on the other hand, catered only to a local market.

Members of the major guilds were likely to be affected materially by the successes or failures of the city's foreign policy, and only they would have the external resources and experience to make them useful in this sphere. These factors, and not merely the greater weight of their economic power within the city, made it inevitable that members of the major guilds would generally have a dominating voice in the councils of government, no matter what concessions might from time to time be made to appease the demands of other sections of the population.

The guild with the most prestige in the thirteenth century was the *Arte di Calimala,* which was principally engaged in the import, finishing, and export of fine cloth, but not in its manufacture. Those who belonged to the Calimala imported their cloth from Flanders, where it had been manufactured from English wool. Before Genoese galleys established a regular service to Flanders in 1278, Flemish cloth had to be brought overland through France, and indeed it was purchased there, during the great fairs in the county of Champagne. The art of the Calimala was the process by which the rough Flemish cloth was transformed into fine material and dyed to make a luxury product very much in demand, notably in eastern markets.

Members of the Calimala guild were thus vulnerable to disturbances both in the countries from which they imported and in those to which they exported. In the Chronicle of Giovanni Villani, himself a member of the Calimala guild, there is a dramatic description of two events in 1291: the loss of Acre in Syria, which he calls "the source and port for all kinds of merchandise from East and West," and the arrest of all Italian merchants in France. Villani draws attention to the connection between these events and to their impact upon Florentine trade: "It is noteworthy," he says, "that between the loss of Acre and this French pressure, the merchants of Florence suffered great damage and loss of property."[14]

The wool guild numbered among its members the greatest merchant-capitalists of the fourteenth century. They enjoyed the usual benefits of a guild, and their constitution (*Statuti*) embodied regulations protecting them against competition, insured the quality of their products, and promoted an *esprit de corps*. When the major guilds gained a dominant position in the government of the city with the establishment of the Priors in 1282, the gain was of particular significance for the future of the wool guild, enabling the most powerful economic group in the community to protect its interests through the city's political institutions.

Only a small minority of those engaged in the activities of a major guild enjoyed the benefits of full membership. These are spoken of in the statutes as *artifices pleno jure*. The rest were *subpositi* (subjects). Not being full members of the guild, the *subpositi* did not enjoy the political rights of citizenship; they were merely inhabitants. The *subpositi* of the wool guild were subject to arrest by a special police created by the guild and to imprisonment in its own jail in the wool palace (*Palagio della Lana*), whereas a citizen would be arrested by an officer of the *podestà* and placed in the communal prison (*stinche*). There was no appeal for the subjects of the wool guild from its jurisdiction to the communal courts; the guild had its own chief magistrate, whose court was their final recourse. Like the *podestà* of the commune, the guild's chief magistrate was a non-Florentine and so was called the *Ufficiale Forestiere* (foreign officer).

The inequality embodied in the structure of the major guilds, and of the wool guild in particular, existed despite the egalitarian implications of the Ordinances of Justice. Under the latter, members of even the minor guilds had been made eligible to the highest offices. The discrimination against magnates was justified by the argument that it was necessary to make all citizens subject to the communal courts and obedient to the single authority of the city. But the Ordinances applied only to citizens. The weavers, fullers, and dyers were despised as persons who had no claim to citizenship. Many, indeed, were recent immigrants from the country. It was not difficult for the masters of the guild to drive a wedge between their subjects and the members of the minor guilds. All that was necessary was to remind the latter that to retain the reputation of citizens, they must avoid association with the proletarians of the wool guild.

The wool guild was a State within the State, as were all guilds to some degree in Florence and elsewhere, but the disproportionate size and power of the wool guild make it a special case. An institution employing a quarter of the population, which could not be called to order for its practices of employment, was able to extract special privileges from the body politic. For example, it was immune from the jurisdiction of the communal office (*della Grascia*) that supervised markets, prices, and wages. The wool workers were left to the mercies of their masters.

Twice in the fourteenth century, in 1342 and in 1378, the subjects of the wool guild challenged the system. The carders, dyers, and fullers formed their own guilds and on the strength of these claimed citizenship. They also declared their independence from the jurisdiction of the wool guild and of its hated magistrate, the *Ufficiale Forestiere*. Both these attempts to obtain freedom from the wool guild occurred during the two major political revolutions of the century: the first in the time of the tyranny of the duke of Athens in 1342 and the second as part of the uprising of the *Ciompi* (wool workers) in 1378. The timing of these attempts confirms the fact that the institutions of the wool guild and of the city were inextricably intertwined: the one could not be shaken without shaking the other.

The Companies

Within the various guilds, the Florentines organized private companies, especially for carrying out distant enterprises. The participants, grouped around a nucleus from a single family (the Bardi, the Peruzzi, the Frescobaldi, et al.), agreed to divide the profits, in proportion to their respective investments, after a term of three or four years, but usually the company was immediately reconstituted, with perhaps some change in the participation. At the end of the thirteenth century, there were some eighty companies in the Calimala guild. The participants in a particular company might, however, belong as individuals to different guilds. In this way, the company could command the expertise of specialists in a variety of trades and professions. This was especially important for the companies engaged in the purchase of English wool. The payments owing to England for the wool were balanced by the obligations owed by England to the Papacy, and the handling of the financial transactions in both directions required a banking service. Florentine companies like the Bardi and the Peruzzi provided this, thus combining banking with the textile business. The same companies made enormous loans to the king of England.

The kingdom of Naples was another important field of investment for Florentine companies. We have already seen that the Angevin conquest was financed by Florentine bankers. They continued to loan to King Charles, and to his successors, for military and other enterprises. In return, the Florentine companies obtained the right to import and export throughout the southern kingdom. They engaged, not only in banking, but in the grain trade (vital to assure Florence its food supply), in the extraction of raw materials, the manufacture and sale of woolen cloth and silks, the sale of cloth from Flanders as well as from Florence, the import of products from the Levant, the supply of furs and amber, and of precious stones to the Angevin court, of timber for the Neapolitan navy and merchant marine, of food and clothing for the army. Florentines filled the offices of the civil administration. They obtained judicial posts from which it was possible for them to look after their economic interests.

The exploitation of the kingdom of Naples, the profits gained from service as the pope's bankers, and from the far-flung operations of the textile trade, are a necessary part of the explanation of the rapid growth of Florentine wealth and power in the fourteenth century. They are also necessary for understanding the concentration of wealth in Florence and the growing power of the companies within the city's political system. The great test of the city's political system cannot be adequately explained without them.

Political and Economic Crises: 1339–1343

Communal government was everywhere breaking down under the weight of internal divisions and the mounting cost of defense against external rivals. Popular government had given way to the rule of one man—the *Signore*—not only in Lombardy but in the nearby Tuscan cities of Pisa and Lucca. Against the threat which the Ghibelline tyrants of these cities posed to Florence, the Florentines had more than once invited a member of the Neapolitan royal house to assume the *Signoria* of their city. In 1341 another crisis prompted them to turn once again to that quarter for help. This was to be their one experience of despotic government, and the story is worth telling for it shows how the institutions of popular government could break down even in a city which boasted of its devotion to freedom. It is true that the despotic regime lasted for less than a year and that Florence, unlike most of the cities of northern and central Italy, was able to restore and maintain the structure of republican institutions, but these considerations do not deprive the Florentine case of general significance. Indeed, we may hope to gain a better understanding of the general tendency toward despotism by examining the special case of Florence where it was reversed.

The crisis arose out of contention over Lucca. After the death of its tyrant, Castruccio Castracane in 1328, the Florentines entered into an alliance with Naples, Verona, and others against the emperor. All the allies gained their objectives except Florence, which was to have acquired Lucca. Instead Lucca fell into the hands of the man who had made himself *Signore* of Verona: Mastino della Scala. He illustrates the growth of signorial power in Lombardy for he had already subjected ten neighboring cities to his dominion. He offered to sell distant Lucca to the Florentines if they would assist him in the conquest of Bologna. The Florentines preferred war.

To finance the war "ten wise merchants of the major companies" were given full powers to adopt necessary measures. They doubled the rate of most of the *gabelles*, the indirect taxes on which Florence usually depended for revenue. Even the increased *gabelles* did not suffice and so, Villani says, the ten "took it upon themselves to furnish the money for this enterprise for the duration" in a series of 100,000 florin loans.[15] The companies raised a third of these loans from their own coffers and obtained the remaining two-thirds from their fellow citizens, who were levied in accordance to their wealth. The commune promised to pay fifteen percent interest. If the citizen did not have the ready cash to lend, one of the companies would advance it for him and collect the fifteen percent from the commune plus five percent from the citizen. This profitable scheme was successful in financing the war. After the first hundred thousand was spent, another loan was floated, so that each month Florence was able to send their Venetian allies the money necessary to maintain the cavalry and infantry.[16]

The Venetians, however, had no interest in pursuing the war for the aggrandizement of Florence and in 1338 made a separate peace with the lord of Verona before Florence had acquired Lucca. Florence was forced to accept an unsatisfactory peace with him in the following year. Collapse of this war effort as well as the bankruptcy of Edward III financially exhausted the major financiers of Florence, especially the Bardi and Peruzzi. A recent historian has interpreted the armed insurrection led by the Bardi in 1340 in this larger context: the Bardi were motivated by the immediate purpose of avoiding bankruptcy and could not see how to do this except by overthrowing the government.[17] The attempt in 1340 failed but it helps to explain the crisis of the following year when Florence was too slow to anticipate Pisa in taking Lucca. Mastino della Scala, facing revolt in Parma, had offered to sell Lucca to Florence or Pisa, but the popular government of Florence could not move with the speed of signiorial states in the game of territorial expansion.

The Florentines now turned to the very emperor, Ludwig of Bavaria, against whom the allied war of 1332 had been fought. The betrayal of Guelf principles destroyed the old alliance with the Angevins and provoked an anti-Florentine reaction in Naples. There was a run on the Florentine banks, which the king did nothing to stop. The Buonaccorsi failed and carried some of the smaller Florentine companies down with them. The big three—the Peruzzi, the Bardi, and the Acciaiuoli—held, but as the panic spread, they turned for salvation to a military savior in the person of Walter of Brienne, who from past Angevin enterprises in Greece bore the now empty title duke of Athens.

Athens's original commission, dated 31 May 1342, was to serve as Protector and General for the limited period of one year. On 8 September, however, a coup d'etat took place, and his new commission made his rule absolute and permanent. In fact it lasted less than a year, until August 1343. So strong was the Florentines' love of liberty that they were able to reverse the almost universal tendency to surrender to signiorial rule. An analysis of the elements originally behind the duke and of those eventually involved in his overthrow seems however to yield a more consistent explanation of Florentine political taste.

The duke of Athens was encouraged to execute his coup d'etat, Villani tells us,[18] by some of the nobility who wanted the Ordinances of Justice abolished, by the companies who wanted to be relieved of the obligation to pay their debts, and by the *popolo minuto*, tired of the war and of the taxes imposed to pay for it. With his new powers, Athens was able to satisfy his supporters' demands. He signed a peace with the Pisans on 9 October (leaving Lucca in their hands). He broadened his support at the bottom of the social scale by authorizing the fullers and dyers of the woolen industry to form their own guild. The Bardi, exiled since the abortive uprising of 1340, were invited to return. The companies were granted a three-year moratorium on their debts.

The satisfaction of particular grievances did not, however, provide a solution to the problem of the city's finances. Its debt had grown to 800,000 florins by 1342 from a mere 50,000 at the beginning of the century. More than half of the debt was owed to those who had made loans (*prestanze*) at fifteen percent. The drastic measure adopted by Athens on 20 November was to suspend the interest payments. This was a measure that hit both individual citizen bond-holders and the companies that had participated in the loans.[19]

Having reduced the flow of payments out of the treasury, Athens next introduced an equally radical measure to increase the flow of revenue into it. The city ordinarily obtained most of its revenue from the *gabelles* (indirect taxes on imports, etc.). These, however, were now yielding only 200,000 florins, as compared with 300,000 a few years before. Athens resorted to a source that had been rarely attempted in the past: the *estimo,* a direct assessment on capital and income.

The same men who had lost the interest owing to them on their loans to the city were hit again by the direct tax on their capital and income. They had allowed the suspension of their political liberty but took a different attitude toward the duke's fiscal policies.

The duke of Athens was not overthrown by a spontaneous uprising of the people. Three separate conspiracies prepared the action, and the leadership of each came from the big merchant-banking families. A provisional government of Fourteen, including both nobles and *popolani,* was established, but it was composed almost entirely of directors or shareholders of the companies.

Representation of the nobility offered the prospect that they might recover access to high office denied them by the Ordinances of Justice. Spokesmen of the middle and minor guilds responded by demanding a return to the Ordinances, and on this issue the provisional government of the Fourteen foundered. On 24 and 25 September 1343 a pitched battle took place. The leader of the party favoring the nobility was Piero dei Bardi, the man who had led the conspiracy against the old regime in 1340 and who had been a supporter of the duke of Athens. The *popolano* party was led by a Medici. The nobles were decisively defeated; twenty-two palaces belonging to the Bardi were sacked and burned. Other noble families, such as the Frescobaldi and the Donati, were exiled for fresh conspiracies.

After their brief encounters with monarchical and aristocratic rule, the Florentines returned to their so-called popular regime. This involved once again the exclusion of both the nobility and of the woolen workers, whose guild was abolished.

Consolidation of the Public Debt: The Monte

The *popolano* government had to face the fiscal problem that Athens had only postponed. First they recognized the public debt, which Athens had in effect repudiated. Then, in 1348, they created a novel institution: the *Monte Comune*.[20] In it the previous debts (*prestanze, gravezze, decimi,* etc.) were consolidated. The new consolidated public debt carried an interest rate of only five percent, as compared with the old fifteen percent, and the notes issued by the new institution were made negotiable. The *Monte*—what in later centuries would be called a state bank—gave the investing classes a permanent stake in the Florentine state; in the long run, it provided economic and political stability.

In the shorter run, however, the decisions of the government spelled disaster for the old companies and their way of doing business. The moratorium that Athens had granted to save them from their creditors was not renewed. They could no longer look forward to extravagant returns on loans to the treasury. Now they were exposed to the full force of their creditors' demands. The Peruzzi were the first to fall, followed by the Acciaiuoli, the Bardi, and many smaller companies and individuals. On the other hand, capitalists who had made their entry into the financial world more recently, like the Medici and the Strozzi, found it possible to adapt to the new fiscal system.

Oligarchy in Florence and Venice

The men who governed Florence between 1343 and 1375 turned to new devices for the security of the regime. A law of 1346 provided that

> no naturalized foreigner, if he, his father and grandfather had not been born in Florence or in its *contado*, could hold any office, even though he had been eligible and had in fact been elected.[21]

Villani tells us that the real motive for this was to exclude the "new men," who had been immigrating in large numbers from the countryside, on the pretext that there might be some Ghibellines among them. A measure of 1347 excluded any Ghibelline from being elected if he, his father, or any relative since 1301 had been a rebel against the commune and required proof that he was a true Guelf. "There is no law more dangerous to the Republic," Machiavelli commented, "than one like this, which concerns actions so far in the past."[22] It put a powerful weapon into the hands of the faction in power. During most of the years between 1343 and 1375 Florence was in fact ruled by a faction—led by the Albizzi—which was able to keep control by making use of anti-Ghibelline laws like those described above.[23] A troublesome critic could always be denounced as a "Ghibelline."

Another device by which the Albizzi suppressed opposition was the Admonition. By a vote of four of the six captains of the Guelf party, any citizen might be warned (*ammonito*) not to accept office. Based upon anonymous accusations of Ghibellinism and offering no opportunity for trial, this procedure was more efficient than that which had required trial in the communal courts.

Thus the government "of the people" that the Florentines had established in the thirteenth century came to be dominated in the middle of the fourteenth century by a faction through the instrument of a party.

The justification offered was that the Guelf party was the only guarantee of religion and liberty. Defenders of the regime could point to the communes in Lombardy and in Tuscany that had been overthrown by a Ghibelline despot.

Venice, the one republic in the north that did survive the general tendency toward despotism, is often seen as an opposite to Florence. While Florence was marked by contentiousness, popular government, and frequent revolutions, Venice was known for its conservatism, its aristocratic exclusivism, and the stability of its constitution.

The basic institution in Venice from the end of the thirteenth century onward was the Grand Council. Before this, Venice was theoretically governed by an elected *doge* and by a popular assembly, but in fact the *doge* dared not act contrary to the advice of the leading men, drawn from the prominent families who controlled the assembly. This was the outcome of the last violent revolution, in 1172, when the *doge* was assassinated. The powers of the *doge* were also limited by various councils; the largest was the Grand Council, which before 1297 numbered as many as five hundred.[24]

Between 1297 and 1323 the structure of Venetian government was further modified and given the form that would remain unchanged for five hundred years. The powers of the *doge* were even more carefully defined, and the assembly of the people sank into insignificance. Between these two extremes, the Grand Council had its membership enlarged to between one and two thousand. In 1323 it was declared that membership in this body should be limited to those nobles whose ancestors had already been represented in it. This is the meaning of the term *serrata* (literally: lock-out). The Senate and the other councils were elected by and from among the members of the Grand Council.

The Venetian system thus limited office to the nobility, while the Florentine Ordinances of Justice, adopted in the decade that saw the beginning of the Venetian reforms, made the nobility ineligible for the highest offices in the Florentine state. On the surface, the two republics were moving in opposite directions.

In fact, however, the Albizzi in Florence had managed to keep control in the hands of those who were being called a "second nobility" of wealthy and aristocratic *popolani*. And if *poplano* status was a mask for aristocratic behavior in Florence, the reverse could be said of Venice. "For," as Machiavelli pointed out:

> the gentlemen of Venice are so more in name than in fact; for they have no great revenues from estates, their riches being founded upon commerce and movable property, and moreover none of them have castles or jurisdiction over subjects, but the name of gentleman is only a title of dignity and respect, and is in no way based upon the things that gentlemen enjoy in other countries.[25]

Both republics, then, were dominated by a minority of wealthy merchants.

Another similarity may be seen in the devices adopted by the two regimes for eliminating unwanted opponents. The Venetian Council of Ten, which acquired such notorious fame for its practice of passing judgments on the basis of anonymous denunciations, was exercising a function essentially similar to that exercised by the captains of the Florentine Guelf party. The Venetian institution is more famous, perhaps because it lasted so much longer and perhaps because it came to use its power to control the conduct of domestic and even foreign affairs.

Though elective office in Venice was open only to those who called themselves nobles, offices in the bureaucracy were open to non-nobles, provided they were *cittadini originarii*. In this restriction we may detect the fear, so strongly felt in Florence, that "new men" might undermine the institutions of the republic.

In Florence, however, a reaction against the Albizzi faction and against the tyrannical practices of the Guelf party set in. During the years 1375–1378, "new men" were dominant in the councils of government. These were the years of the "War of the Eight Saints" against the papacy, a war that the exponents of traditional Guelf principles could hardly have been expected to lead.

The conclusion of the war was followed by the revolution of the *Ciompi* in 1378, and this by three years of a so-called democratic regime, based on the lesser guilds. The Albizzi and other leaders of the Guelf party were meanwhile in exile. When they returned in 1382, they were able to construct a regime quite different from that of the period 1343–1375.

The regime established in 1382 lasted until the advent of the Medici in 1434, or, if we consider that the Medicean regime was not a reversal but a perfection of its principles, until the end of the republic in 1532. From 1382 onward, political power was openly concentrated in the hands of the wealthy men who were members of the major guilds. Since the representation of minor guildsmen was sharply restricted, first to three and then to two in a priorate of nine, it was no longer necessary to prevent such elements from acquiring a dominant position through constitutional means, and thus no longer a need for "anti-Ghibelline" laws or for the admonitory machinery of the Guelf party.

The number of men from the major guilds who participated in the priorate in the years after 1382 was unusually high; at the same time participation from the middle and lesser guilds was restricted. We should not, therefore, speak of Maso degli Albizzi, the most influential figure of the regime, as a tyrant, but we can say that the stability of the regime rested on an exclusivism like that of the Venetians, even though the Florentine exclusivism was less complete and less durable.

The Florentine Territorial State

Cities like Florence originally sought to extend their jurisdiction, as we have seen, to the boundaries of the *contado*, which coincided approximately with those of the bishop's diocese. Soon, however, the commune began to annex neighboring land to the *contado*. When—in 1125—the Florentines conquered Fiesole, on the hill above them, they added its *contado* to their own. In the fourteenth century they expanded its boundaries up the Arno, at the expense of Arezzo, and down the Arno by annexing the diocese of Prato and a large part of Pistoia's diocese, as well as places that had belonged to the diocese of Lucca— though the attempt to conquer Lucca itself, during the wars of the decade 1332–1342, was a failure.

Beyond the bounds of the expanded *contado*, the Florentines conquered territory that they designated as belonging to their *distretto*. Whether a given place was assigned to *contado* or *distretto* seems to have been determined by administrative considerations or else by the original terms of annexation. Territory added to the *contado* was administratively annexed to one of the four quarters into which the city proper was divided. Annexation to the *contado* therefore meant treatment according to the Florentine laws governing the rest of its *contado*, including subjection to the *estimo*, the direct tax on real estate. Communes of the *distretto* retained the privilege of being governed by their own laws.

By 1427 Florentine territory as a whole covered 11,000 square kilometers, but of this only 4930 square kilometers belonged to the *contado*. Some of the increments had been very large; the addition of Cortona had added about 350 square kilometers; that of Volterra, 800; that of Pistoia, almost 900. The largest additions were those of Arezzo in 1384 with about 1500 square kilometers and of Pisa in 1406 with 2000 square kilometers. Florence now possessed almost all the northern half of Tuscany; in all Tuscany, the only important states still independent were Siena and Lucca. The duchy of Milan was not as extensive: only 7200 square kilometers (in 1542); the Genoese republic even less so: 6000 square kilometers.[26]

When a whole city-state like Pisa or Arezzo entered into the Florentine dominion, it brought with it its own very considerable *contado*. Or rather, the disposition of that *contado* was part of the process of effecting the subjection of the parent city. The future of the ex-subjects of a conquered city may be illustrated by the arrangements worked out with Castiglione, a dependency of Arezzo until the latter's surrender to Florence on 27 October 1384. The new status of Castiglione was set forth in a document dated 10 December. Thereafter the inhabitants and territory of Castiglione were to enjoy the protection of Florence. To assure this, the Florentines would send a *podestà*, who must be a Florentine and a Guelf, to serve a six-month term, with both civil and criminal jurisdiction (with *imperium merum et mixtum*). But the *podestà* was to swear, upon entering upon his office, to respect the present and future statutes of Castiglione, and his stewardship was subject to audit by judges elected by his subjects at the end of his term. He was to be paid by the Castiglionesi, but elected by the Florentines, from among members of the major guilds or the independently wealthy. Florence was to impose no tax. Castiglione would elect its own priors and other officials, and make its own laws, provided only that they not conflict with the present contract. Castiglionesi were to be treated in Florentine territory like Florentine citizens, except that they must recognize the jurisdiction over them of their *podestà*.[27]

The contract between Castiglione and Florence shows that the Florentines were willing to make concessions to their prospective subjects in order to detach them from their recent Aretine rulers. The whole Aretine *contado* was similarly reorganized under contracts that bound its villages and castles to Florence instead of to Arezzo.

The Distribution of Wealth in Florence and Its Territory

A detailed assessment (*catasto*) of the wealth of Florence, its *contado* and district was carried out in 1427. The fortunate survival of this vast mass of data and its analysis with the aid of computers by Herlihy and Klapisch has provided us with a profile of Florence's economic and social structure that is statistically based as no profile of any other community before the industrial revolution can be. The authors have been able to offer, among other things, tables showing the distribution of wealth within Florence and between Florence and its dominions.[28]

Within Florence, 14 percent of the households had no reportable property and another 31 percent none that was taxable after deductions. At the other end of the social scale, 1 percent (100 families) possessed more than 25 percent of the total wealth of the city and one-sixth of the wealth of the whole territory. This one percent owned more than all the inhabitants of the six secondary cities and more than the 37,000 families living outside town walls. Two-thirds of the wealth of the territory was owned by the 14 percent who resided in Florence.

The advantage of residing in Florence is revealed by the figures that show the average Florentine household possessed property valued at 1022 florins (before deductions), while the average household in one of the secondary cities possessed only 257 florins' worth (four times less), and the average rural peasant household possessed about 60 florins' worth. The rural peasant was thus, on the average, twenty times less wealthy than the Florentine city-dweller. Such averages of course conceal the concentration of wealth within Florence; if we took this into consideration, the contrast between the peasant and the wealthy Florentine would be even greater.

Only a quarter of the real estate of the *contado* was still in the possession of those who resided there (the *contadini*); something like three-quarters of it belonged to Florentine residents. If we include the district beyond the *contado*, Florentines had come into possession of 51 percent of the whole. This percentage rose even higher in the course of the fifteenth century. But real estate was not the favorite form of Florentine investment.

Taking Florence, its *contado* and district together, Herlihy and Klapisch report (Table 29) that the 14 percent of the population that lived in Florence owned, in addition to the 51 percent of the real estate of the whole, 78 percent of the personal property (movable wealth, i.e., commercial and industrial property), and ninety-nine and seven-tenths of the public debt.

The figures on the proportion of urban wealth invested in commercial and industrial property show how economic domination accompanied political domination. In Florence 59.6 percent of the wealth was invested in movable property, as compared with 42.7 in Pisa, 33.5 in Arezzo, 27.1 in Pistoia, etc.

The Venetian Territorial State

Until the opening years of the fifteenth century, Venice refrained from acquiring territory on *terra firma*, but upon the dissolution of the Viscontean empire (see below), the whole area between the Tagliamento, the Adige, and the Alps fell into Venetian hands, including the cities of Vicenza and Padua. Eventually Venetian dominion extended to within 32 kilometers of Milan at Lodi. The appearance of this vast Venetian territorial state was the major novelty on the Italian landscape in the fifteenth century.

The Venetians adopted a policy similar to that of the Florentines with regard to conquered cities. Local autonomy was conceded to them but was subject to Venetian intervention. The subject city was deprived of its *contado,* and the Venetians established elaborate regulations to protect the communities in the *contado* in the enjoyment of privileges guaranteed to them.

The Venetian and Florentine systems of territorial rule were both put to the test by the shocks of the French invasions, as Sergio Bertelli has pointed out. Pisa took the opportunity to rebel against Florence in 1494, Arezzo in 1501. The cities subject to Venice rebelled in 1509:

> Three different cases, but with three identical results. Each time we find the citizens of Pisa, of Arezzo, of Verona, of Padua, of Vicenza rising against the dominant city; each time we find the *"contadini"* of their respective *contadi* breaking away from their respective cities, in favor of Florentine or Venetian dominion.[29]

The Viscontean State

The territorial state in northern Italy was, except in the case of the Venetian Republic, the creation of signiorial governments. The largest and the most enduring was built by the Visconti of Milan in the fourteenth century. Under their Sforza successors, it lasted until it was taken over in the sixteenth century, first by the French and then by the Spanish.

Communal government had already given way to the signiorial by the middle of the thirteenth century, but the significant process of expansion began with the accession of Azzone Visconti in 1329. During his ten-year rule, Azzone was able to extend his dominion to Como, Lodi, and Vercelli, all in 1335; to Piacenza in 1336; and to Brescia in 1337. The process continued under his successor, the Archbishop Giovanni, who acquired Asti in 1342, Parma in 1346, Alessandria and Tortona in 1347, and Bologna in 1350.

The wealth of Milanese resources and the unlimited power which the Visconti had arrogated to themselves explain the rapidity of the Visconti advance only in part. Account has also to be taken of the decadence of communal government. It was in the hands of a narrow oligarchy and torn, like Italian cities elsewhere, by faction. Under an inequitable system of taxation, it was difficult to find the revenues necessary for defense.

The Visconti promoted the image of being above faction and of being the defender of the people. He had no toleration for opposing factions or for those who were reluctant to pay taxes, but he did offer order, peace, and security. There were partisans of the Visconti in every city, ready to argue the advantages that Viscontean rule would bring. Surrender to the Visconti was a confession of the failure of communal government and not merely the result of external force.

Gian Galeazzo Visconti (1378–1402) embarked upon a course of aggrandizement that came close to creating an Italian kingdom. He began in 1387 with the conquest of Verona. Gian Galeazzo's diplomatic strategy was an obvious but successful one. Behind the back of the Scaligers, he secured the alliance of the Carrara of Padua and then took possession of both Verona and Vicenza, obliterating the Scaliger State. Next it was the turn of the Carrara in Padua. This time Gian Galeazzo made an alliance with Venice for the partition of the possessions of the Carrara that lay between them, securing Padua for himself, and rewarding Venice with an area north and west of Venice known as the Trevisan Mark, which Cangrande had once conquered for Verona.

Gian Galeazzo's conquest of Verona, Vicenza, and Padua was something more than the addition of three cities (with their subject territories) to his dominions. He had within a few months eliminated two of the largest and oldest signiorial states of northern Italy. After his death, as we have seen, these cities fell to Venice. The process by which the lesser states were swallowed by the greater was not easily reversible; it may therefore be said that Gian Galeazzo was largely responsible for creating the system that emerged in the fifteenth century in which political power in Italy was distributed among five territorial states: the kingdom of Naples in the south, the papal states and the Florentine Republic in the center, the duchy of Milan and the Republic of Venice in the north.

The outcome was not what Gian Galeazzo had intended. The logical end of his career would have been the creation of a monarchy for all of Italy north of Rome. Instead, he was driven, either by his own ambition or by the resistance of the Florentines, to extend his dominion across the mountains into Tuscany. His influence was strongly felt in Pisa and Lucca, where—in both cases—communal had given way to signiorial government. By 1399 Gian Galeazzo took over Pisa directly by purchase from the incumbent ruler, and later in that same year he acquired the city of Siena by the outright gift of its citizens. The Pisans had had no choice in the decision of their *Signore,* but the Sienese had retained their representative institutions; moreover, a choice was presented to them: either to make peace with Florence, whose expanding territory threatened

Siena with encirclement, or to seek the protection of Gian Galeazzo. By a majority vote in their General Council, they chose the latter course.

The terms[30] under which Gian Galeazzo acquired dominion over the Sienese Republic are interesting; indeed the Sienese were able to attach conditions to their surrender. These were drawn up in thirty-two *capitoli*, or articles, which were then approved by Gian Galeazzo with some modifications on 11 December 1399 and ratified by the General Council of Siena on 26 December by a vote of 347 to 102. Gian Galeazzo's dominion was thus limited by a formal constitution. By the first of the articles of 1399, Gian Galeazzo agreed that the government of Siena would remain in the hands of its Priors and of its Captain of the People and that these officers would retain the powers they possessed before the transfer of dominion, except for what was specified in the subsequent articles.

One of these had to do with taxation. It promised that the duke would not levy any tax or other imposition upon the citizens or inhabitants of the city, the *contado*, or the district of Siena. (The Florentines likewise refrained from taxing the subjects of their district.) Another article provided, however, that a ducal officer must be present at sessions of the city's treasury officials, to "keep record of all revenues and expenditures of the Commune, and to make sure that receipts and payments of money are in order."

Supervision of foreign relations was assured by the installation of a ducal chancellor, who, alongside the city's own chancellor, must sign all letters and decrees issued in the name of the Priors.

Supervision of local government was further provided for by the presence of a lieutenant representing the duke. The lieutenant was to be present at all functions of the commune and at all meetings of the Councils, although he was to "have only two votes in any of these meetings of Priors and Councils, so that his two votes will count no more than those of two Priors."

Gian Galeazzo was given the appointment of the governors of castles and fortresses in the *contado* and district, and the Sienese can hardly have been surprised by this, since the purpose of the whole negotiation had been to make the duke responsible for their defense. What is striking is the benefit the Sienese expected to gain from the arrangement. By Article XX:

> The duke shall be obliged to preserve, defend and maintain in their obedience all those lands, castles and places in the *contado* and district presently in the obedience of Siena, and indeed to increase the city's powers and jurisdiction over all of these to the extent they should be. He shall not sell, or otherwise transfer the city of Siena, its *contado* and district, or any of the lands, castles and places above-mentioned.

Thus, by the very act in which they signed away their independence, the Sienese contrived to stipulate that the city would retain its district as well as its *contado* and that with the help of their new ruler their jurisdiction over their subjects would become even more complete. The Florentines and the Venetians, as we have noted, sought to deprive their subject cities of their *contadi,* hoping in this way to make the latter dependent on the metropolitan city and at the same time to weaken the subject city. In his arrangement with Siena, Gian Galeazzo took an exactly opposite course. The tendency toward centralization seems in this case to have been much stronger in the policy pursued by the two republics than in that of the duke of Milan.

The relations between Siena and Gian Galeazzo were further defined by the additional Ordinances he issued on 16 March 1400 to govern the conduct of his lieutenant. He was to attend all city Councils, but to be "the last to offer his counsel, because, if he were the first, the citizens might out of fear or respect refrain from giving their real opinions." He was to see to it that no action contrary to the ordinances, statutes, or customs of the city was taken. He was not to accept gifts of wood, wine, grain, or other things from the citizens; on the contrary, he was to pay what he owed in *gabelles* like everyone else and so were his officers and soldiers. The Florentines must have been mistaken when they described as a tyrant the man who required his lieutenant to protect his subjects' freedom of speech and to guard their constitution against violation! The promises made in these Ordinances were, of course, an uncertain guarantee of their being observed in fact and we shall never know how good Gian Galeazzo's promises would have turned out to be, since he died in 1402, too soon to provide an adequate test. Nevertheless, what these documents make clear is that he and his advisers were interested in the principles that should govern the relations between central and local government. This comes out clearly in the Ordinance that provided:

> In matters concerning the Commune and the City, and not the State, (the Lieutenant) shall let the citizens do as they wish in accordance with their own ordinances and customs.

The explicit distinction between the State (*stato*) and the City seems to justify Burckhardt's famous assertion that something new in history had made its appearance: the State as a calculated conscious creation, as a work of art. We must however observe that the conception is restricted to the central government and that the same restriction applies to the rest of Gian Galleazzo's dominions, old and new. They were a collection of cities rather than a State in the modern sense. The only institution they shared was Gian Galeazzo himself. Each of the original fourteen (eventually twenty) cities under his dominion proclaimed him its *Dominus (Signore).* Each, like Siena, agreed in its contract with him that he might be represented by a lieutenant.

Gian Galeazzo did not attempt, as had Florence and Venice, to broaden the base of the central government at the expense of the cities. On the contrary, he sought to exercise power indirectly over the countryside through these cities. He did have a ducal chancery, and he did establish certain councils with competence over more than one city. Such administrative institutions do not necessarily qualify even as embryonic elements of the modern, centralized, territorial State. To see in Gian Galeazzo the precursor of Napoleon is to overlook the work of the French Revolution. Gian Galeazzo began the building of the cathedral of Milan which Napoleon carried to completion, but Gian Galeazzo never contemplated conferring a common citizenship upon his various subjects, nor did he dream of giving his collection of cities a common legal code. To find his legislation, indeed, one must consult each city's collection of statutes. To have effect in all his dominions, an act of Gian Galeazzo had to be enacted and registered among the statutes of each city separately.[31]

Florence under the Medici, 1434–1494

The glories of Florence in the fifteenth century have prompted students to wonder if they were in some way attributable to an economic or political revolution. It is now agreed, however, that her economic and political institutions remained essentially what they had been since the thirteenth century. When Cosmo de' Medici, returning from exile in 1434, inaugurated Medici rule, he did so without assuming a ducal title like the Visconti in Milan. He preferred to exert his power through the old republican institutions.

The problem was how to assure stability in a republic whose offices were filled by a system of elections by lot. The solution was to authorize the officials (*accopiatori*) to hand-pick the names to go into the election bags. Later, in 1458, a Council of One Hundred was established, with responsibility for everything to do with elections, taxes, and the raising of troops. The executive was still further strengthened against the old legislative councils by the creation of a Council of Seventy. Thus between 1434 and 1494 the Medici had managed to make their regime stable by means that, without abolishing the republic, made a mockery of its representative bodies. The purpose of the new Medicean councils was recognized by the Florentines when, after repudiating Piero de' Medici in 1494, they abolished all of them together on 11 November 1494.

The End of the Florentine Republic

The ease with which Piero was overthrown is evidence of weakness in the regime, but the immediate cause came from without rather than from within. It was the French invasion and Piero's surrender of Florentine territory that brought about his repudiation. His patrician opponents, declaring that the Medici had in fact been tyrants, aimed to restore the pre-Medicean republic, but the advocates of a more popular regime insisted upon a new constitution, which was finally adopted on 24 December 1494. Its chief novelty, the Great Council, superficially like the Venetian institution, was composed of all who themselves, or whose ancestors, had filled one of the important offices. The *Signoría,* a Council of Eighty, and other magistracies were elected by the Great Council. To be enacted, a law had first to be proposed by the *Signoria,* then approved by the Eighty, and finally voted by the Great Council. This body, though it provided opportunity for broader political participation than any previous regime, was still representative of only a small fraction of the population of the city. It does not justify description of the regime as democratic.

The circumstances after 1494 in any case provided no fair test of a Florentine government, whatever its structure. For the restoration of Pisa and her other lost territory, Florence was dependent on France, and therefore isolated from the league of Italian states formed to expel the invader. The city was torn between the followers of Savonarola and the patrician party. His execution in 1498, however, did not change the situation of Florence, which continued under Soderini to find herself isolated. When the French were forced to withdraw from Italy in 1512, Florence was obliged to accept a return of the Medici to power.

The Medici were again expelled and the republic proclaimed once more in 1527, but the rapprochement between the Emperor Charles V and the Medici Pope Clement VII meant that Florence was restored to the Medici in 1530, this time for good. Alessandro was installed as head of the republic by the emperor in October 1530 and made duke in 1532. He was succeeded by Cosmo I (1519–1574), first as the Duke of Florence (1537), then as the Grand Duke of Tuscany (1569). With this development, we can say that the era of the city-state came to an end for Florence.

The End of the Era of the City-State

The outcome of the wars which had begun with the French invasion of 1494 was the Spanish domination of the Italian peninsula. Ferdinand of Aragon had added Naples to his dominion in Sicily; the French had replaced the Sforza as the rulers of Milan; the Sforza were restored by Spanish armies, but eventually Milan, too, became one of the dominions of Charles V. After the sack of Rome in 1527 by imperial troops, the papacy was no longer able to play the politically independent role of the past. Within Tuscany, Siena was occupied by the Spanish in 1530. They were driven out by the French in 1552, but in 1555 the French garrison and the restored republic were obliged to surrender to the combined forces of Charles V and of Duke Cosmo. Charles's son, Philip II, governed Siena as imperial vicar until 1557, when, in return for support against the French, he transferred Siena and most of its territory to the possession of Cosmo. Republican institutions survived in Lucca until 1799, but with the people (after 1556) excluded from government.

Of the five territorial states that dominated the peninsula in the fifteenth century only Venice remained outside the Spanish orbit. The powerful position that she occupied in the sixteenth and into the seventeenth century, exerting a magnetic attraction to the advocates of republicanism in the seventeenth century and later, makes it necessary to qualify the suggestion that the era of the city-state was everywhere ended in the sixteenth century. Yet if we look at the rest of Italy, and especially if we look beyond Italy, and take note of what happened to the towns of Castile, forced to surrender their autonomy to the crown in the third decade of the sixteenth century, it seems fair to conclude that these years did indeed mark the end of an era.

Notes

1. Henri Pirenne, *Histoire Economique et Sociale du Moyen Age*, ed. Van Werveke (Paris: Presses Universitaires de France, 1963), 17.

2. *Ibid.*, 27.

3. Bartolo da Sassoferrato, *Consilia, quaestiones et tractatus*, X (Venice, 1602), fols. 103vo–104ro, quoted by Sergio Bertelli, *Il potere oligarchico nello stato-città medievale* (Florence: La Nuova Italia, 1978), 5.

4. Daniel Waley, *The Italian City-Republics* (New York: World University Library, McGraw-Hill, 1969), 60.

5. Paolo Brezzi, *I comuni medioevali nella storia d'Italia* (Turin: Edizioni Radiotelevisione Italiana, 1959), 32.

6. Bertelli, *Il potere oligarchico*, 26.

7. Quoted by Waley, *City-Republics*, 59, from a translation by C. C. Mierow of the text in the *Monumenta Germaniae Historica, Scriptores*, XX, 396–397.

8. E. Jordan, *Les origines de la domination angevine en Italie* (Paris: Picard, 1909), 556–558.

9. The text was published by Francesco Bonaini in the *Archivio Storico Italiano*, n.s., t.I, pt. 1 (Florence, 1855).

10. In the Statuto del Capitano, quoted by Gaetano Salvemini, *La Dignità Cavallaresca nel Comune di Firenze* (1896), republished with his *Magnati e Popolani* (Turin: Einaudi, 1960), 398.

11. Waley, *City-Republics*, 35.

12. Bertelli, *Il potere oligarchico*, 44.

13. David Herlihy, "The Family in Renaissance Italy," *Forums in History* (St. Charles, Mo.: Forum Press, 1974), 4.

14. Giovanni Villani, *Cronica*, VII, chapters 144 and 146. Originally *Croniche di Giovanni Villani* (first published Venice, 1537); cited from Florence edition (Giunti, 1587).

15. *Ibid.*, XI, chapter 49.

16. *Ibid.*; see also Armando Sapori, *La crisi delle compagnie mercantili dei Bardi e dei Peruzzi* (Florence: Olschki, 1926), 109–110.

17. Sapori, *La crisi delle compagnie mercantili*, 118–120.

18. Villani, *Cronica*, XII, chapter 1.

19. Marvin Becker, "Economic Change and the Emerging Florentine Territorial State," *Studies in the Renaissance*, 13 (1966), 8; Sapori, *La crisi delle compagnie mercantili*, 148.

20. Becker, "Economic Change," 30.

21. Villani, *Cronica*, XII, chapter 71.

22. Machiavelli, *Discourses*, Book III, chapter iii.

23. Gene Brucker, *Florentine Politics and Society, 1343–1378* (Princeton: Princeton University Press, 1962), especially p. 117, but I am indebted to him for this whole section.

24. Frederic C. Lane, *Venice and History* (Baltimore: Johns Hopkins Press, 1966), 286.

25. Machiavelli, *Discourses*, Book I, chapter 55.

26. David Herlihy and Christiane Klapisch-Zuber, *Les toscans et leurs familles* (Paris: Ecole des Hautes Etudes en Sciences Sociales, 1978), 110. The figure of 11,000 square kilometers for the Florentine territory is arrived at by starting from E. Conti's estimate of 4930 square kilometers for the *contado*, which according to Herlihy and Klapisch-Zuber covered only 42 percent of the whole. The comparative figures for other city-states are drawn from Julius Beloch's *Bevölkerungsgeschichte Italiens,* III (Berlin and Leipzig: W. de Gruyter, 1937–1961).

27. Bertelli, *Il potere oligarchico,* 34.

28. Herlihy and Klapisch-Zuber, *Les toscans,* chapter ix, 241, is devoted to the distribution of wealth.

29. Bertelli, *Il potere oligarchico,* 38.

30. The text of the articles, in my translation, may be found in Gordon G. Griffiths, "The State: Absolute or Limited?" in R. M. Kingdon, ed., *Transition and Revolution* (Minneapolis: Burgess, 1974), 32–36.

31. F. Cognasso, "Lo stato di Gian Galeazzo," chapter xxxi of his book on *I Visconti* (Milan: dall'Oglio, 1966), and his "Istituzioni Comunali e Signorili" in the *Storia di Milano,* Vol. VI, Part III (Milan: Fondazione Treccani degli Alfieri, 1955).

Chapter Four

THE SWISS AND GERMAN CITY-STATES

Christopher R. Friedrichs

Central Europe has long been a land of cities. From Roman times onward, urban life has been a distinct feature of civilization in the Germanic lands that stretch from Switzerland northward to the Baltic Sea. A few cities of the Roman era have sustained their existence in an unbroken line down to modern times. Others trace their origins to the medieval epoch. By the High Middle Ages hundreds of cities dotted the Germanic region, serving as centers of commercial, cultural, and religious activity.

All these cities had certain things in common. They all conformed to a basic physical pattern: each city consisted of a dense cluster of dwellings and public buildings enclosed by a high wall, or in some cases, by a complex system of fortifications. They were all characterized by distinctly urban forms of economic activity, such as regularly-scheduled markets, and by distinctly urban forms of economic organization, such as guilds. Each city had a population consisting mostly though not entirely of *Bürger* (citizens)—a designation that distinguished its bearers both from the urban lower class and from the great mass of rural inhabitants. And each city had a system of government based not on rule by hereditary noblemen but on rule by oligarchic, elected city councils.

It is scarcely surprising that the Germanic cities should have had so much in common. The very term city—*Stadt* in German—referred not to some vague criterion of size or function, but to the possession of specific privileges of self-protection and self-administration which set any city, no matter how small, clearly apart from the ordinary villages of central Europe. These privileges were granted or confirmed by feudal overlords in the form of one or more charters, and these charters were always regarded as the most important and treasured documents in a community's possession.

Of course there were great variations in size and importance among the cities of the Germanic world. The largest among them in the late Middle Ages had populations approaching 40,000; the smallest had under 1,000 inhabitants. Yet in their physical structure, their economic system, and their legal and social organization, all the Germanic cities displayed striking similarities—and continued to do so until the end of the eighteenth century, when the double impact of the industrial and French revolutions began to transform urban life in central Europe beyond recognition.

Among these hundreds of Germanic cities of the pre-modern era, however, a certain group stands out as having enjoyed a uniquely great degree of political independence and influence. In Switzerland these cities were the urban *Orte*— in modern terms, the urban cantons. In Germany proper they were the *Reichsstädte*, or imperial cities. What set these cities apart from hundreds of other cities in central Europe was the fact that they owed no obedience to a local or regional overlord. In fact, they recognized no overlord other than God and, in most cases, the Holy Roman Emperor—and this gave them vastly greater freedom than most Germanic cities, both in the way they governed themselves and in the way they related to the outside world.

But were they city-states? There can be little doubt that this term is correctly applied to the seven Swiss free cities: Basel, Bern, Fribourg, Lucerne, Schaffhausen, Solothurn, and Zürich. One need only consider the four criteria listed in the prologue to this volume. First, each urban state had a distinct urban core, the city itself. Second, each enjoyed particularly great opportunities for economic self-sufficiency, made possible by its control over a substantial hinterland. Third, all shared a fundamental sense of common culture and historical tradition which linked them to each other. And, finally, by the end of the Middle Ages all of them had become politically independent. By the fifteenth century they had successfully broken away from the Holy Roman Empire, yet their membership in the Swiss confederation was voluntary in origin and limited in effect; not until the nineteenth century did Switzerland evolve into a true unified state in a modern sense.

But what of the imperial cities, the *Reichsstädte*? There were about eighty of them, and they included most of Germany's leading urban centers in medieval and early modern times: Augsburg, Cologne, Frankfurt am Main, Hamburg, Lübeck, Nuremberg, Regensburg, Strasbourg, and scores of others. Like the Swiss free cities—some of which, in fact, had originally been *Reichsstädte*— they met almost all the critera that define city-states. Each one had a clearly demarcated urban core, and each enjoyed considerable economic autonomy— although some were more successful than others in acquiring direct political control over a territorial hinterland. All shared a common language and traditions, leading to extensive political, economic, and social contacts among them. But they never achieved, nor even attempted to achieve, quite the same degree of independence as was acquired by the Swiss cities. For the German imperial cities openly acknowledged and accepted the Holy Roman Emperor as their overlord. Their aim, in fact, was never to be independent, but to be accepted as politically equal in status to the more than two hundred duchies, counties, bishoprics, abbeys, prelacies, and other units which also belonged to the Holy Roman Empire.

In this essentially they succeeded. The princes of the Empire could never quite accept the thought that the cities were their political equals, but in fact the imperial cities, or at least the greatest of them, were increasingly able to assert a status of virtual equality with the secular and ecclesiastical principalities. But what exactly was implied by that status? Were the estates of the Empire, including the cities, sovereign states, or were they merely subordinate parts of a sovereign whole? Even after 1648, when the Peace of Westphalia attempted to answer these questions more precisely than ever before, the status of the estates continued to perplex political theorists—as it continues to puzzle historians today. Consider the explanation provided by Samuel Pufendorf, one of the leading political thinkers of the late seventeenth century:

> Germany has its particular Form of Government, the like is not to be met with in any Kingdom of Europe, except that the ancient Form of Government in *France* came pretty near it. . . . The Estates of Germany, some of which have great and potent Countries in their possession, have a considerable share of the Sovereignty over their Subjects: and tho' they are Vassals of the Emperor and Empire, nevertheless they ought not to be consider'd as Subjects, or only as potent or rich Citizens in a Government; for they are actually possess'd of the Supreme Jurisdiction in the Criminal Affairs; they have Power to make Laws and to regulate Church Affairs, (which however is only to be understood of the Protestants) to dispose of the Revenues arising out of their own Territories; to make Alliances, as well among themselves as with Foreign States, provided the same are not intended against the Emperor and Empire; they may build and maintain Fortresses and Armies of their own, coin Money, and the like.[1]

It might be argued that, as estates of the Empire, the *Reichsstädte* cannot rightly be regarded as city-states. But to say this would miss the point of German politics before 1800. For far from detracting from their status as city-states, the existence of the Holy Roman Empire was, in fact, what made it possible for the imperial cities to achieve and maintain that status. The constitution of the Empire, complex and cumbrous as it was, protected the cities from being absorbed by their aggressive and expansive territorial neighbors— ambitious states-in-the-making like Brandenburg-Prussia, Saxony, Bavaria, Württemberg, and Baden. When the Empire was finally abolished in the early nineteenth century and Germany was reorganized into a mere 41 states, only four city-states managed to survive: Hamburg, Bremen, Lübeck, and Frankfurt am Main. All the rest were swallowed up by the territorial states from which the Empire had long and effectively protected them.

The Holy Roman Empire underwent extensive changes, both geographical and institutional, from its origin in the ninth century until its dissolution in 1806. In the early Middle Ages it encompassed virtually all of central Europe and much of Italy as well. By the end of the fifteenth century, however, its effective power was confined to the area north of the Alps. In 1648 what had long been true in fact was confirmed in law: Italy, Switzerland, and the northern Netherlands were excluded from the Empire. Still more territory was lost in later years as Louis XIV began to push the frontiers of France steadily eastward to the Rhine. The institutions of the Empire also underwent constant evolution, and the change was not always linear: the power of the emperor himself, as well as that of the imperial diet and bureaucracy, waxed and waned in an irregular pattern through the centuries.

Under such circumstances, it is hardly surprising that the status of individual cities was also subject to fluctuation. Most of the free cities of Germany and Switzerland had established their autonomy by the fourteenth century. Yet there remained countless anomalies. Consider the great city of Hamburg: although for all practical purposes it had long since become independent of its feudal overlord (the king of Denmark), it was definitively recognized as an imperial city only in the seventeenth century. It was also possible for a city to lose imperial status, the most spectacular example being Strasbourg, which was annexed by the French crown in 1681.

The central European city-state was essentially a Swiss and German phenomenon. On the fringes of this area, however, lay some other communities which might well be added to the list of city-states. To the southwest, for example, lay the French-speaking city of Geneva. Medieval Geneva was a provincial city of the duchy of Savoy, ruled by a Savoyard bishop. In the 1530s, however, Geneva expelled its bishop and asserted its free status—a status which it retained for three centuries. Although Geneva allied itself with some Swiss cantons, it did not become a canton itself until 1815. To the northeast lay another free city, Danzig. Like most commercial cities in the Baltic region, Danzig was essentially a German community without being part of the Holy Roman Empire. From 1454 onward Danzig was formally subject to Poland, but in actual fact the city enjoyed almost complete autonomy until it was absorbed by Prussia in 1793. (A brief reminder of Danzig's earlier status was to come in 1920 when it was established as a free city under protection by the League of Nations. But nineteen years later Danzig fell, as free cities had so often before, under the invasion of a powerful neighbor.)

Somewhat harder to classify are certain great cities of the Low Countries. In the thirteenth and fourteenth centuries the three leading cities of Flanders— Bruges, Ghent, and Ypres—had acquired such extensive grants of autonomy that they almost functioned as independent city-states. Yet they never completely escaped from subordination to the counts of Flanders, and their subsequent overlords—first the dukes of Burgundy and then the house of Habsburg—successfully strove to whittle away their privileges. One final effort by the city of Ghent to revolt against its princely rule ended abruptly in 1540, when Charles V revoked the city's privileges and reduced it to submission. A similar pattern was evident elsewhere in the Netherlands. The city of Groningen, for example, had broken away briefly from its overlords in the late Middle Ages and effectively ruled the surrounding countryside; by the sixteenth century, however, the city came under direct Habsburg control. It is true, of course, that the northern Netherlands as a whole were liberated from Habsburg rule later in the sixteenth century. But the cities of this region—even powerful commercial centers like Amsterdam—were firmly integrated into the provincially-organized system of the Dutch Republic and enjoyed no further opportunities to assert themselves as city-states.

We must turn, then, to Germany and Switzerland to find the most abundant and long-lasting examples of European city-states north of Italy. Before we proceed to describe their attributes and examine their political, economic, and social structure, we must take a closer look at the way in which these cities acquired their particularly autonomous status.

Historical Framework

The Holy Roman Empire was founded in the year 800 with the coronation of Charlemagne by Pope Leo III. The Carolingian empire soon disintegrated, however, and from the point of view of German history the refoundation of the Empire by Otto the Great in 962 is almost more important. By then the Empire no longer included France, but it still encompassed a huge part of central Europe and northern Italy. Although Otto and his successors strove to assert their authority over the whole region, they were forced to share power with a number of great vassals, especially the German dukes. Some dukes tried to assert more authority than the emperors could accept. Thus, the history of Germany in the next few centuries was dominated by constant struggles for power between the Holy Roman Emperors on the one hand and some of their greatest vassals on the other. These struggles were soon complicated by the involvement of the Church, which turned against the emperors in the late eleventh century. They were further complicated by the occasional transfer of the imperial crown from one great family to another, which always required a reshuffling of alliances.

The imperial struggles brought endless warfare and disruption to central Europe—but they also gave many smaller political units the chance to enhance their own power by playing off the interests of one great dynasty against another. Among these lesser beneficiaries of the imperial wars, especially in the twelfth and thirteenth centuries, were dozens of German cities which took advantage of the conflicts to assert their own political autonomy.

There was no single way in which the city-states of central Europe acquired their free status: indeed, almost every one did so in a slightly different manner. Nor was there ever complete agreement about which cities had or had not achieved free status. But the main patterns by which cities arrived at this point are clear.

A few cities, such as Aachen and Goslar, enjoyed imperial status by virtue of the fact that they had served as centers of royal administration in Germany from Carolingian or slightly later times. Many other imperial cities had once belonged to a territorial overlord but had succeeded in liberating themselves from his control. Among them were a number of episcopal seats, including some of the oldest urban communities in central Europe—cities like Augsburg, Basel, Cologne, Speyer, Strasbourg, and Worms. As centers of both ecclesiastical authority and secular administration (for a bishop generally ruled over part of his diocese as a secular overlord), these cities attracted large settlements of merchants and craftsmen. In many German cities, beginning in the twelfth century, these traders and artisans began to form communes, associations of citizens committed to securing a greater degree of self-government from their municipal overlords. In some episcopal cities, however, the members of the commune were not content with this—they attempted instead to free themselves entirely from the bishop's control by appealing over his head to the emperor. Often the emperor was responsive to such an appeal, especially when, as was generally the case between the late eleventh and the late thirteenth century, the emperor was engaged in a conflict with the Church.

Intervention by the emperor, however, did not necessarily make the city into a *Reichsstadt* in one step. In Augsburg, for example, Emperor Frederick Barbarossa granted a charter in 1156 that guaranteed the citizens specific rights of self-government but still recognized the bishop as the city's overlord. Even the more extensive charter of privileges granted by Emperor Rudolf of Habsburg in 1276 continued to recognize the bishop's position. It was only in 1316, when Emperor Ludwig the Bavarian granted the citizens a charter that made no reference to the bishop's authority, that Augsburg could be said to have definitely become an imperial city.

It was not only episcopal cities which might come under the emperor's direct authority; other *Reichsstädte* had previously stood under secular overlords. Most of the cities in this group passed to the emperor as the result of complex dynastic accidents. Among these cities were those which had been acquired or founded by the great ducal house of Zähringen. The emperors had invested this dynasty with authority over a large part of southwestern Germany and western Switzerland. But in 1218 the last of the Zähringer dukes died without heirs, and the family's possessions reverted to the emperor—including the cities they had acquired, such as Zürich, and the cities they had founded, such as Rottweil and Bern.

But the largest group of imperial cities consisted of towns which, after being founded or nurtured by one imperial dynasty within its own territorial domains, suddenly achieved free status when the dynasty itself collapsed. Beginning in the late eleventh century, the great house of Hohenstaufen built up control over large parts of southern Germany—an activity which was accelerated when the family came to occupy the imperial throne, as it did for most of the period from 1138 to 1254. Throughout this era the Hohenstaufens were active in developing old towns and founding new ones in the lands they ruled in southern Germany. In 1254, however, the Hohenstaufens' power came to a sudden end, and the Empire was plunged into twenty years of interregnum while various princes competed for election as emperor. During this period the Hohenstaufen towns grew accustomed to governing themselves—and when at last the interregnum ended in 1273 the new emperor, Rudolf of Habsburg, eager to bolster support for his shaky regime, made it a policy to guarantee these cities their imperial status.

Simply to have imperial status recognized, however, did not necessarily make a city free in the fullest sense. For the medieval emperors took their position as municipal overlords seriously. They expected to receive tax payments from the cities, though often this claim met with little success. There was, however, a more profitable way to exploit a city financially, by "mortgaging" the whole community to some local prince or nobleman. In return for a cash payment, the emperor would place the city—with its revenues—in the hands of the nobleman, where it remained until the emperor or, often enough, the citizens themselves found the money to buy back the city's freedom. Not until the end of the fourteenth century did this practice die out. And even in cities that had been spared this indignity—such as those that had received a charter specifically protecting them from being mortgaged—there were other ways in which the emperor could exert direct control. For example, in his capacity as the city's overlord, the emperor would appoint an imperial representative as the city's highest official (generally known as the Ammann, Vogt, or Schultheiss) and reserve for his own courts the disposition of capital cases. In many cases it was only when the city had acquired—by petition or purchase—the right to name its own candidate as imperial representative and the right to use its own courts to try capital cases that it could truly regard itself as a free city.

The amorphous and varied ways in which the imperial cities had acquired their free status led to much confusion about which cities were actually included in their number. Similar confusion arose concerning some of the secular and ecclesiastical principalities of the Empire. The most famous attempt to codify an exact list of imperial estates was undertaken at the imperial diet of Worms in 1521. The *Matrikel* drawn up on that occasion recorded a total of 81 princes, 83 ecclesiastical rulers, 145 counts and lords, and 85 imperial cities.[2] Yet the list was not entirely reliable. Its main purpose was to specify each estate's obligations in terms of men and money for a proposed imperial army, and it was thus in the emperor's interest to list as many estates as possible—especially wealthy cities, even if their free status was debatable. Included, for example, were cities like Göttingen, which had never even made claims to imperial status.

A more reliable list of imperial cities can be assembled for the period after the Thirty Years War: when the war ended in 1648, there were 65 imperial cities.[3] This list did not remain constant, however. The eleven Alsatian cities—Strasbourg and ten much smaller towns—were taken over by France, which also acquired the Burgundian town of Besançon. Two other minor cities were annexed by powerful neighbors within Germany itself. A total of 51 free cities survived to the end of the Empire.

Of the 65 free cities recorded in 1648, only fourteen lay north of the river Main; the vast majority were located in southern Germany. To their number

INSET: LAKE OF CONSTANCE REGION

ABBREVIATIONS

Aa Aalen	Gi Giengen	Nd Nordhausen	So Solothurn
Ba Basel	Go Goslar	Nö Nördlingen	Sw Schweinfurt
Bh Buchhorn	He Heilbronn	Of Offenburg	Ub Überlingen
Bi Biberach	Is Isny	Pf Pfullendorf	Wa Wangen
Bo Bopfinger	Ke Kempten	Ra Ravensburg	We Weil der Stadt
Bu Buchau	Kf Kaufbeuren	Rn Reutlingen	Wm Wimpfen
Di Dinkelsbühl	Li Lindau	Ro Rothenburg ob der Tauber	Wn Windsheim
Es Esslingen	Lt Leutkirch	Rt Rottweil	Ws Weissenburg im Nordgau
Fb Fribourg	Lu Lucerne	Sf Schaffhausen	Wz Wetzlar
Fr Friedberg	Me Memmingen	SG Schwäbisch Gmünd	Ze Zell am Harmersbach
Ge Gengenbach	Mü Mühlhausen	SH Schwäbisch Hall	

Map 5: *The Free Cities of Central Europe (1789)*

should be added the seven Swiss city-states, by then completely independent of the Empire but still linked economically and culturally to many of the south German cities. The main reason for this preponderance of free cities in the south Germanic region was, as we have seen, the fact that so many cities had been founded or nurtured by the Hohenstaufen dynasty, whose territorial domains lay mostly in the south.

Urban life was equally vigorous in northern Germany, of course. Nothing illustrates this better than the power and solidarity of the Hanseatic League, the great commercial alliance to which about seventy Baltic and North Sea towns actively belonged in the late Middle Ages.[4] But almost all of these member communities were territorial towns, ultimately subject to the authority of a local overlord; only a handful—such as Lübeck, Hamburg, and Bremen—were autonomous city-states. As the territorial rulers in northern Germany grew increasingly vigorous in demanding revenues and obedience from their subject towns, more and more Hansa cities were forced to withdraw from the League. In short, an alliance between free and subject cities became increasingly difficult to maintain—and this fact, as well as changing commercial patterns, contributed to the disappearance of the Hanseatic League by the seventeenth century.

Of course the imperial cities also had an overlord, the emperor. But by the end of the Middle Ages it had become increasingly unnecessary for the emperors to involve themselves closely in the political and fiscal affairs of the imperial cities. For one thing, the imperial title had become virtually hereditary in the house of Habsburg. Under the constitution of the Empire, as it had evolved during the Middle Ages, the position of emperor was elective; when one emperor died, his successor was chosen by the seven electoral princes of the Empire. For two centuries after the fall of the Hohenstaufen, these princes had switched from one dynasty to another in choosing new emperors. But after the mid-fifteenth century, their choice always fell on the head of the house of Habsburg. As a secure political and economic base, the Habsburgs could rely on their huge territorial holdings in southwestern Germany and Austria and, after 1526, in Bohemia and Hungary as well. They were scarcely as dependent on the revenues and political support of sixty or seventy imperial cities as, for example, their penurious ancestor Rudolf I had been in the late fourteenth century.

The cities grew increasingly independent in their actions. Only a few went so far as to break away from the Empire altogether in order to join the Swiss confederation. After all, most imperial cities saw in the Empire exactly the bulwark they needed to defend urban autonomy from the expansionist activities of neighboring princes. But many of the cities themselves became increasingly expansionistic during the late Middle Ages. In the fourteenth and fifteenth centuries most of the imperial cities began to display the characteristics of true city-states. They formed alliances with other cities or friendly princes to wage war on territorial rulers whose policies they feared. They engaged in massive building projects to make their walls and fortifications impregnable to surprise attack. And, above all, one imperial city after another began to take over large sections of the surrounding hinterland, buying up villages from bankrupt noblemen and turning the peasants into their own subjects. The magistrates of a city like Nuremberg or Ulm, themselves rulers over thousands of rural subjects, could take an increasingly detached view of their allegiance to the emperor.

Perhaps nothing makes this clearer than the conduct of the imperial cities during the Protestant Reformation. Emperor Charles V was an ardent Catholic, bitterly opposed to the great movement of religious reform launched by Martin Luther in 1517. Yet a majority of the imperial cities—including almost all of the major ones—supported the Reformation and introduced Protestant practices at a very early stage. Indeed, the very word *Protestant* alludes to the "protestation" against the emperor's religious policies submitted by five princes and fourteen imperial cities at the diet of Speyer in 1529. Some cities, to be sure, adopted the Reformation more hesitantly than others. And in 1548, shortly after Charles had achieved his one major victory in his struggle against the German Protestants, most of the imperial cities half-heartedly accepted the "Interim" settlement by which the emperor attempted to restore religious uniformity. But their allegiance to this measure soon wore out, and when the Habsburgs finally agreed in 1555 to let each imperial estate chose between Catholicism and Lutheranism, most of the imperial cities adhered to the new faith.

The emperor was somewhat more successful when he intervened to change constitutional arrangements in the imperial cities. Most of these cities in the sixteenth century were governed by councils which included representatives both from the craft guilds and from wealthy "patrician" families. Charles V suspected, not without reason, that one cause of the Reformation's success in these cities was the political influence of the guilds, whose members tended to be more radical in religious matters than the wealthier strata of citizens. Between 1548 and 1552 Charles sent commissioners to about 25 south German imperial cities to promulgate new constitutions which would eliminate guild representatives from positions of political power. These measures did not achieve their intended effect—for even with more exclusively "patrician" councils, almost all of these cities remained loyal to the Reformation. But the new constitutions did remain in effect—partly because the patricians themselves found the new arrangements more agreeable and partly because guild members did not fight to retain their political power as passionately as they had fought to introduce the religious reforms.

Until the Empire ended in 1806, the emperor's ultimate authority over constitutional arrangements in the imperial cities remained unquestioned. But the reforms imposed by Charles V represented the last such intervention on a large scale undertaken at the emperor's own initiative. In fact the emperors became increasingly respectful of the cities' traditions. Even during the Thirty Years War (1618–48), when dozens of Protestant imperial cities took part in hostilities against the Catholic Habsburgs, the emperors generally confirmed the political and religious liberties of the cities they reconquered. As a rule, the emperors of the seventeenth and eighteenth centuries intervened in a city's political affairs only when asked to do so by one of the parties to a civic dispute. There were many such disputes, and the emperors often appointed commissioners to resolve a civic conflict by clarifying or reformulating the city's constitutional arrangements. But the initiative for such intervention came increasingly from the cities themselves. Sometimes a particularly bitter dispute would erupt into violence. But more often the availability of the emperor as an arbiter or court of last resort made possible a peaceful resolution of what might otherwise have developed into an open fight. And this, in turn, contributed to the continuing political independence of the German free cities. For after all, as the examples of Sumer, Greece, and Italy make clear, few things make a city-state more vulnerable to aggression by a powerful neighbor than a state of internal conflict.

Some imperial cities were the victims of aggression—above all the Alsatian towns which fell to France under Louis XIV. But most imperial cities retained their autonomy until the Empire itself collapsed, although there were moments of danger. In 1686 the king of Denmark suddenly tried to exercise his long-dormant overlordship over Hamburg and mounted a campaign against the city. And in the early eighteenth century both Augsburg and Ulm faced a possible loss of independence when Bavarian troops occupied them during the War of the Spanish Succession. But these threats, and others like them, could be overcome—if not by force, then by diplomacy—as long as the overall structure of the Holy Roman Empire remained intact.

In the end, France did bring to a close the age of German and Swiss city-states—though scarcely in a way that Louis XIV might have envisioned. With the beginning of the French Revolution, radical ideas spread quickly throughout Germany, leading to ever more criticism of the tradition-bound, oligarchical systems of government typical of the imperial cities. More important was the way in which Napoleon redrew the map of central Europe, eliminating the Holy Roman Empire and assigning most of its smaller units to larger states like Bavaria and Württemberg. For, after Napoleon had been defeated, nobody attempted to restore the complicated patchwork of late eighteenth-century Germany; only four of the German city-states survived after 1815 and eventually they, like the other states of Germany, were absorbed into the Prussian-dominated German Empire. The Swiss city-states were also deeply affected by the Napoleonic era, for the Switzerland that emerged in 1815 was much closer to a modern state than the loose confederation which Napoleon had invaded in 1798. True, some relics of the old city-state constitutions persisted in the Swiss city-cantons until 1848 and in the four free cities of Germany until 1871. But eventually the great political trends of the nineteenth century—written constitutions, universal male suffrage, and above all national unification—eliminated these anachronistic vestiges. Today nothing survives of the central European city-states other than their physical remains (much decimated by war and modernization)—and a wealth of proud historical traditions.

Physical and Geographical Attributes

At the core of every central European city-state was the city itself, a cluster of public and private buildings clearly demarcated from the surrounding countryside by a wall. In their physical appearance, the free cities of Germany and Switzerland differed little from territorial cities subject to a local overlord; it was their political system and their relationship to the land outside the walls that most clearly differentiated them from subject cities.

The free cities of central Europe were small by modern standards. The largest was probably Cologne, with a population of some 30,000 in early modern times. Nuremberg was typical of the large free cities: its population was about 20,000 in 1500, and it measured less than two kilometers from one end to the other. To walk across the whole city might have taken twenty minutes, though a wagon or coach would have needed more time to negotiate the narrow streets. A small city like Kaufbeuren, whose population amounted to some 3,000 souls in the seventeenth century, was scarcely 500 meters across. A few free cities were even smaller.

What distinguished a city from a village was not its size but the nature of its privileges, and among the first privileges any city sought was the right to build a wall. A high wall, punctuated only by carefully-manned gates, made it possible for the city to regulate the flow of people and goods in and out of the community, and to defend itself from all but the most ambitious attacks. Most German and Swiss free cities underwent their most rapid growth between the thirteenth and fifteenth centuries, and many of them had no sooner completed one wall than they found it necessary to build another one somewhat farther out. After the end of the Middle Ages, however, these cities tended to become more stable in size. Few extended their walls outward between 1500 and 1800, though many embellished their walls with additional bastions and outworks.

The complexity of the wall system depended on the size and wealth of the city concerned. The walls of little Dinkelsbühl could have been scaled by someone using a high ladder—so long as the watchman was out of sight. Mighty cities like Nuremberg, Hamburg, and Cologne, however, had massive fortifications that were adequate to deter any military storm. The old walls have survived in some German and Swiss towns, but in most cases they were destroyed when the cities underwent a new wave of growth in the nineteenth century.

Modern imagination sometimes exaggerates the density of construction inside medieval towns—in fact almost every city had some gardens and open market places. But it is true that buildings inside the walls were closely clustered together. Towards the center of town were the major public buildings: the city hall, perhaps some guild halls, the "Stube" where wealthy patricians met socially, and—dominating all—the principal church or (in episcopal seats)

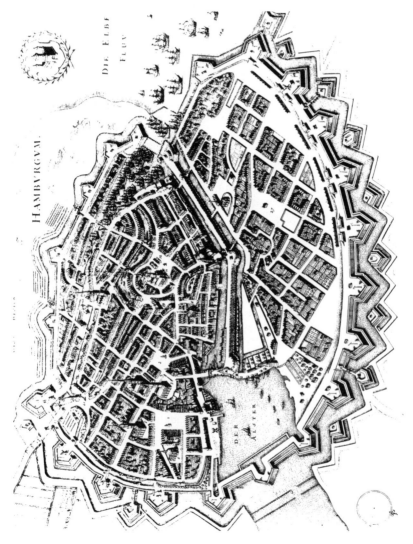

Illus. 7: *Plan of Hamburg*

the cathedral. Scattered throughout the city were lesser churches, some warehouses and granaries, many taverns, perhaps some monasteries, and always the "hospital," that is to say, the city almshouse. But the overwhelming majority of buildings consisted of private houses—generally high buildings with a narrow front to the street and a tiny garden or courtyard behind. There were no separate places of business in the German or Swiss city; instead, every citizen carried out his trade—banking, weaving, shoemaking, or whatever—from his own house. The bottom floor or floors would be used as a shop or workshop, and the family, its servants, and perhaps some lodgers would dwell in the floors above.

Each central European city had a narrow strip of land outside the walls, the *Stadtmarkung*, in which it enjoyed complete authority. Here might be located a few additional houses, some water mills, a few gardens, and sometimes a sanatorium for lepers or other incurables. But what distinguished the city-states from territorial cities was their attempts, often successful, to gain control of a much wider band of territory outside the city limits. A territorial city, itself subject to a noble or princely overlord, could scarcely attempt to gain authority over the surrounding villages. But a free city could.

In most cases the acquisition of such territories dated back to the fourteenth and fifteenth centuries. Surrounding any city in central Europe were dozens of villages, each normally under the control of a seigneur, or lord of the manor, who in turn owed allegiance to a greater nobleman or prince. As in all of feudal Europe, the seigneur functioned not only as landlord but also as chief administrator and judge in minor cases. But "higher jurisdiction," for instance over capital cases, was reserved to the true overlord.

In the late Middle Ages, many of the petty knights and lords of central Europe were falling into debt—generally due to the Germanic practice of dividing land equally among all heirs, which split noble holdings into inadequate parcels. Typically, an impoverished knight might borrow money from a citizen of the neighboring town, putting up one of his manors (or part of a manor) as security. When the debt came due, the knight could not pay—and the citizen acquired the rural holdings. In other cases, a seigneur might attempt to solve his problems by getting inscribed as an urban citizen himself, thus bringing his manors under the city's authority. In yet other cases, the city itself, or a municipal institution such as the hospital, would engage in systematic purchases of rural holdings. In all events, by the end of the Middle Ages many cities or their citizens had acquired extensive control over manors in the surrounding countryside—and with this came the control of day-to-day administration and the rights of lower jurisdiction.

Often the urban-owned manors were scattered throughout the countryside; in any given village some peasant holdings might belong to the city while other holdings belonged to rival seigneurs. A few cities, however, succeeded in gaining full control over large areas of contiguous manors. When this happened, the city concerned was generally not satisfied with the rights of lower

Illus. 8: *View of Lübeck*

jurisdiction—it would attempt to assert full legal authority over the district. Of course the previous overlord might protest, even by force. But if the city were successful in defending its claims, it could establish a true urban territory.

Take, for example, the case of Rothenburg ob der Tauber. By the beginning of the fifteenth century, Rothenberg had acquired full or partial possession of more than a hundred nearby villages, controlling a contiguous area of over a hundred square miles. To provide protection from marauding freebooters, a wall of earthworks and hedges was constructed around the whole area. At first this hedge-wall was perceived strictly as a device for military protection—but over the centuries it came to be regarded as a boundary marking the limits of Rothenburg's full legal authority. As the neighboring overlords had only few holdings within this area, they gradually gave up trying to oppose the city's growing claims to complete authority. Thus, by the end of the Empire, Rothenburg had acquired an extensive urban territory under its full control.[6]

The urban territories varied considerably in size. The largest by far was that of Bern, which covered close to three thousand square miles in western Switzerland. This territory included a number of smaller cities which had accepted Bern as their territorial overlord. The next largest Swiss city-state was Zürich, though its territory was but a quarter the size of Bern's. In Germany the largest urban territories were those of Ulm and Nuremberg, each with areas of four to five hundred square miles, followed by such cities as Rothenburg, Schwäbisch Hall, and Rottweil.

The size of the territory, however, bore no systematic relationship to the wealth or the importance of the city. Some of the smallest city-states ruled over a respectable amount of territory, while some of the greatest did not. Take Augsburg, for example: although many Augsburg patricians had country estates, the city never succeeded in establishing a territory of any note, for the regional magnates (the duke of Bavaria to the east and the bishop of Augsburg to the west) remained far too powerful. There were even some areas within the walls of Augsburg that stood under ecclesiastical rule and were not, strictly speaking, subject to the city council's authority. Yet Augsburg was always one of the great urban centers of Germany, and in the sixteenth century it was probably the wealthiest city in the Empire. Obviously its wealth was not dependent on full political control of the agrarian hinterland; it came instead from commerce, investment, and finance.

The fact that some city-states failed to develop full-fledged territories should not obscure the degree of influence which each of them exerted over its rural hinterland. The free cities invariably served as crucial markets and sources of capital for the agrarian regions that surrounded them. For a long time they also served as important sources of capital, goods, and services for the neighboring princes. This began to change in the seventeenth and eighteenth centuries. Inspired by absolutist and mercantilist notions, the German princes strove to make their states economically self-sufficient—following much the same ideal that had traditionally animated city-states in central Europe and elsewhere. To implement such aims, the princes promoted the development of their own residential cities: Munich, Stuttgart, Karlsruhe, Düsseldorf, and the like. The growing economic (and cultural) importance of these cities, reflecting as it did the growing strength of the princely states themselves, epitomized the threat which confronted German city-states in the eighteenth century—and to which most of them succumbed in the nineteenth century.

Citizenship and Social Structure

The most fundamental aspect of the social structure of the Germanic city-state was the threefold division of its inhabitants into citizens, non-citizens, and rural subjects. The citizens, or *Bürger*, were the permanent, privileged members of the urban community; the non-citizens were tolerated outsiders who participated in the city's social and economic life only by permission of the magistrates. In many cases the legal status of non-citizens was less secure than that of the city's rural subjects, who, at least, often enjoyed the secure tenure of their peasant holdings.

The concept of citizenship in the Germanic cities went back to the twelfth century, when the inhabitants of many communities began to form communes, or *coniurationes*. The inhabitants of the community, hitherto individual subjects of an overlord, would take an oath of solidarity to press collectively for a guarantee of their economic and legal rights. Citizenship—that is to say, membership in the commune—would be carried on by inheritance in the male line from one generation to the next. In addition, outsiders might be admitted to citizenship if they had sufficient wealth or skills to make them desirable members of the community; the right of citizenship would then pass to their descendants as well.

Only adult males were considered citizens in the full sense, although their wives, widows, and daughters enjoyed a status of passive citizenship that guaranteed them the full protection of the city's laws. Typically, the son of a citizen would assume the full status of *Bürger* in his twenties, when he was ready to marry, establish a household, and practice a trade. What made citizenship so desirable was the fact that most crafts or retail activities could be carried out only by citizens. This also meant that citizenship was not a highly exclusive category—everyone from merchants and professionals to humble weavers and cobblers was included among the *Bürgerschaft*.

There were, of course, subgroups within the citizenry. In smaller cities these groups were generally unofficial; people simply knew who the "better," more "honorable" members of the community were. The larger the city, however, the more formalized the status boundaries became. In seventeenth-century Frankfurt, for example, the citizens were divided into five official strata: 1) patricians; 2) non-patrician magistrates and merchants; 3) distinguished retailers and professionals; 4) common retailers and craftsmen; 5) unskilled workers, such as coachmen and day-laborers.[7] Only a large city like Frankfurt could produce a true "patriciate"—a social group consisting of the descendants of old merchant families who now held themselves aloof from trade and tried to be accepted as minor noblemen. But every city had a group of citizens whose social superiority was understood and accepted by all.

A few non-citizens were also persons of wealth and prestige, for many towns granted residence-permits to a few wealthy rentiers, merchants, and professionals who wanted to live there but still retain citizenship in their home communities. Most non-citizens, however, were powerless and property-less people at the bottom end of the social ladder: alien apprentices and journeymen, servants, beggars, casual laborers, and the like. This does not, of course, include the apprentices or journeymen who were the sons of local citizens. They were simply in training until they were old enough to establish themselves as craft-masters and citizens in their own right. But it does include the huge number of people who arrived in most German cities to work as journeymen or servants on a temporary basis. Their presence in the city was tolerated only as long as their labor was useful. Some were lucky and eventually got accepted as citizens. Most did not.

Certainly citizenship involved clear economic and social advantages. To be the citizen of a free city was a proud boast, and one not lightly surrendered. But there is little evidence that the Germanic city ever commanded the depth of personal loyalty which, say, the Greek city-state evoked from its citizens. Many people in the sixteenth or seventeenth century were content to die for their religion—but not many would willingly give their lives for their city. In the fall of 1681, as the army of Louis XIV marched toward Strasbourg, the magistrates of that free city consulted a representative group of 300 citizens about whether or not to submit to French annexation. There was much heated talk about saving the city's honor by offering at least a token resistance—but when it came to an actual vote, all but one of the citizens consulted voted to submit to the French king.[8]

One reason for this less than total commitment to one's own city-state lay in the fact that extensive mobility and intermarriage took place between different communities. Young men often left their hometowns in search of new opportunities elsewhere, and if one could display adequate wealth or credentials, he would generally be accepted without much ado as the citizen of another town. Young women of citizen families were often married off to men of compatible social rank in another city. But perhaps the most important factor in moderating the degree of loyalty citizens felt towards their city lay in the great disparity of wealth and influence which was visible even within the ranks of the citizenry itself.

Social differences were acute in all the German and Swiss cities. They were most acute, however, in the largest cities, where capitalism had achieved its earliest advances. Capitalist activity not only created huge mercantile fortunes, it also frequently reduced craftsmen from independent producers to virtual wage-laborers, dependent for employment on the great merchants. Consider, for example, the disparity of wealth in sixteenth-century Augsburg. In 1527

Augsburg's leading family, the Fuggers—international merchants and bankers to the house of Habsburg—calculated their net worth at over 2 million guldens, probably the greatest fortune of their age. At the same period, fully 54 percent of the Fuggers' fellow citizens were inscribed in the tax rolls of Augsburg as "have-nots"—people who may have been able to live off their income but had so little actual property that it rated no assessed value.[9]

In a smaller city, differences were not quite so extreme. In Nördlingen, for example, the tax register for 1579 records only 1 percent of the 1,541 citizens as "have-nots," and the city's richest citizen was worth only 21,000 guldens. Even so, great disparities were evident here as well: 10 percent of the citizens, for example, owned fully 60 percent of the community's wealth.[10]

Yet there was one factor which, at least for a time, moderated the effect of such disparities and retarded the emergence of rigid class lines. That was the great extent of social mobility that could take place in urban society. The cities were, after all, places of opportunity, where hard work and a shrewd marriage might enable a modest craftsman to move up in the world, or at least enable his children to do so. Even the lordly Fuggers of the early 1500s were but two generations removed from the simple weaver Hans Fugger, who immigrated to Augsburg from a nearby village in 1367.

It is no accident that the Fuggers' spectacular rise took place in the fifteenth century, a time of enormous growth and enterprise in almost all the Germanic cities. Enjoying as they did a virtual monopoly on both commercial activity and the production of goods, the cities tended to welcome newcomers and encourage economic activity in every sphere. Beginning in the sixteenth century, however, things began to change. Like the Italian city-states, many German and Swiss cities began to suffer economically as the center of commercial gravity shifted from the middle of Europe to the Atlantic seaboard. Proto-mercantilist princes and noblemen encouraged their rural cottagers to engage in weaving and other crafts which had formerly been the almost exclusive preserve of urban artisans. In addition, many German cities suffered from the massive taxes and "contributions" levied during the Thirty Years War of 1618–48 and the French and Turkish wars of the late seventeenth century. In this general environment of economic stress, the society of the free cities tended to become more and more rigid and less and less open to change. Magistrates grew fearful of admitting aliens to a community whose existing citizens were already finding it hard to make a living. With the decline of economic opportunities, social mobility leveled off, and it became harder and harder for citizens to enter the charmed circle of patricians or "honorables" who dominated the city's life. For some citizens of the free cities, the revolutionary changes of the early nineteenth century meant the collapse of an old way of life; for many others, however, they signified a new era of long overdue economic and social opportunities.

Many cities had a large number of subjects outside the walls. Except in the case of Bern, whose territory included some smaller cities as well as many villages, a city's subjects generally consisted almost wholly of rural peasants. Some were tenants of individual citizens who owned country estates; others were tenants of the city itself. But either way, their relationship to the urban seigneur probably differed little from the relationship they might have had with a noble or ecclesiastical one. Life was always an endless round of inadequate harvests and burdensome dues and fees. The peasants knew the city well, for many went there to market and some went there to seek employment. But their status as the city's subjects gave them no special advantages if they sought to be admitted as citizens. After all, applicants with special skills were normally favored, and the range of artisan skills that could be acquired in the village was limited indeed. Altogether it can scarcely be argued that German or Swiss peasants gained any noticeable benefits from being subjects of a city-state.

Functions

The original and principal function of the central European city-state was economic: to protect and promote the capacity of its citizens to engage in trade and production in such a way that the greatest possible amounts of profit would remain within the hands of the community itself. This, after all, was the reason why communes were organized in the twelfth century; by making the overlord deal with the town as a whole rather than with individual subjects inside it, the early communards tried to limit his power to interfere directly with their economic activities. It was certainly far better for the citizens to negotiate a lump-sum tax payment each year, and allocate it among themselves, than to have the ruler's bailiff pry into the individual activities of each household as he collected taxes from door to door. Similar motives lay behind the effort of many towns to assert their status as free cities, for the distant emperor, though he might still extract obedience and levy taxes, was even less able than a local ruler to interfere with economic activities on a day-to-day basis.

From the very beginning, the cities assumed wide governmental functions. After all, by building walls, allocating internal taxes and undertaking to regulate trade, a town might succeed in getting rid of alien officials—but the more fully it succeeded in doing so, the more fully the town itself assumed responsibility for the governmental services previously provided by the ruler. Above all, this involved the maintenance of law and order and the defense of the community from outside attack—the classic functions of government in its most minimal sense. For the Germanic city-states, this was only the beginning. Economic activities had to be supervised so that enterprise would be rewarded yet unfair competition prevented. Weights, measures, and monetary exchange had to be regulated so that people would trust the city's markets. Foreign merchants had to be admitted and controlled. Disputes about property and debts had to be adjudicated. Grains had to be stockpiled—an almost sacred duty of governments in pre-modern Europe—so that bad harvests would not be followed by starvation and riot. And if the city acquired a rural territory, agencies had to be established to carry out most of these same functions on the village level.

Finally, the spiritual needs of the inhabitants had to be satisfied and their moral behavior regulated. Scarcely ever—either before or after the Protestant Reformation—were civic officials willing to leave these matters entirely in the hands of the church. Instead, civic and church officials collaborated, often uneasily, in attempting to regulate the spiritual and moral lives of the community.

It is clear that the fundamental raison d'etre of the city-state lay in its capacity to serve the economic interests of its citizens. Yet even in the earliest days of the communes these interests were never quite uniform. A handful of citizens might be engaged in long distance trade, and they looked to their community to support their enterprises abroad while guaranteeing them considerable economic freedom at home. No great merchants, however, were likely to prosper unless their community included a much larger group of people engaged in ordinary retailing, service trades, and craft production. These were the people, after all, who provided an immediate market for imported products and, even more important, who manufactured goods for export. The interest of these lesser citizens was summarized by their persistent demand for a *bürgerliche Nahrung*—a decent livelihood, to be achieved both by protecting them from exploitation by the richest local merchants and by limiting excessive competition among themselves.

During the era of general economic expansion, which lasted from the late fourteenth to the late sixteenth century, most city-states were able to balance these conflicting demands from different sectors of the citizenry with some success. Gradually, however, it became harder and harder to do so. In the smallest cities, where long distance trade became negligible, the protection of *bürgerliche Nahrung* became the community's only policy—which often accelerated the trend to economic stagnation. In larger cities, the interests of commerce were more likely to prevail, leading to a conflict of interests between the merchant oligarchy and the mass of ordinary citizens. In the very largest city-states, however, a third pattern often emerged. Most of these cities were still centers of vigorous commercial activity—but political authority was often in the hands of patricians who became increasingly contemptuous of trade and saw the government chiefly as an instrument to promote their own aristocratic pretensions. By the end of the eighteenth century, the city-states rarely served the economic interests of a significant body of citizens—let alone non-citizens and rural subjects. To a large extent, the system that Napoleon destroyed (at least in Germany) had already lost its reason for existence.

Organization

In theory all male citizens, as juridical heirs of the original commune, had an equal right to participate in the political life of the city-state. In actual fact this was never the case: all the German and Swiss city-states were ruled by a narrow elite. On a symbolic level, the tradition of equal participation by all male citizens was often maintained. Many cities, for example, had periodic ceremonies in which all the citizens renewed the oath that had first been sworn when the commune was founded. In many places a "large council," representing a wide segment of the citizenry—or even an assembly of all male citizens—would be summoned on occasion to be informed or consulted about crucial developments. But in practice real power was always vested in the hands of a much smaller group.

These cities were oligarchic rather than democratic in their political system. The medieval and early modern mind recoiled at the notion that people could be governed by their social inferiors. What is surprising is that each of the central European city-states retained its oligarchic form of government right down to the end of the eighteenth century. Some cities were annexed by a neighboring ruler, but not one city-state ever fell into the hands of a local despot or dynast who converted temporary political authority into hereditary rule by his family. The cities might have powerful personalities who dominated the politics of their time—men like Heinrich Toppler in fourteenth-century Rothenburg or Jacob Sturm in Reformation Strasbourg. But they always exercised authority as members or agents of a city council. The essential principle that political power was to be shared by a group of magistrates rather than vested in a single man was never undermined.

The exact structure of government was different in each community, resulting as it did from centuries of local evolution. But almost every city had a council (or group of councils) that exercised all political authority. The name of the council varied from town to town—it might be called the *Rat*, the *Magistrat* or the *Senat*—as did the number of members: for a small town, fifteen members might be typical, while a large town like Frankfurt had forty-three. The council was often divided into "benches," with one bench enjoying more authority or prestige, or had a smaller "privy council" which functioned as the executive committee. A city rarely had just one mayor. Typically there might be two or three *Bürgermeister,* who assumed the actual duties of office on a rotating basis. In some cities the principle of rotation was extended to the council itself: in Zürich, for example, there were two separate councils of 24 members each, one of which sat from December to June and the other from June to December. Possibly the most complicated system was that of Strasbourg. There was a Council of Thirteen (for foreign and military affairs), a Council of Fifteen (for domestic affairs) and a Senate (for legal decisions). Some members of the Thirteen and Fifteen sat in the Senate, and all three of these bodies came together to constitute the supreme Magistracy, known curiously as the Senate-and-Twenty-One.

Election to the council, or councils, took place in a number of ways, but never was it thoroughly democratic. Generally it involved a disguised form of co-optation. For example, when a vacancy occurred the "large council" might be permitted to chose which existing council members should serve as "electors" to choose their new colleague. Once elected, a council member generally served for life. One important variation, however, was introduced in many cities during the fourteenth century. This was the system under which the city's guilds were able to select a given number of council members. In theory this should have made the composition of city councils more democratic, but in actual fact the guilds almost invariably selected their most wealthy and prestigious members, so that councils with guild representatives often differed little from those with only merchants or patricians as members. Charles V succeeded in eliminating the guild-representation system in numerous cities in the mid-sixteenth century, although it persisted in some places—including some of the Swiss cities—down to the end of the *ancien régime*.

Whatever their composition, the councils of the Germanic city-states enjoyed almost complete authority over both citizens and subjects. In some cities, as we shall see, citizens' deputations won the right to scrutinize and criticize certain council decisions, but the power of these deputations never increased over time and very often decreased. Crucial decision making about every aspect of the city-state's existence was always vested in the magistracy itself. In addition to carrying out legislative and administrative functions, the council normally also functioned as the city's highest court. Jurisdiction over lesser cases was sometimes delegated to a lower court, but major civil and criminal cases were decided by the magistrates themselves; indeed, it was members of the council who normally sat behind a screen and gave instructions as suspected criminals were interrogated or tortured.

Subordinate to the magistracy was a municipal bureaucracy, ranging in prestige and salary level from legal consultants and city clerks down to watchmen and beadles. An additional bureaucracy supervised affairs in the rural districts. As usual in pre-modern Europe, the villagers enjoyed considerable rights of self-administration over matters of scant interest to their seigneurs: which fields to leave fallow, when to plant or harvest, and the like. But the city's administrators were there to deal with criminal matters, to settle property disputes, and, above all, to assure prompt payment of taxes and dues.

In addition to the bureaucracy, the magistrates were also served by a civic militia, sometimes commanded by professional officers but always composed of citizens themselves. Patrol and watch duties were handled on a rotating basis, but the whole militia could be called out when danger threatened. No city could hold out forever against a major army, but with the aid of its militia and fortifications a city could ward off surprise attacks and at least force an opponent to mount an expensive and time-consuming siege.

In some cities, membership in specific militia units was a source of great pride and identity for citizens; on rare occasions, as in early eighteenth-century Frankfurt, the militia companies even developed into vehicles of political protest. But for most citizens a far more important organization was the *Zunft*—the guild or craft association. Sometimes members of more than one craft were grouped together into a single guild; nor were guilds always confined to craftsmen. Normally, however, the term *Zunft* referred to organizations that grouped together all those citizens who were engaged in a single craft. The original purpose of the guilds was economic: to protect the reputation and well-being of each craft by enforcing uniform standards of production, by controlling the admission of new members, and by preventing non-members from engaging in competition by practicing the same trade. But the well-being of the craft was also to be protected in more general ways—for example, by upholding standards of decency and good behavior among members and their families. Inevitably the guild came to operate as a framework for the whole social life of its membership. Often larger guilds even erected a *Zunfthaus* in which meetings were held and social activities took place.

In the fourteenth century the guilds in many German cities became a focus for political activity and often succeeded in asserting a right to be represented in city governments. The political powers of the guilds, however, rarely survived to the eighteenth century. In the mid-sixteenth century the system of guild representation was overturned in many cities by direct imperial decree; elsewhere it was more gradually undermined. In some cities the term *Zunft* itself was replaced by the politically less evocative term *Handwerk*. But as social and economic organizations the guilds continued to function—subject to control and supervision by the magistrates—until the end of the Empire.

Merchant guilds also existed in many cities, but they never acquired the degree of cohesion and control that characterized the craft guilds. The more individualistic nature of mercantile activity made it harder to impose the rules and standards of uniformity which were the essence of the guild system. This is not to say that joint enterprises among merchants were unknown. The Great Ravensburg Trading Company, for example, was an association of merchants from ten different Swabian cities who engaged in trade with Italy, the Low Countries, and Eastern Europe throughout the fifteenth century. But most of the truly great mercantile undertakings—such as those of the Fuggers or the Welsers in Augsburg—were one-family affairs.

Some of the guilds' purely social functions were provided at the upper levels of society by exclusive fraternal organizations or drinking-societies (*Trink-stuben*). But the main function of these organizations was to make clear to all which families should be considered members of the social elite. In the largest cities these organizations took the form of highly restrictive patrician societies; it was generally necessary for a family to have dispensed entirely with commercial activity and to live off rents in "aristocratic" style to be admitted to such a society. In some cities, such as Frankfurt, the power to fill most seats on the city council devolved upon these patrician societies. In Nuremberg, however, there was a striking variation on this system—the city had no patrician societies as such, but the "dance statute" of 1521 specified which families might attend balls at the city hall, and this in turn made clear which families counted as patricians and could place members on the city council. Smaller cities, of course, had to draw on a wider spectrum of citizens—including merchants, professionals, and even some distinguished artisans—to make up the social and political elite. But the larger a city became, the more likely it was to include a clearly-defined non-commercial patriciate which dominated social and political life, while the community's commercial vitality depended on a slightly less prestigious stratum of active entrepreneurs.

Membership in the guilds and corporations was normally confined to members of the citizenry. But there was one institution that encompassed virtually all inhabitants of the city-state, citizens and subjects alike. This was the church. Except for Jews—who were allowed to live, heavily taxed and confined to a ghetto, in some cities—every inhabitant of the city-state was a Christian and thus, by definition, a member of the church. Not only did the church conduct the ceremonies associated with the crucial rites of passage—baptisms, weddings, funerals—but it also administered the endless cycle of ordinary worship and special festivals deemed necessary for the spiritual well-being of individual Christians and of Christian society itself. In addition, many service institutions, such as hospitals, orphanages, and schools, had been founded by the church as part of its mission in society.

In theory the medieval church was an organization whose institutions were separate from those of civil society. In actual fact the institutions of the church were closely intertwined with those of the city-state, and they became even more so during the late Middle Ages. During the course of the fourteenth and fifteenth centuries, urban magistrates became increasingly involved in such "ecclesiastical" matters as the appointment of parish priests and the administration of schools and hospitals. To some extent this reflected the attempt by city councils to assert their control over every aspect of life in the city-state. But in addition, as the laxity and corruption of the late medieval clergy became increasingly apparent, there was a growing concern among many citizens that the city-state was in danger of losing God's favor unless conditions in the church were set aright. The free city, as an unusually distinct political and social organism, was widely understood to be a "sacred corporation," whose existing freedom and prosperity depended on God's continued grace. Thus, if the city strayed too far from God's will, it was not just individual sinners but the community as a whole that might be visited with divine retribution.[11]

Attitudes like this help explain why the Protestant Reformation of the early sixteenth century evoked such particular fervor in the city-states of Germany and Switzerland. Though the impetus for reform generally came from the lower orders, the magistrates were quickly persuaded that adoption of the Reformation would be useful, both to appease the will of the people and to satisfy the will of God. In addition, though by adopting the Reformation they ran the risk of antagonizing the emperor, the magistrates could also complete their long-standing program to assert control over ecclesiastical institutions. In all those city-states that adopted the Reformation—and this included virtually all of the larger ones—not only the church itself but also such institutions as schools and hospitals came under the complete control of the magistrates. In matters of theology and morals the opinions of the Protestant clergy were treated with deep respect, but in the last analysis the ministers served at the magistrates' pleasure and stood, like every other member of the civic bureaucracy, in a position of direct subordination to the city council.

The only exceptions to this rule were the city-states that remained Catholic—a few large cities, like Cologne, and a number of smaller ones. Here, as in other Catholic districts, the regenerated church of the Counter-Reformation struggled to reform its clergy and to assert its authority and independence from secular rulers. But even in the Catholic city-states the aggressive church of the Counter-Reformation made no effort to involve itself seriously in those areas of concern traditionally reserved to secular authorities. Catholic as well as Protestant theologians taught their flocks from Romans 13 that "the powers that be are ordained by God." It was a lesson that magistrates of both faiths rarely let their subjects or fellow-citizens forget. To the end of the *ancien régime,* each city-state continued to be dominated by a small group of men who were convinced of their God-given duty to rule justly but firmly over all the citizens and subjects entrusted to their care.

Political Life

Great as the magistrates' authority was, it did not always go unchallenged. Many of the central European city-states experienced a vigorous and conflict-ridden political history. Political life in the free cities bore little resemblance to that of Western society of modern times. There was no mechanism for the orderly alternation of power between different political groups or parties which advanced different programs or espoused competing ideologies. The medieval and early modern concept of urban government was rooted in the assumption that magistrates always ruled in the interests of society as a whole, arriving at their decisions not through a process of conflict and choice but through the habit of determining and acting on a consensus. For the most part, rulers and ruled alike accepted this as the basis for the magistrates' authority. When, however, a substantial body of citizens decided that the magistrates were no longer acting in accordance with the common good, political conflict was likely to break out.

Most of this conflict took place among the citizens themselves. Only occasionally did non-citizens or rural subjects challenge the authority of the magistrates—although when they did, they were apt to do so in a particularly violent form. A number of imperial cities felt the impact of the great Peasants War of 1525 when rural subjects rose against their overlords in many parts of southern and central Germany. In urban territories, as elsewhere, the uprisings were directed chiefly against new or excessive forms of economic exploitation, although the religious passions of the early Reformation period added to the fervor with which some peasants attacked their overlords. In a few city-states, such as Rothenburg, the peasants and their sympathizers within the urban population actually seized control for a brief period before being suppressed.

Switzerland experienced its greatest peasant revolt in 1653, instigated chiefly by rural subjects of Lucerne and Bern. Here, too, the peasants rose not to proclaim a new social order but to protest the erosion of what they considered their traditional rights and freedoms. These revolts were all crushed by authorities using the customary combination of false promises and military force. Peasant subjects, though entitled to paternalistic government, were not felt to have any legal or moral justification for rising against legitimate authority, and magistrates had few scruples about the means of suppressing their revolts.

Disturbances among the citizens were a somewhat different matter. Extensive as their powers were, the magistrates were always held to be ruling on behalf of the citizenry as a whole. So when the citizens became sufficiently exercised, their demands had to be taken seriously—especially since they could, and sometimes did, appeal over the heads of their magistrates to the emperor himself. Frequently it was the introduction of a new and unprecedented tax that triggered the citizens' outrage. Meetings and demonstrations might be followed by the formation of a citizens' committee which would demand the right to be consulted about municipal affairs. Or the citizens would press for a restructuring of the council itself. Often they succeeded.

The first great wave of citizen uprisings began in the fourteenth century, touching by far the majority of the Germanic free cities. These uprisings have come to be known as the "guild revolutions," for it was generally the merchant and craft guilds which spearheaded the opposition to existing patrician councils. In one city after another, the guilds actually won the right to fill a given number of council seats. But this did not necessarily mean that power passed to the lower orders of society; generally the "guild members" of the council were prosperous merchants or unusually wealthy artisans. Even the revolutionary council which governed Lübeck from 1408 to 1416 did not differ too greatly in its social composition from the council it temporarily replaced. But such movements did demonstrate vividly that existing magistrates could not take their power entirely for granted.

Another major round of citizen disturbances was associated with the Reformation. In many cities the magistrates, fearing an open conflict with the emperor, were hesitant about religious reform—until they were pressured into more radical measures by the citizenry as a whole. Nor were these disturbances limited to religious issues alone. In some cities the peasant revolts of 1525 stimulated citizens to revolt as well, demanding economic and constitutional reforms; many of these demands were met, only to be rescinded by the magistrates once the danger of widespread revolt had passed. In 1528 Lübeck again became a center of revolutionary activity. The formation of a citizens' "committee of sixty-four" to press for religious reform eventually led to the establishment of a new regime which not only completed the Reformation in Lübeck but also, in attempting to improve the city's commercial position, got Lübeck deeply involved in a struggle over the succession to the Danish crown. The traditional regime was not restored to power until 1535.

Some historians have suggested that the Reformation era represented the last period during which citizens played a dynamic part in the political life of the German cities; thereafter, it is argued, the magistrates became increasingly autocratic in their methods of government and the citizens lapsed into passive obedience. This, however, was not the case. It is true that the magistrates in many of the free cities, influenced by absolutist trends in the neighboring princely states, asserted their political primacy in increasingly authoritarian terms. There were certainly cases in which magistrates referred to their fellow-citizens as "subjects"—a term which would have been almost unthinkable in German or Swiss cities during the Middle Ages. But the citizens did not willingly accept any attempts at political subjugation. Quite the contrary, until the very end of the old Empire there continued to be outbreaks of conflict between citizens and their magistrates.[12]

Some cities still experienced real—though short-lived—revolutions. In Frankfurt, for example, mounting resentment about the magistrates' failure to reaffirm the citizens' traditional privileges culminated in 1614 when the patrician council was pressured to resign. It was replaced by a magistracy under the control of Vincenz Fettmilch, a confectioner. Cologne experienced an equally sweeping revolution in the 1680s. What began as a citizens' investigation of corruption among the magistrates finally led to the complete overthrow of the council and the appointment of an entirely new one under the leadership of Nikolaus Gülich, a petty retailer. Such outright revolutions, it must be added, were invariably doomed to failure: the emperor could not tolerate the total overthrow of existing authorities and always used his influence to make sure the traditional councils were restored. Fettmilch, for example, was arrested by moderate fellow citizens after only seven months of power; Gülich was overthrown after two years. When citizens remained somewhat more moderate in their demands, they could often count on support from the emperor. An outbreak of conflict between citizens and magistrates generally led to the appointment of an imperial commission, which investigated local circumstances and often insisted on sweeping reforms before the magistrates were reconfirmed in their power.

In the Swiss city-states, of course, the magistrates were quite safe from this form of intervention. The tightly-knit Bernese patriciate could rule over city and territory without answering to anyone. Even in Germany magistrates generally enjoyed a free hand in ruling over their cities. At a time when territorial princes were imposing closer and closer controls over the administration of their territorial cities, the imperial cities enjoyed a remarkable degree of independence in running their affairs. But to the very end of the Empire, the magistrates had to take into account the fact that an excessively high-handed way of ruling might unleash an unwelcome cycle of citizens' protests, imperial intervention, and edicts of reform. Thus, the latent political power of the citizens, and of the emperor himself, though not a factor in the day-to-day or year-to-year administration of the German city-states, always loomed in the background as an ultimate form of control over the behavior of the magistrates.

Foreign Relations

Three major concerns were likely to shape the relationship between a Swiss or German city-state and other political entities. The first was the need to assert and protect the city's free status. The second was the desire to acquire and then to defend the city's territorial possessions. The third was the need to promote and protect the rights of merchants and other citizens doing business away from the city. In the pursuit of these objectives, the city-state was drawn into relationships—sometimes hostile, sometimes amicable—with other city-states, with neighboring principalities and sometimes with more distant states. In addition, there were times when relations between an imperial city and its own overlord, the emperor, could take on the form of relations with a foreign power.

The desire to protect its own independent status was usually the first and most important issue to involve a city-state in relations with its neighbors. Typically, an adjacent principality would threaten the city's freedom, using some jurisdictional dispute or other legal issue to justify an attack on the city. The danger was particularly acute if the principality concerned had been the community's overlord before it achieved free status, for there might be residual rights or claims which could be cited in support of an invasion. Some nascent free cities lost their independence to an aggressive neighbor; others just barely managed to save themselves. For centuries the annual "pig sermon" in Nördlingen commemorated the occasion in 1440 when a squealing pig had supposedly alerted the citizens just in time to ward off a surprise attack by the neighboring counts of Oettingen. This marked the last time the counts attempted to take the city by force, but for centuries legal disputes, especially concerning the villages over which both sides claimed authority, embittered relations between the city and its noble neighbors. Much greater cities could also be threatened by neighboring powers. As late as 1686 the city of Hamburg had to ward off a bombardment by the king of Denmark, who attempted to reassert his long inactive status as the city's overlord.

The city-states were not confined to passively defending themselves from attack. Conflicts with neighboring princes might also be exploited as a means of undertaking territorial expansion. The city of Esslingen, for example, had a long history of conflicts with the neighboring counts (later dukes) of Württemberg, which dated back to the city's attempt to seize land from the counts in the Middle Ages. In 1312 Esslingen took advantage of Emperor Henry VII's struggle with the counts to occupy Stuttgart and a number of other Württemberg cities. By 1316, however, Esslingen had been forced to return these acquisitions, and in later centuries the tables were turned. Completely surrounded by

Württemberg territory, Esslingen suffered recurrent periods of economic harassment by its neighbor, including a blockade of all trading from 1541 to 1557.

In struggling to protect themselves from their neighbors and to add to their own domains, the cities did not always work alone. Frequently—and especially in the late Middle Ages when urban expansion was at its most vigorous—the cities entered into leagues and alliances with each other. The most important of these was the league of Swabian cities. This alliance was founded in 1376 by fourteen south German cities to protect their independence both from ambitious neighboring princes and from the emperor himself, whose policy of mortgaging cities to local rulers gravely threatened the cities' security. Soldiers of the league inflicted a humiliating defeat on knights led by the count of Württemberg in 1377, and the number of cities belonging to the league rapidly increased to about forty. In 1388, however, the league was defeated in the battle of Döffingen and soon afterwards the alliance had to disband. It was not the only such alliance, however. A league of Rhenish cities flourished contemporaneously with the league of Swabian cities, and in the fifteenth century smaller alliances of south German cities were formed from time to time to combat princely foes like the counts of Württemberg and dukes of Bavaria. From the early sixteenth to the early seventeenth century, representatives of the central and south German city-states met almost every year to conduct a *Städtetag*, a conference at which they deliberated on political, economic, and other matters of mutual concern. The very fact that such assemblies were held illustrates the differences in political consciousness (and opportunities) between the city-states and the territorial cities of the Empire.

An association of somewhat different character was the Hanseatic League: it was organized primarily to secure commercial privileges and trading monopolies for merchants from member cities who did business in the Low Countries, England, Norway, and elsewhere in northern Europe. The Hansa consisted primarily but not exclusively of north German cities; some cities in the Netherlands, Scandinavia, and the eastern Baltic region were also included. Moreover, the German members included both free and territorial cities. Even so, during the late Middle Ages the Hansa was able to pursue effective collective policies in pursuit of economic advantages for merchants from the member cities. The pinnacle of its power was probably reached in 1368–70, when virtually all the member cities joined in a successful war against the king of Denmark. A century later the league was still able to wage an equally determined war against England. By the sixteenth century, however, the Hansa was in decline. Regional princes, such as the dukes of Pomerania, were increasingly determined to control their own territorial cities, and this made it harder and harder for subject towns to function effectively as members of the Hanseatic alliance. This factor, combined with the overall changes in the trading patterns of northern Europe, contributed materially to the eventual collapse of the Hanseatic League as a political and economic force.

An even more durable form of association was represented by the Swiss confederation. Its formation was a matter of long evolution; only in 1513 did the confederation reach its full complement of seven city-states and six rural cantons. Nor did membership in the confederation mean that all the cantons acted in concert. Throughout the Middle Ages, the territorial ambitions of individual cantons led them into separate alliances or conflicts with neighboring states—and sometimes into conflicts with each other. But dangers to the confederation as a whole—such as the threats posed to Swiss autonomy by the house of Habsburg or, in the late fifteenth century, by the dukes of Burgundy—usually drew the cantons into close and effective military cooperation. A last threat to the confederation's solidarity came during the sixteenth century when religious conflicts of the Reformation era brought Catholic and Protestant cantons into bitter conflict with each other; in fact, the Reformer of Zürich, Ulrich Zwingli, died in a battle between his city and five Catholic cantons. But eventually the need to protect their collective autonomy from outside enemies proved more decisive for the cantons than any territorial or religious disputes among them. By the time Switzerland's independence was recognized in the Peace of Westphalia (1648), the solidarity of the confederation and cooperation between its urban and rural cantons could be taken for granted.

The religious disputes which nearly undermined the Swiss confederation also had profound effects on the relations between the German city-states and other political units. In the 1530s, for example, almost twenty free cities (along with a few territorial cities which still enjoyed quasi-autonomous status) joined a dozen princes to form the Schmalkaldic League, an alliance dedicated to protecting the Protestant cause. Although this league disbanded after Charles V won a decisive victory over its members in 1547, the tradition of forming alliances for religious purposes persisted. Sixty years later seventeen imperial cities joined the Protestant Union of 1608, whose formation aggravated the tensions which eventually led to the Thirty Years War. During the war itself, many Protestant cities were drawn—voluntarily or otherwise—into military alliances against the house of Habsburg.

None of these alliances ever included all of the imperial cities. Some cities remained Catholic; others were religiously divided; still others, though Protestant, avoided commitments that would place them in direct opposition to the emperor. There was one cause, however, which united all the imperial cities in the sixteenth and seventeenth centuries: the effort to gain recognition as fully equal participants in the meetings of the imperial diet. In the Middle Ages there had been some diets to which the cities were not even summoned. By the sixteenth century, this was no longer the case: the college of imperial cities was regularly represented, along with the college of electors and the college of princely estates (secular and ecclesiastical). Yet there remained considerable ambiguity about whether votes by the college of cities were necessary and of equal weight as those by the other two colleges. This ambiguity was cleared up by the Peace of Westphalia, which granted the college of cities equal voting rights—and by implication guaranteed the cities a legal status equal to that of the other estates of the Empire.

The imperial cities had long struggled to achieve this status. Yet the Peace of Westphalia was, for most of them, a hollow victory. For by 1648 most of the imperial cities were past their economic or political prime. It is true that most of these cities had escaped outright plunder or destruction during the Thirty Years War—but only by making huge "contributions" to the invading armies, burdening the cities with debts that crippled most of them economically for decades to come. Under such circumstances, the possibility of engaging in any kind of meaningful "foreign relations" disappeared. During the Middle Ages, great urban alliances like the Hansa or the league of Swabian cities had waged vigorous wars in pursuit of their political or economic aims; in the Reformation era the cities could still function as major participants in religious alliances. But after 1648 few imperial cities could have mustered enough funds or troops to defend themselves—let alone to participate meaningfully in an alliance with other political units. Nor, in fact, was there any longer much need for them to do so. The treaties of Westphalia brought religious peace to the Empire, and thereafter the Protestant cities had nothing to fear from the imperial house of Habsburg. Quite the contrary, they looked confidently to the emperor himself and to the institutions of the Empire to protect them from the increasingly ambitious dukes and princes of the age of absolutism. Their continued status as city-states depended, in fact, more and more on the continued existence of the Empire. And when it disappeared, in 1806, most of the city-states disappeared as well. Only the Swiss urban cantons and four free cities in Germany lingered on as reminders of an earlier era.

Conclusion

The history of the central European city-states spanned more than half a millennium. Most of them emerged as free cities in the twelfth or thirteenth century; the majority lasted until the beginning of the nineteenth. During that time, most of these cities exhibited a striking degree of institutional stability. In terms of political practices, economic organization, even physical appearance, a city like Zürich or Hamburg would have seemed very similar in 1750 to the way it had been in 1350. Some of this stability, of course, was the product of stagnation. By and large the end of the Middle Ages was a period of economic expansion, social mobility, and political flexibility in the central European city-states. Later centuries, however, brought economic contraction to most of these cities, and with it came an increasing constriction of economic and political opportunities. But even in those cities which continued to thrive economically, the outward forms of life remained almost unchanged.

All this was shattered in the early nineteenth century. One reason was the collapse of the institutional framework in which most of the city-states had functioned. With the abolition of the Holy Roman Empire, almost all the German city-states were quickly absorbed into territorial states like Bavaria and Württemberg, most of which had long been hoping for an opportunity to annex their urban neighbors.

But the disappearance of the city-states in central Europe was due to more than just the collapse of the Holy Roman Empire. Some of them, after all, did survive the Napoleonic era—only to lose their distinctive characteristics as city-states a few decades later. For in fact the German and Swiss city-states must be seen as part of a broader urban civilization which was swept away by the political and economic changes of the nineteenth century.

There were thousands of cities in pre-modern Germany and Switzerland. What made the city-states unique among them was the fact that they had achieved such extensive privileges of self-government and self-administration as to make them politically and economically almost autonomous. But privileges of some degree or other were characteristic of all cities. Indeed, citizenship itself was a privilege, which conferred on those individuals who possessed it the right to live, marry, practice a trade, and play at least some political role in the community.

The liberal economic and political doctrines which gradually triumphed in the nineteenth century swept away the whole framework of privileges on which urban civilization in central Europe had been based. No longer could magistrates decide who could or could not live in the community. Citizenship became national, not local: anyone could move anywhere and take up any craft or work in the pursuit of economic opportunity. Industrialization both required and in turn was promoted by *Gewerbefreiheit,* the freedom to practice any trade. In place of specialized journeymen traveling from town to town until they received permission to settle down, the nineteenth century witnessed the mass movement of unskilled laborers from the countryside to take up work in booming factory towns. And along with the freedom of movement for individuals came freedom of movement for goods: customs barriers, like citizenship, were transferred from the local or regional to the national level.

In this context, the whole notion of cities as privileged corporations which could control the movement of people and goods in and out of their walls became meaningless (as did the walls themselves, many of them torn down early in the nineteenth century). And with the erosion of privilege as a defining characteristic of cities in general, the particularly privileged city-states could never have retained their special characteristics. There was, to be sure, some resistance to the new trends. Hamburg, for example, only consented to join the German customs union in 1881—ten years after it had become part of the German Empire. But inevitably the former city-states of central Europe came to lose their distinctive character. In modern Germany nothing but history distinguishes former free cities like Cologne or Frankfurt from erstwhile subject cities like Stuttgart or Munich. The city-states of central Europe could not have survived the civilization that had created them.

Notes

1. Samuel Pufendorf, *An Introduction to the History of the Principal Kingdoms and States of Europe, Made English from the Original High Dutch*, 9th ed. (London: J. Knapton, 1728), 281.

2. The list appears in Herbert Grundmann, ed., *Gebhardts Handbuch der deutschen Geschichte*, 9th ed., vol. 2 (Stuttgart: Union Verlag, 1970), 769–784.

3. Listed in Günter Buchstab, *Reichsstädte, Städtekurie und Westfälischer Friedenskongress: Zusammenhänge von Sozialstruktur, Rechtsstatus und Wirtschaftskraft*, Schriftenreihe der Vereinigung zur Erforschung der neueren Geschichte, 7 (Münster: Aschendorff, 1976), 219–220.

4. Philippe Dollinger, *The German Hansa*, trans. D. S. Ault and S. H. Steinberg (Stanford, Calif.: Stanford University Press, 1970), ix–x, lists some 200 towns whose merchants were associated with the Hansa at some point between the fourteenth and the sixteenth century. But only about seventy of these towns were full, active members of the League (p. 88).

5. Since no systematic censuses were conducted before the early nineteenth century, population figures for central European cities must generally be extrapolated from other sources, such as parish registers, tax records, and so on. Estimates for the population of most German cities in pre-modern times will be found in the multivolume series founded by Erich Keyser, ed., *Deutsches Städtebuch* (Stuttgart: Kohlhammer, 1939–1974).

6. See Herbert Woltering, *Die Reichsstadt Rothenburg ob der Tauber und ihre Herrschaft über die Landwehr* (Rothenburg: Verein Alt-Rothenburg, 1965), 13–69.

7. The Frankfurt "police ordinances" of 1621, 1671, and 1731, which specify the division of citizens into five categories, are summarized in more detail by Gerald L. Soliday, *A Community in Conflict: Frankfurt Society in the Seventeenth and Early Eighteenth Centuries* (Hanover, N.H.: University Press of New England, 1974), 62–63. There were some minor changes between 1621 and 1731.

8. Franklin L. Ford, *Strasbourg in Transition, 1648–1789* (Cambridge, Mass.: Harvard University Press, 1958), 47–49.

9. Wolfgang Zorn, *Augsburg: Geschichte einer deutschen Stadt*, 2nd ed. (Augsburg: Hieronymus Mühlberger, 1972), 174; Friedrich Blendinger, "Versuch einer Bestimmung der Mittelschicht in der Reichsstadt Augsburg vom Ende des 14. bis zum Anfang des 18. Jahrhunderts," in Erich Maschke and Jürgen Sydow, eds., *Städtische Mittelschichten* (Stuttgart: Kohlhammer, 1972), 32–78, esp. p. 71.

10. Christopher R. Friedrichs, *Urban Society in an Age of War: Nördlingen, 1580–1720* (Princeton, N.J.: Princeton University Press, 1979), 103–106.

11. The arguments in this paragraph and the next draw heavily on the influential work of Bernd Moeller, *Imperial Cities and the Reformation*, trans. H. C. Erik Midelfort and Mark U. Edwards, Jr. (Philadelphia: Fortress Press, 1972).

12. This point is argued more fully in Christopher R. Friedrichs, "Citizens or Subjects? Urban Conflict in Early Modern Germany," in Miriam U. Chrisman and Otto Gründler, eds., *Social Groups and Religious Ideas in the Sixteenth Century*, Studies in Medieval Culture, 13 (Kalamazoo, Mich.: The Medieval Institute, 1978), 46–58, 164–169.

Chapter Five

THE HAUSA CITY-STATES FROM 1450 TO 1804

Robert Griffeth

The Hausa of modern northern Nigeria and southern Niger constitute one of Black Africa's largest populations. They share a very old common historical tradition, and they speak and write in a language which has spread widely across West Africa's vast grasslands as a result of the vigorous commercial enterprise of their long-distance traders. They are also among the most fully Islamized of sub-Saharan Africa's peoples, although the vitality of pre-Muslim Hausa customs and beliefs remains strong in their culture down to the present day. But of all the features of Hausa civilization that have come to symbolize their distinctive way of life, those associated with the great walled cities of Hausaland's core territories are central.

For nearly three hundred and fifty years (ca. 1450–1804) Kano and Katsina, Daura, Gobir, and Zauzau (Zaria) as well as many similar, if smaller, expressions of the urban phenomenon flourished as sovereign city-states within the general milieu of an evolving common Hausa culture. As in the cases of city-states in antiquity and Western Europe's late medieval and early modern experience, the Hausa urban polities were almost continuously challenged and disturbed by powerful imperial neighbors; they also spent a great deal of their energies in competing and warring with each other. At the same time, each possessed that essential special feature of all city-states: those who constituted the local community—rulers, citizens, and subjects—regarded themselves as sovereign, as belonging wholly to a place and a defined social unity which commanded their highest allegiance. While recognizing and affirming the cultural ties which knit them to all other Hausa, they nonetheless prized most their independence and often struggled mightily to insure that it remained unfettered by encroachments from foreign kingdoms and neighboring Hausa alike. The walled cities were thus more than symbols of independency and places of refuge in stressful times: the walls enclosed that space, that almost sacred terrain, within which each member of the community could affirm and secure his or her status in the best of times as well as the worst. For a Hausa to say "I am a Katsinawa" or "I belong to Kano" was to express one's ultimate loyalties and pride of identity.

The origins and early development of Hausa city-state civilization are both ancient and poorly known.[1] The first adequately documented instances of city-states *in situ* appear only near the end of the first millennium A.D. While both physical evidence and oral tradition speak of cities and their rulers as early as the eleventh century, the fully developed Hausa city-state civilization is known in fair detail only from the mid-fifteenth century. By that time the written accounts begin to reflect the strongly Islamic features which have come to characterize certain key groups of the population. The internal vigor of the strongest states, coupled with the declining powers of their formerly potent Songhay (western) and Bornuese (eastern) imperial neighbors, caused the seventeenth and eighteenth centuries to be a period when the Hausa city-states reached their full flowering as sovereign entities. Local production and foreign commerce both grew dramatically. Great market centers flourished and expanded, particularly at Kano. Hausa merchants penetrated new commercial zones far to the west and south. The socio-economic structures within individual states grew increasingly complex and specialized. And all exhibited greater signs of Islamic influence in the patterns of intellectual and cultural life as well as in government.

This great age of city-state dominance ended abruptly during the years 1804–1812 when the Fulani, a distinguishably foreign people who had entered Hausaland from the far West African grasslands as cattleherdsmen over the previous four to six centuries, organized and successfully carried out a revolution based on Islamic reformism (*jihad*) that finally and definitively swept away the cherished local sovereignty of the most important Hausa states. In their place the new Fulani rulers established a Muslim imperial government, the Caliphate.[2] The city-states became provincial capitals (emirates) owing allegiance and paying regular taxes to the Caliph, who ruled from the new imperial city of Sokoto. This Hausa-Fulani empire, as it came to be called, pursued a campaign of imperial expansion that extended far beyond the frontiers of traditional Hausaland. It became, in fact, one of the largest and most powerful states of nineteenth century Africa. When it, too, fell victim to foreign rule under British and French conquerors in the early years of the present century, the result was not a restoration of quasi sovereignty to the old Hausa city-states. The British, in particular, ruled their new Nigerian colony (to which Hausaland was amalgamated as a major region) by maintaining and attempting to modernize the Fulani-created administrative apparatus. One consequence was an even greater diminution of local city-state autonomy than had occurred during the precolonial era. This expanded and colonially shored-up Hausa-Fulani Caliphate and emirate system of government was itself badly shattered in January, 1966 when the last ruler, Sir Ahmadu Bello, Sardauna of Sokoto and Premier of the Northern Region, was assassinated in the course of the first Nigerian coup d'etat.

Most standard accounts of Hausa history have paid scant attention to the pre-1804 city-state period. Those three and one half centuries extending from the successful introduction of Muslim influence to Hausaland up to the Fulani *jihad* are usually depicted as an era of unrelieved internal competition and warfare during which time the Hausa states more often than not suffered from the depredations and tribute exactions of powerful neighbors. Historical interest has also focused on the theme of West African Islamic development in which the seventeenth and eighteenth centuries are regarded as a time of Hausa religious and cultural regression from what were the sound Islamic beginnings of the fifteenth and sixteenth centuries.[3] From this perspective the city-state period is merely a long, painful time of transition when the potentially civilizing forces of Islam are kept in check by endemic political disorder and the resurgence of local, pagan traditions: "good" Muslims were forced to bide their time, mute their discontents, and await the chance to put things to right which they did finally when the Fulani reformers coalesced into a potent new revolutionary party.

As in many other instances, this view of Hausa history demonstrates once again the high order of preference shown by historians for the study of powerful centralized states and empires with emphasis placed upon the spread of "universal civilizations" such as Islam. The achievements, and setbacks, of societies which exist on smaller political scales and which assert local, "particularistic" cultural traditions command a lesser share of attention and interest. This essay will attempt to shift that unequal balance of attention and interest by treating the relatively long age of developed Hausa city-state culture as a notable achievement worthy of study in its own right.

Geographical Setting and Hausa Pre-State Developments

Hausaland proper, that core area within which Hausa speech, society, and culture leading to the establishment of those urban concentrations known as *birni* (pl. *birane*), gradually developed in the well-watered grassland zone of modern northwestern Nigeria and southern Niger. This zone, bordered by the Sahara on the north, is part of a vast territory called by Arab geographers the *bilad al-Sūdān*, "Lands of the Blacks," and spans the continent in the vicinity of ten to fifteen degrees north latitude from Ethiopia to Senegal. Except for the northern-most limits of the Sahel (the last latitudinal zone in which farming is possible before entering the desert itself) no pronounced geographical features separate Hausaland from similar grasslands that encircle its eastern, western, and southern flanks. Stream and river courses maintaining annual flows intersect it; and generally speaking, the whole of the region is capable of supporting settled farming communities.. This ecological condition has existed throughout historical times and is certainly the basis upon which cereal agriculture (millet and sorghum predominate as staple food crops), cotton and indigo cultivation, and animal domestication spread. The first Hausa settlements were in all likelihood small family-managed farms which grew over time into more densely populated villages (*gari*) of extended kin. Some few of the *gari* subsequently enlarged their territories while preserving at their centers the nuclei of the first *birane*.

Scholarly controversy has enveloped the discussion of Hausa *birane* origins. The most popular view until quite recently was based largely upon the preserved Hausa written accounts and scraps of information taken from the reports of medieval travelers. This view asserted that the Hausa oral accounts were formally written down by literate Muslims some two hundred or so years ago and that they embodied an amorphous legendary tale of a founding ancestor, Abayajidda, a foreigner from the central Arab lands of the Near East, which reflected a Muslim bias that vastly postdated the actual establishment of Hausa culture. In order to grapple with this complicating element, some scholars have chosen to strip the accounts of what they regarded as merely legendary (that is, the stipulated facts contained in the written accounts) while at the same time proceeding to argue that Hausa culture of the present day is very old—some would assert two to three millennia. Archeological evidence is almost wholly lacking to support this argument, but speculations based upon the comparative study of the languages spoken in the Central Sudan are made to give secondary support to the concept of an ancient Hausa culture that evolved over many hundreds of years prior to the present millennium. To the extent that foreign influence was thought to have played a significant role in this basically indigenous development, it was seen to have come from the north, the Saharan lands of the Tuareg nomadic peoples.

This general view has been termed by Professor J. E. G. Sutton, in a recent reconceptualization of the whole problem, as the "orthodox" view of Hausa beginnings.[4] Sutton, who feels that the written record must be taken far more seriously as an historically accurate description of "true" Hausa origins, argues that the record itself in combination with a more precise understanding of linguistic evidence reveals "the clear message . . . that Hausa expanded from east to west across the savanna belt of Northern Nigeria. And the relative homogeneity of the language and culture within this vast zone indicated that the spread is quite recent (within the present millennium, say)." Further, Sutton argues that while the written sources are clearly idealized, they do represent real historical developments that "enshrine the vague memory of how Hausaland and 'Hausaness' began from a series of small centers and hill-bases on its eastern side" which subsequently were extended to the western Hausa areas of Zamfara and Gobir by the seventeenth century.[5]

Sutton's reformulation of the question is very convincing. It identifies Hausa language directly with its closest set of neighbors, the tongues spoken by the Teda-Daza peoples of the Lake Chad region. It conforms the direction of movement of peoples in this whole region—basically an east to west migration—to the evidence presented in the oral and written accounts. And, Sutton's postulation of a more recent date (during the present millennium) for the emergence of a homogeneous Hausa culture, including the foundation of the

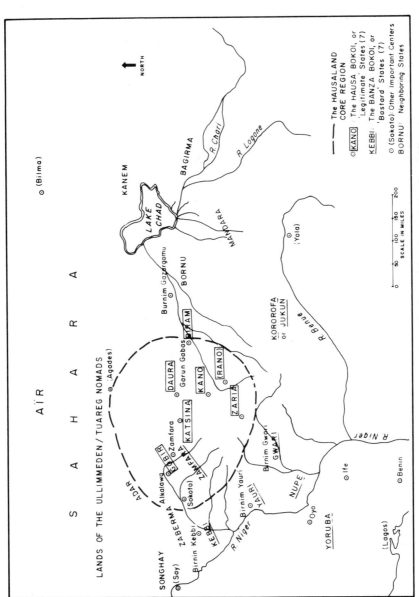

Map 6: *The Hausa and Their Neighbors (Modern Northern Nigeria and Southern Niger)*

nuclear Hausa states, also accords well with both the traditions and the Muslim elements contained within them. Using Sutton's guidelines, we shall now turn to the Hausa oral and written accounts themselves in order to chart Hausa city-state beginnings.

Foundations of the First City-States

In the Legend of the Queen of Daura and Abayajidda the Hausa possess one of Africa's most elaborately developed epic tales of origin. The story seeks to explain the circumstances surrounding the founding kingly lineages in each of the original seven *birane* and the relation of these states to nearby neighbors. It places heavy emphasis on the unity of Hausa culture despite the obvious disunity of the city-states in the political sphere. The tale also reflects many elements of formal Islamic story-telling, the main purpose of which is to link the distinctly non-Arab Hausa to the old centers of Muslim civilization in the Near East. There are many versions of the Daura Legend, each differing from the others in important matters of detail and chronology; but, all versions preserve the key features mentioned here.[6]

Abayajidda (or as he is known in the commonest of the versions, Abuyazidu) was a son of Abdulahi, King of Baghdad. He quarreled with his father, left Baghdad with a large company of followers, journeyed west, and finally arrived in the Bornu kingdom (located on the western edge of Lake Chad), Hausaland's strongest and nearest imperial neighbor. The Bornu *Maï* (ruler) saw that his visitor was very strong and commanded a great following of armed horsemen. He thereupon arranged for the marriage of his daughter, the Princess Magira, to Abayajidda. Subsequently, the *Maï* asked Abayajidda for the loan of his horsemen in order to conduct a campaign against Bornu's foes. In exchange for this the *Maï* promised that upon his return from battle he would install his son-in-law's lieutenants as princes in the country. This promise proved to be a skillful deceit as the *Maï* intended to use his newly enlarged army to attack and kill the newcomers. Warned of this treachery by his wife, Abayajidda and Magira fled to the west, soon arriving in the first of the Hausa territories, Daura, at the site of Birni Gabas ta Buram. There he left his Bornuese wife and journeyed on farther with one of his concubines to Birnin Daura.

Upon his arrival he was extended hospitality by an old woman named Waira. He asked her for water and received the reply that water was available only on Fridays as there was a great and menacing snake who dwelt in the well and prevented the people from drawing water on all the other days of the week. So Abayajidda took a bucket and went to the well to see for himself. When he let the bucket down, the snake appeared; but Abayajidda drew his knife and cut off the snake's head. The following morning, which was Friday, the townspeople came to the well and saw the body of the slain snake. The Queen of Daura, who was summoned, asked her people who had killed the snake. Many lied and claimed credit for the act. She then asked for the snake's head, and none who had spoken could produce it. Waira then spoke and said that her visitor, a man who had arrived the night before on an animal "which was like a horse and yet was not a horse" had gone to the well for water. She reasoned that it may have been this visitor who slew the snake. Abayajidda, when summoned, produced the snake's severed head.

Then the Queen said that she had promised half her kingdom to any who could rid her domain of the snake's menacing presence; but Abayajidda asked instead that she marry him. And so he remained with the Queen of Daura as her husband along with the concubine who had accompanied him. Thereafter he was called by the name Makassarkin (snake-killer) and it was to him that the people were asked to bear their news. The concubine bore a son who was called Mukarbigari. Then the Queen of Daura bore a son whose name was Bawogari. Upon his father's death, Bawo became the ruler (*sarkin*, pl. *sarki*) in his father's place.

Bawo in his turn had six sons. These were Gazaura who succeeded to the Daura kingship and Bagauda who founded Kano State; Gunguma who became king of Zauzau (Zaria) and Duma, King of Gobir; Kumayau established his rule over Katsina and Zamna Kogi over Rano. These six were all descended from three of Bawo's wives, each pair from a common mother. Together with a son of Abayajidda's Bornuese wife, Magira, who had remained at Gabas ta Buram (Biram), these offspring of a common grandfather are regarded by the Hausa as the founding ancestors of the Hausa Bakwai, or the "true and legitimate Hausa Seven." A parallel line of descendants from Abayajidda and his concubine through her son, Mukarbigari, went on to found seven other states, the "bastard or illegitimate Seven," termed the Banza Bakwai. These latter include most of the kingdoms which flank Hausaland to the south and west and are usually identified as Zamfara, Kebbi, Nupe, Gwari, Yauri, Yoruba, and Kwararafa. References to them appear constantly in the Hausa traditions and written records with principal emphasis placed on their inferior status within the immediate Hausa cultural world.

Two of the Hausa Bakwai, Kano and Zaria, developed especially rich local traditions which cast considerable light on critical features of city-state growth. Kano, though frequently locked in fierce competitive struggle with Katsina, appears to have been the first state to have created an effective army used to enlarge and consolidate the territory under its control. By the seventeenth century, Kano had also become the major international market center of Hausaland (a position which on earlier occasions was held by Katsina), the main terminus for the trans-Saharan trade routes coming down from North Africa. And, finally, Kano also developed as the most important center of Muslim culture in Hausaland. Not only had its rulers and noble classes converted, but Kano also had a large population of foreign Muslims, among whom the Wangara (Mande-speaking merchant groups from the Western Grasslands region of the middle and upper Niger river) are credited with first introducing the civilization of the Prophet to Hausaland.

Zaria, the most southerly of the Hausa Seven, records in its traditions two matters of great interest in the process of city-state growth. First, its deep association with the tradition of wall building under its great sixteenth century monarch, Queen Amina, who is credited with introducing techniques of construction widely imitated throughout the region. Second, the practice of slave-trading, as its position closest to the non-Hausa stateless peoples ideally located it for that purpose.

Of the remaining traditional Hausa Bakwai, Katsina—Kano's principal competitor—most clearly developed into the strongest state in the early part of the period. Rano remained a small state, virtually disappearing from the record by the seventeenth century. Daura and Biram, the original *birane* of tradition, were continuously subjected to the influence of the Bornu empire and did not become in either scale or political and economic importance the equal of Kano, Katsina, and Zaria. Gobir, the seventh of the leading states, has a history that sets it apart from the other six. As the most northerly of the Hausa core states, its development is inextricably intertwined with the affairs of the desert nomads of Aïr. In a sense, Gobir was the gateway kingdom through which merchants plying the desert trade had to pass before entering the densely settled Hausa core. By the same token, it had also to serve as the first line of defense for all the rest from the possible depredations of the nomadic Tuareg. The Fulani revolution originated in Gobir at the end of the city-state period and thus its political role in nineteenth century Hausa-Fulani history is central. Finally, the state of Zamfara, often spoken of in the traditions as numbering among the Hausa "bastard Seven," lies more within than outside Hausaland proper. It, too, experienced periods of relative strength and importance, although it never achieved the status or power of either Katsina and Gobir which border it.

Three main factors appear to have operated during the early state-formation period in Hausaland which helped create conditions favorable to the emergence of the city-state pattern. First, excepting Gobir, the region remained relatively isolated from the principal centers of imperial power. In the far Western Sudan, the ancient Ghana kingdom was invaded in the eleventh century by the armies of the Maghrebian Almoravid state and its effective power base destroyed. Not until the 1300s did a new and enlarged empire, Mali, replace it. Even then Mali's interests were concentrated in the middle Niger and Western Saharan areas. Such contacts as Mali did have with Hausaland came in the form of Mande-speaking Muslim traders and missionaries who peacefully settled as foreigners in the Hausa towns. To the east, on the far side of Lake Chad, the old Kanem kingdom's energies were absorbed by the need to defend itself from the nomadic Bulala warriors of the desert. Only in the course of the fourteenth century did the rulers of this state physically relocate their capital to the south and west of the lake, creating the new Bornu kingdom. The Bornu *Maï*'s, as they acquired full control of their new lands, frequently took to interfering in the affairs of their Hausa neighbors. But this capacity only developed in the fifteenth and sixteenth centuries.

This relative isolation seems also to have applied to the international trading situation. From the Western Sudan the major trans-Saharan trade routes struck directly northwards toward the Maghreb while the eastern routes, leading out from Kanem/Bornu, traversed the desert to Libya in the north and the Upper Nile in the east. To the extent that Hausaland was integrated into this vast, Muslim-dominated international trading network, it was as a receiver of goods that had first passed through the Malien and Bornuese imperial market centers or as a supplier of locally manufactured articles, particularly indigo dyed cotton cloth. In the fifteenth century both Katsina and Kano were beginning to attract an increasing volume of the trans-Saharan trade, a development which was in later centuries to make these cities commercially dominant throughout the Sudan.

Before that happened, however, Hausaland was to experience in a much more direct way the influence of reborn imperial power. The Songhay empire, successor to Old Mali, appeared on the scene in the middle of the fifteenth century and, from its imperial cities of Gao and Timbuktu, rather regularly entered into the affairs of the Hausa, breaking down the long period of relative isolation. Similarly, from the east, Bornu developed a much greater capacity to intervene in Hausaland and often did so by demanding tribute from the Hausa kings. But by this time the core *birane* had evolved into a fairly strong set of city-states, each protected from all but the most serious armed invasions by its ring of defensive walls. Despite foreign meddling, the city-state structures remained intact as autonomous political entities, so that by the end of the sixteenth century, when Songhay power was crushed by the invading forces of a Moroccan army and Bornu became much troubled by both internal difficulties and external threats, the Hausa states were freed to enter upon their great age of independent development.

A second factor which helped to foster a city-state rather than a highly centralized pattern of political organization in pre-fifteenth century Hausaland may be linked to the area's rich agricultural potential. As was the case in nearly all West Africa's grassland farming populations, the oldest Hausa chiefly offices were identified with the control and use of land by small nuclear units that were knit together by the ties of kinship. Chiefs were either heads (*gidaje*) of patrilinear family groups occupying a common territory or were religious officials charged with performing the cycle of ritual observances regarded as necessary to insure the success of the agricultural enterprise. These latter chiefs were called *sarki noma*, kings of farming. When more extensive powers became attached to certain chiefs or when others were appointed or elected to perform specialized duties and functions (such as leaders of the hunt, war leaders, and so forth) kinship terminology was frequently retained. This close interconnection between kin-based social organization, control and use of arable land, and the exercise of ritual functions was the invariable base upon which more elaborate forms of political office grew. As some of the original farming hamlets became the nuclei of the *birane*, each consisting of many different kinship units as well as immigrant settler groups, the old patterns still remained to command the loyalties and to focus the cultural outlook of the ruling groups. This great resilience of traditional Hausa culture subsequently proved capable of confronting, domesticating, and assimilating even so alien a cultural force as Islam when it first appeared in fourteenth century Hausaland.

While the relative isolation of early Hausaland from the main centers of imperial power and international commerce may help to explain why the small farming communities were able to evolve a common, if decentralized, pattern of agriculturally based culture, a third major factor must be identified as the main impetus that led to city-state development. That factor is, in the broadest sense, a sustained growth of Hausa productivity both in agriculture and craft industries. As indicated earlier, Hausaland is located in an exceptionally fertile region of the West African grasslands; but it is not the only such area. The characteristic modes of local subsistence production and the types of social organization which they evoked show considerable uniformity throughout the _bilad al-Sūdān_ from Lake Chad to the Senegal. But only in Hausaland does a true city-state pattern emerge early and endure late. All available evidence seems to point to a genuine growth of the economy based upon greater efficiency in the traditional modes of production; the larger economic surplus which resulted enabled specialized classes of artisans (weavers, dyers, metalsmiths, leather-workers) to devote their time exclusively to craft production, a mode which often flourishes best in an urban setting. The growth of urban concentrations, the core _birane,_ in turn attracted large numbers of immigrants who swelled the ranks of city-dwellers living under the political control of the traditional Hausa _sarki_ and their officials. Note however that none of the _birane_ originated as market centers servicing the international trade. That pattern typified the imperial states whose emperors drew their wealth from taxes levied upon the trade. The reverse development occurred in Hausaland where first the individual states grew large and then attracted the attention of the international merchant community and finally surpassed the old imperial market cities as the main destinations of the trans-Saharan and internal West African traders alike. It is interesting to note that this gradual shift took place roughly contemporaneously with the rise of North European dominance over the world's maritime commerce, although the two developments are not connected.

Historians frequently find it necessary, or convenient, to explain any major historical phenomenon by reference to at least three factors, as has been done here to account for the appearance of the Hausa city-states. In the eyes of the Hausawa, on the other hand, the story is recounted rather differently. At the conclusion of the lengthy, imprecisely documented formative period to which their Legend of Daura and Abayajidda refers, each Hausa comes to regard his or her identity as the consequence of belonging to a very specific place and a well-defined social entity: to the _birni,_ whose walls enclose the sacred original center as well as provide protection in troubled times; to the rulers whose positions and status are legitimized by the places they occupy in an elaborately hierarchical social structure derived from ancestral kin-relatedness; to a style of life covering everything that possesses deep local roots from work to worship. In a word, sovereignty comes to describe for each Hausa that most cherished of all values: the sense of belonging to a finite place with known boundaries, to a community of persons—both citizen and subject—beyond which no higher authority is recognized. At this point historical tradition is not the common story of all Hausa. History becomes the individual histories of the Hausa *Bakwai,* the original Seven, and of the lesser states. The most recoverable of the early histories begins with fifteenth century Kano which also supplies the bulk of the evidence for the seventeenth and eighteenth centuries.[7] Even so, the main distinguishing characteristics of all Hausa city-states, large and small, reveal common elements sufficient to make reasonable a collective description of them.

This collective description will be treated under four broad categories: physical appearance and territorial configuration; social and economic organization; political structure and office-holding; and, cultural institutions, with particular reference to the role of Islam.

Physical Appearance and Territorial Configuration

A Hausa city-state comprised the whole of that territory within which the inhabitants recognized the sovereign power exercised by the ruler who resided at its capital. While the range in size varied from as much as 10 to 13,000 square miles for large states such as Kano and Zaria, many of the smaller states could claim no more than a few hundred square miles. The largest part of the population within each lived in hamlets and small towns, close to its agricultural domains. But each citizen's eyes were turned by loyalty and the formal links maintained by the ruler's officials to the seat of power, the capital city.

The capital *birni,* its massive earthwork walls often encircling a number of square miles, contained the ruler's residence and the walled compounds (*gida*) of his senior officials; the main market; workshop areas where the artisans and craftsmen plied their specialized trades; residential quarters and compounds of the Hausawa citizenry; wards occupied by resident foreigner groups; and substantial open space. Much of the open space was under cultivation since protected fields and gardens supplied food for the city-dwellers on those many occasions when the *birni* was under attack and siege. Carefully maintained water wells were strategically located throughout the various quarters; and the garden plots and fields were planted adjacent to marshy ponds and drainage sumps.

Systematic archeological survey work has yet to be undertaken on the Hausa *birane.* Consequently, the various stages of growth that they experienced are known mainly through traditional attributions to the reigns during which one or another prominent feature of wall and building construction occurred. However, two clues are provided from careful examination of their sites. First, the main core *birane* are located near abundant and easily workable sources of iron-stone, thus providing an essential natural resource for one of the main craft industries. In the case of Kano, the iron-stone is found in hills that subsequently were enclosed by the girdling walls. Second, particularly fertile garden soils with access to perpetual water supplies are invariably present. Oral tradition adds a further dimension to these two features by stressing that original townsites were found in the vicinity of the great *iskoki* (traditional Hausa nature spirits which are still the object of worship by non-Muslim Hausa).[8]

The walls reflect the beginnings of the city-state system since they were clearly designed as defensive fortifications. The *Kano Chronicle* states the time in which this tradition was begun as the eleventh century when Gijimasu, the third *Sarkin* Kano, assembled the people to begin construction of the walls. They were completed by his son, the fifth *Sarkin,* Tsariki, and were entered through eight different gates. Later North African visitors such as Leo Africanus, in the early sixteenth century, remarked on the great scale achieved by subsequent additions to the Kano walls. By the early nineteenth century, when the English explorer Major Dixon Denham came to Kano for a prolonged stay, we discover that Kano's walls have reached a length of nearly fifteen miles in an irregular oval shape and contain fifteen entry gates.[9] They had been built up to heights of over thirty feet with dry ditches dug on both the inner and outer perimeters at the base. The gates were constructed of heavy wood covered with sheet iron and were large enough in height and width to permit horse mounted soldiers to pass easily through. Guard houses flanked each gate, and observation posts and low towers were situated at intervals along the wall.

Tradition also records that a great period of wall building all over Hausaland occurred during the late fifteenth and early sixteenth centuries, inspired largely by the female ruler of Zaria, Queen Amina.

Aside from market areas and mosque sites, most structures within the city walls conformed to a single pattern that was most elaborate in the cases of the ruler's palace and the residences of high court officials and wealthy merchants and was repeated in a less grandiose fashion for the dwellings of the lesser citizenry and resident foreigner groups. The basic unit of this pattern was the mud-walled compound (*gida*) whose internal spatial arrangements mirrored Hausa social structure. The pattern applied equally to the smaller towns and farming hamlets of the city-state's rural countryside, except that these would not always have the encircling defensive walls around the whole.

Each *gida* was entered through a forecourt, the openings to which were off-set so as to conceal the main interior from passersby on the street. Flanking the entryway were areas where unmarried sons had their huts. In the same forecourt area the slave quarters were adjacent to the place where horses and donkeys were tethered. To penetrate the large inner court one continued through a partitioned access hut, its openings also off-set to further obstruct the view from either the street or forecourt. At the center of the inner court, the compound head (*maigida*) had his dwelling surrounded by the huts, cooking areas, and granaries of his wives. In spaces radiating out from the *maigida*'s hut

Illus. 9: *A Hausa Town View*

the other male heads of families residing in the compound had their living quarters, similarly encircled by the huts of their wives. Common bathing and latrine areas were located at the rear of the inner court, screened off by mat walls and partitions. In the case of a particularly prosperous *gida,* a well might also be maintained within the walls.

The *gida*'s labyrinthine entry pattern reinforced the Hausa social practice of *kulle* (wife-seclusion), while the flanking arrangement of the interior court huts reflected the hierarchical organization of the various polygamous family groups, single adults, and slaves who together made up the residential unit. The entryway space (*zaure*) served the additional crucial function of providing a gathering place for males. Here male neighbors greeted each other and socialized; during the dry season men also plied their craft activities, particularly weaving, in the *zaure.* Rich merchants or important administrative officials might have a separate audience room that was more private than the *zaure,* and was located closer to, or within, the inner courtyard; but, for most of the citizenry, the compound's entry-space held the most important Hausa social activities: men's talk and men's work. Should a compound contain but one outside opening, it was regarded as housing a single social unit under the control of the senior male, regardless of how many actual domestic groups lived within. Were a second or more doorways cut through the walls, these would be reckoned as constituting evidence of additional social units for purposes of census, taxation, and the like.

Three other types of structure—or defined space—complete the physical layout of the large *birane* and smaller towns alike. The first of these is the market which, in the capitals, was a very large, centrally located place that might include sheltered stalls under mat roofing, permanent mud-brick buildings, and large open—but carefully staked out—spaces assigned to purveyors of goods who attended the market daily. The second characteristic structure was the mosque. Each quarter of the main cities would surely have its mosque, often more than one. In many instances the mosque would consist of little more than an arrangement of stones laid out on the ground with its eastern alignment containing a niche indicating the appropriate orientation toward Mecca for the recitation of daily prayers. In other cases the mosque would be more elaborate, sometimes an enclosed area with muezzin's tower for calling the faithful to prayer. Such mosques might possess areas shaded by trees or mats where the *mallams* (Islamic religious teachers) held classes for young boys and serious older students. Although the evidence is not wholly clear, it would appear that the construction of grand central mosques (such as had taken place in the imperial states of Mali and Songhay in their cities of Timbuktu and Jenne) did not occur until the nineteenth century under the Fulani rulers. The clear assumption is that during the city-state period the ruler's palace and the central market served as more significant physical landmarks than did the mosques, even in the largest cities. The third characteristic of the *birni* consisted of specialized wards or quarters. Some of these were places devoted to particular

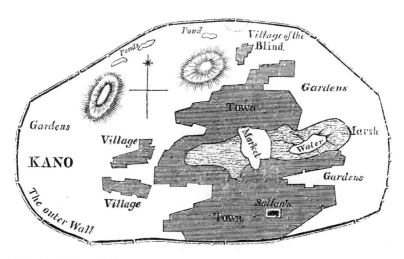

Illus. 10: *Plan of Kano*

crafts, such as the indigo dyeing pit areas or the forge and smithy works of the metalsmiths. Others were special villages for the blind or lepers. Strangers' quarters, as for instance dwellings occupied by long-distance foreign traders who swelled the cities' populations to nearly twice their resident size during certain months of the year, were a bit different from the *gida* pattern of the Hausawa.

These characteristic features of the great *birane* were, ideally, repeated in the provincial towns, the *gari*. On more modest scales the *gari,* too, were encircled by earthwork defensive walls. Each had its market of either the periodic (meeting on regular cycles of every fourth, fifth, or seventh day) or daily type. Mosques with their resident *mallams* and members of the main craft guilds would be found there, too. But standing at the center of the *gari*'s area would be the *gida* of the governor or provincial administrator of the district. This official's role would be to oversee (to rule) the ward heads of the *gari* and to command, protect, and tax the farming hamlets where the overwhelming majority of the population resided. The village and town areas were clearly defined territories, each possessing its known share of the city-state's rural domains. So clear was the pattern that the Fulani rulers of the nineteenth century were able to allocate the *gari* as "fiefs" to the aristocrats who came to rule Hausaland after the *jihad*. The British, in their turn, formalized the *gari* as the smallest units of local administration and simply assimilated this traditional form of territorial organization into their structure of colonial overrule.

The principal variation from this pattern of territorial organization that linked the humblest farmer to the king concerned the uncultivated wastelands and fields that were regularly allowed to lie fallow. While these lands unquestionably belonged to the city-state, they served as pasturage for the cattle-keeping Fulani. Very often the farmers encouraged the pasturing of cattle on fallow fields and exchanged surplus grain with the herdsmen in return for milk, meat, and the recognized benefits of soil revitalization through animal manuring. Whereas town-dwelling Fulani were assimilated into the structure of government and controlled under Hausa *sarki* in the same fashion as any other foreigner group, the pastoral Fulani (*Fulanin boroje*) continued to live among the farmers while obeying the dictates of their nomadic leaders (*ardo*). They remained little influenced by Hausa social, political, and cultural (e.g., Islamic) institutions so long as the focus remained the economic symbiosis described here. Eventually, of course, the pagan pastoral Fulani joined with their Muslim, town-dwelling brethren (the *Fulanin gida*) in the jihadic revolution that swept the Hausa *sarki* from power.

In summary, nothing about Hausaland's physical location nor its socio-economic development up through the city-state period appears to distinguish it sharply from other West African grassland societies. Adjoining territories in the Chadic east and Niger west were similarly fertile and open. The peoples of both areas practiced an agriculture and developed craft industries comparable in character to those of the Hausa. Herdsmen, more often than not pastoral Fulani, practiced a system of economic exchange with the farmers based upon occupational specialization and this pattern extended right across the *bīlad al-Sūdān* from Senegal to Chad. Even at the level of territorial organization and systems of local government, considerable similarities can be found to have existed between the Hausa and, for example, peoples such as the Malinke of the Upper Niger valleys. But of all these regions, only Hausaland evolved and nurtured the city-state society to a high level, whereas its neighbors early found themselves subjects of imperial overlords.

In an effort to understand why this development occurred, let us now turn to a brief consideration of the second general descriptive feature of Hausaland in the city-state era—its social and economic organization.

Hausa Society and Economy

All Hausa city-states were plural societies.[10] The Hausawa, or free citizenry, formed the largest segment of the population in the city and countryside alike. But in each state—with important internal variations—non-Hausa were both directly incorporated within, or were formally attached to, the rigorously hierarchical Hausa social structure. Ethnicity, defined in this context as full membership in a Hausa patrilineal descent group, represented only one—if usually the most important—ingredient that conferred social status and rights upon both citizens and subjects of the ruler's domain.

Two major groups of non-Hausa were accorded exceptional status. The Fulani pastoralists, whose mode of life required their regular movement over wide areas both within and between states, had to be governed by rules different from those that regulated the affairs of the settled rural and urban populations. The other group consisted of both long-distance traders and Muslim clerics who were foreigners by origin but who came to reside more or less permanently in individual states. Individuals who belonged to either of these prestigious communities were frequently allowed to organize and administer their own internal affairs under the general supervision of the *sarkin*'s officials. Nearly all other persons of foreign origin were absorbed within the basic Hausa social structure as slaves or in other categories of rank and class (e.g., occupational castes and guilds, such as ironworkers) that fell distinctly short of "free" status.

The Hausa ideal of what should constitute a well-regulated social order was based on the primacy of kinship. The humblest farmer (*talakawa*) was linked to the noble classes and his ruler by bonds of shared blood. Males who could lay claim to lineage membership in this fashion (women were regarded as legal minors) constituted the bulk of the free citizen population. However, the socially pluralistic reality which everywhere existed—a reality that militated against strict application of the ethnically defined kinship principle—meant that large numbers of socially useful, occupationally specialized persons of non-Hausa origin had somehow to be grafted upon the kinship structure, especially where their roles in the economic and cultural life of the state were crucial to its success as an enterprise. In some instances this was accomplished by grants of special privilege. But, in many other instances, non-Hausa were directly assimilated into the ethnic social core itself through intermarriage, classificatory redefinition of social status, and incorporation of children born to slave mothers and free fathers. A significant number of such persons ultimately acquired positions in the titled office structure that ruled Hausa political institutions.

Two important features of Hausa culture helped to blur and mitigate the potentially divisive and conflicting elements that made up the pluralistic social organization. The first was the widespread use of a common spoken language. Not only did the rulers and their rural kinsmen address each other in their native tongue; but all other permanent residents of the states used Hausa as well, at least as a second language when conducting their business affairs in the towns and cities or in their relations with state authorities. This was true in all the city-states and could not, therefore, have resulted from the imposition of linguistic conformity by a dominant political power. More likely, a common Hausa speech, remarkably free from the dialectical variation that would have made mutual intelligibility difficult, emerged from the stimulus provided by interstate and international commerce in which so many Hausa participated. A thriving commerce depends in part on the ability of those who share in it to understand one another. Those who originated from, or who came to live within, the most important region for West African interior commerce in the period from fifteenth through nineteenth centuries came to employ Hausa as a commercial *lingua franca*. But whether or not Hausaland's relative linguistic homogeneity is to be explained on the basis of economic factors, the fact remains that such homogeneity did reduce one of the features so prominent in many plural societies: conflict and hostility between those of different languages living under the governance of a common set of rulers.

Islam was the other leading feature of Hausa culture that served to cross-cut ethnic and class distinctions. During the city-state period most, probably the majority, of rural Hausa continued to practice their traditional religion, although incorporating into it selected Islamic elements. Only after the Fulani *jihad* did this basic difference between the religion of the rural Hausa and their rulers provoke general conflict between the two; prior to 1804, however, religious dualism appears to have been generally acceptable to both the sovereign and his subjects since it was the kinship bond which sustained their primary loyalties. Yet from the sixteenth century onward Islam began to provide the dominant cultural orientation for the city-dwelling populations in most of the states. The rulers and a good share of the nobility converted to Islam, a situation which permitted not only amicable, but formal ties to be forged between the ethnically differentiated communities that made up the *birane*. Members of the Muslim learned classes were attached to the courts as titled officials of the state while, at the same time, they were allowed to take very direct roles in the internal governance of wholly Muslim wards and quarters. So long as the leaders of the Islamic communities were willing to accept their status as privileged and protected residents without seriously agitating for the stricter application of Muslim law for all citizens then, clearly, Islamic culture served to mitigate potential conflict. The fact that, following the *jihad,* the learned Muslim leadership was no longer willing to abide what they had come to regard as an intolerable dilution of correct Islamic practice was a major contributing factor to the destruction of the sovereign city-state structure in Hausaland.

It is evident, therefore, that the ideal of kin-relatedness as the basis of citizenship was, throughout the age of city-states, continuously subjected to influences that fostered cooperation among, and helped ward off conflicts between, the diverse groups of differing social origin that together made up the corpus of free citizenry. But the kinship organization remained the bedrock upon which the whole elaborately stratified society rested.

The lowest order of citizens, the peasant-farming *talakawa,* was organized into domestic socio-economic units known as *gandu.* A *gandu* comprised two or more males and their families who jointly operated a farm under the authority of its senior male member who was also the head (the *maigida*) of the residential compound. This individual served as the "legal person" for the whole unit; he bore the responsibility for representing its members before the political authorities, as well as exercising internal control over its affairs.

Within the *gandu* the *maigida* organized and saw to the carrying out of agricultural tasks. He allocated the farm plots, collected and redistributed the harvest, and insured that seed and tools were made available. His overall supervision extended also to any client groups that might be attached to the *gandu* as well as to its slaves, if it owned any. He was responsible for the welfare of its individual members, reconciling disputes between them, and performing those ritual observances—either traditional or Muslim—that formed part of the annual cycle of festivals or other occasions when performance of religious duties was called for. Should the *gandu* flourish and its numbers grow too large, various male members and their families might leave the *gida* to set up new *gandu* which, when sufficiently well-established, would be recognized by the political authorities as separate legal entities. This process of orderly segmentation was assisted by the assumption of hereditary rights over farmland on the part of the sons of the original *gandu* head. This process received formal recognition through the manner in which taxes were levied: tax liability for postadolescent males began when they still resided in their father's *gandu,* and steadily increased through marriage and the enlargement of their families. To meet this tax demand, the father increased the size of his sons' farm holdings (*gayuana*) every year. When sufficient land had been acquired and a compound constructed to house those who worked it, the new *gandu* was entered upon the tax rolls.

Modern studies have shown that this ideal of the *gandu* consisting of the patrilineal descent group continues to hold great prestige in the eyes of the rural Hausa; however, other features of Hausa social life operated to disrupt it. The high incidence of divorce in a setting where polygynous marriage was a universal ideal; patterns of social avoidance between parents and their children and between brothers; strong attachments between matrilineal kin in a fundamentally patrilineal society; and economic differentiation resulting from the adoption of specialized occupations (especially commerce) on a full-time basis—all worked to keep the actual numbers of ideally defined *gandu* low. Since these factors were also present during the city-state period, the presumption is that the basic descent group organization at that time was as open to change and transformation as it was when carefully examined by social investigators of a later period. Far from leading to a break-down of "classical" Hausa social organization, these elements of departure from the ideal could just as well have made their contributions to the well-being of the city-states, for they may have encouraged movement from rural to urban areas and participation in the various specialized social and economic sectors (commerce, craft production, and the Muslim intelligentsia) that gave dynamic, growth-producing qualities to the city-states.

Despite the fluidity of social organization suggested here, the role of the *gandu* head remained central to all those areas where those who came under his authority had need to deal with other social units or with the political powers. First among those responsibilities was making provision for the marriage of *gandu* members. Since unmarried adults were considered to be social outcasts (this was especially true for women), the arrangements necessary to provide a suitable mate (cross-cousin marriages were preferred), to secure the necessary sums for bridewealth payments, to arrange for the remarriage of widows and divorcées (both were known by the common name *bazawara*) all fell within the purview of the *gandu* head. He had, in addition, to insure that taxes, fines, and other official levies were paid; to provision feasts; to transmit communications from the political authorities to the *gandu*'s individual members; and to maintain active social relations with the *gandu*'s neighbors.

While farming was the primary activity of the *talakawa*, craft production and other specialized occupations also formed a major portion of the tasks assigned to each male (women generally did not participate in the agricultural labors although, beyond their domestic and child-rearing roles, they performed specialized craft tasks too). Each man was known by a title that indicated his specialist's role: hunter, fisherman, house-builder, weaver, leather-worker, butcher, porter, herbalist, petty trader, and so forth down a long list. These occupations were performed part-time during the farming season and full-time the rest of the year.

These descriptions of the Hausa *talakawa* obviously differ little from the patterns of social and economic life characteristic of traditional kin-based subsistence societies the world over. But the economic organization of city-state Hausaland had evolved far beyond the traditional subsistence level. Its most distinctive feature was the high degree of labor specialization it had achieved, coupled to a distinct orientation toward production of surplus foods and goods for extensive regional and international markets. The division of labor, and the social forms which it took, were prominently reflected in the presence of craft and occupational guilds.

The artisan guilds possessed their own hierarchies of officials whose chiefs represented their members in the marketplace and with the political authorities. Among the most important craft guilds were those of the ironworkers, dyers, artificers, and leather-workers; specialized occupations included corporate groups of musicians, story-tellers, and prostitutes. In the hierarchical ordering of professions all these were regarded as low in status. The high status end of the occupational spectrum was represented by professions that offered opportunities for acquiring greater personal wealth. Chief among them was that of merchant, whose activities and accomplishments were recognized by the honorific term *kasuwanci*, "successful trading." Together with bankers, brokers, commission agents, clerks, and the like, successful merchants formed something resembling a social class since access to membership in it appears to have been open to individual initiative and was not monopolized by a handful of great families, merchant houses, or a specific ethnic group. The presence of so many foreign merchants in the international trading system of which the city-states formed an integral part must have contributed greatly to maintaining this openness of access. By the seventeenth century the most numerous group among the long-distance traders were the Hausa themselves who in turn pushed the trade routes on toward the forest and coastal regions where they established important Hausa commercial colonies.[11]

Another high status profession comprised the Muslim literate teachers, scribes, and religious officials who, together, were known by the name *mallanci* (corresponding to the Arabic *culema,* "learned ones"). Here again, membership in this "class" was open to aspiring and capable students who had successfully completed the required stages of formal Koranic instruction, regardless of their social origins.

The highest prestige attached to the profession called *sarauta* (ruling), which included not only members of the aristocratic and noble lineages, but free-born and slave office-holders and administrators as well. While nobility was recognized by the title *sarakuna* (chief or ruler), commoner office-holders were called *masusarauta* (administrators). *Sarauta* was regarded by the Hausa as a wholly proper full-time occupation. Needless-to-say, the aristocratic lineages attempted to monopolize high offices by asserting the claim to hereditary rights and by intriguing for the appointment of kinsmen and clients to titled positions where hereditary claims were invalid. As the city-states grew larger and more complex, as competition and warfare between them increased, and as commerce steadily expanded, more elaborate instruments of government were required than could be managed by recruitment from the aristocratic lineages alone. Thus, the *masusarauta* came to form a substantial class of bureaucrats and state officials (which in turn was inherited by and reformed to suit the tastes of both the Fulani and the British rulers of later times). It is equally clear from the histories of the various states that, increasingly, slaves were recruited to fill high offices of the expanding bureaucracy.

Slaves were unquestionably of central importance to the growth and development of Hausa city-state culture. This, in turn, raises major questions: What proportion of the total population was slave? What were their origins? Were they a suppressed lower class, or captives acquired by war, raiding, or purchase? What was the slave contribution to increases in the production of an exportable economic surplus? It is well known that slave labor played a crucial role in basic production, perhaps the predominant one, in the city-states of antiquity. Was the same true of Hausaland? The evidence for the city-state period is inadequate to provide firm answers to these questions. What is known is that the slave component of Hausa society steadily increased throughout the nineteenth century during which the Fulani rulers vastly expanded the slave-raiding enterprise both for the purpose of reexporting slaves in the trans-Saharan trade and, dramatically, to enlarge the labor force at all levels (from agricultural workers to throne servants).[12] But was this true in the pre-*jihad* states?

Demographic estimates can be only wild estimates. The state histories constantly refer to slave-raiding expeditions; to tribute payments paid in slaves; to gifts made by the ruler of one state to another; and to individual slaves, particularly eunuchs, who rendered loyal service to their masters. Therefore, whether or not the slave populations made up ten or twenty or more percent of the total population appears to be less important a question than those relating to how slaves were regarded and employed. As in later times, many were employed within the states while others became unhappy victims of the apparently insatiable demand of Hausaland's North African trade partners for African slaves. Where Islamic law held sway, the offspring of free fathers and slave mothers could—over relatively few generations—acquire their freedom by the process of absorption into their master's kin group. Others secured protection, if not free status, by the services they rendered to their masters.

The answers to the questions posed here seem to suggest that slaves formed a significant, if unmeasurable, stratum of Hausa society throughout the city-state and subsequent periods; that slaves were acquired mainly by raids upon neighboring non-Hausa groups (particularly the small tribal societies south of Hausaland); that slaves did not form a submerged order of ethnic Hausa; and that they were counted among the most valuable possessions an individual or group might own. The value of the slave to the farming kinship unit was that he added to the group's labor force; and, in the case of a woman, that she produced new members for the unit. The special value of the ruler's slaves was built upon the absolute loyalty they owed to their masters in a society where most personal rights were conferred by blood ties. Seen from an economic perspective, slaves undoubtedly added an important dimension to increases in production within the states as well as to the revenues earned when they were sold in international exchanges. On the other hand, nothing in the existing evidence suggests that Hausa society was *fundamentally* a society of masters and slaves. The *talakawa* and other free groups—even when the institution of slavery grew rapidly in the nineteenth century—far out-numbered the slave population.

Rather than slavery, it was a different form of dependent relations that formed the basis of socio-economic bonds in Hausa society. That bond has been referred to as clientship, an intricate and pervasive set of relationships that linked each individual to a superior in a hierarchical order that reached right up to the level of the monarch. So central was clientship to the social and economic relations of the free Hausa and resident foreigner groups of the city-states that many commentators have been tempted to describe both Hausa and the later Fulani-Hausa societies as "feudal."

Sociologically defined, clientship "links individuals of unequal status, fortune, and political position or prospect" in a patron-client relationship that assumes mutual benefits and solidarity of interest between the contracting parties.[13] At the lowest level, such contracts were formed between compound heads (the legal persons of Hausa society) and needy men who received from their patrons protection, housing, food and clothing, plots to farm, and even bridewealth for marriage in return for acting as menial servants to their masters, who also paid their taxes. But the system of clientage extended far beyond this level of vassalage and most importantly characterized the relations between men of independent means: this permitted the client to maintain his *mutumci* (manhood and self-respect) while allowing him to perform political and other forms of service to his lord. At the highest levels of society, including the

Muslim literati and wealthy merchants, clientship was termed *chapka* (allegiance) and indicated the formal respect extended by these persons to their rulers. Another form of clientship was called *barantaka* and was a more institutionalized linkage between economically independent clients and noblemen who held high political office (or the prospect of acquiring it).

These basic forms of clientship evolved during the city-state period. Constant reference to them is made in the traditional histories. What ultimately gave clientship its "feudal" character may have been a product of the later Fulani times when the new rulers rewarded their loyal clients with "fiefs"—possessions that increasingly became attached to hereditary rights (including both land and political offices). During the era of the autonomous Hausa polities, the chief contribution of the system of clientage must surely have been the role it played in the reconciliation of differences between the various groups that made up the plural society. Every free man, regardless of his social or ethnic origin, through the contract systems of *chapka* and *barantaka* found his place and his protection secured within the social order.

While the harmonization of diverse social units was accommodated to the growing economic structure of specialized labor in the Hausa city-states, it was the elaborate political system of titled offices that gave those states their most distinctive character.

Sarauta: The Hausa Political System

Hausa city-state government was formalized by the system of titled offices—*sarautu* (pl. *sarauta*)—within which the noble lineages sought to monopolize high offices by providing the chief candidates for the most important positions including the *sarkin*-ship, provincial governors, military, judicial, and city administrative officials. Each of these titled offices constituted a distinct, insoluble legal corporation with carefully defined rights, powers, duties, and relations to other offices. Each also possessed certain tangible benefits in the form of specially reserved lands, groups of clients and slaves, horses, praise songs, and so forth. Since noble lineages claiming hereditary rights to office often were subdivided into two or more branches, there was intense intralineage competition between the factions for *sarauta*. Some clerical lineages also attained hereditary rights to office, and these came to form a special branch of the nobility.

While kinship served as the basic legitimizing force which strengthened and perpetuated high political office among a small number of aristocratic lineages, the need to staff new offices as the Hausa government grew more complex began to draw commoner clients and slaves into the system. This would appear to have been an early development, for the old state histories refer to slaves and eunuchs occupying the very highest offices of state as early as the sixteenth century.[14] At the same time, the basic kinship ingredient of office-holding made the competition between sublineages (especially the appointment of clients and slaves) the central reason underlying factional politics in the city-state period. The fact that all offices from the *sarkin* downward were also status ranked meant that competition for new, additional, and better titles was equally intense. The ruler used this competition to award titles to lineages that lacked proper hereditary claims and thus reinforced monarchical power through the parallel system of client patronage.

At the apex of the system were the senior titled offices whose occupants constituted a council of state. These included the *Kaura,* the senior military commander, whose policy-making role and administrative duties made him the equivalent of the king's prime minister. A significant aspect of the *Kaura*'s power was his right to allocate the booty gained in war. Ranged under the *Kaura* were a whole series of subofficials—normally drawn from the ranks of the *Kaura*'s kinsmen, clients, and slaves—who acted as advisors, tax collectors, messengers, market overseers, and keepers of estates, compounds, and horses. Next in line of importance was the *Galadima*. He, too, served on the high councils of state but had special responsibility as the king's main deputy in relations with the noble lineages. He presided over meetings of the state's princes and princesses and possessed sole authority for disciplining persons of aristocratic station. His role was central in informing the king about general affairs in the kingdom, and he had direct access to the *sarkin* for that purpose. The *Galadima,* through his numerous subofficials, also administered a major quarter of the *birane* in which his compound was located, as well as outlying territories and provinces that were attached directly to his office.

The other titled offices reserved to the nobly born or their appointed clients concerned both men and women. Among the princely titles the most important was that of *Yerima,* or crown prince and designated successor to the ruler. The office was not based on the principle of primogeniture but was filled on the basis of the ruler's choice ratified by the members of the state council. Other princes of the royal entourage occupied lesser offices, and all had direct relations with the *Galadima* who served as their liaison to the *sarkin*. Chief among the female titled offices was that of the *Magajiya,* the official queen mother, who though never the biological mother of the reigning king was a senior member of the dynastic lineages. She had responsibility for training the princesses and was always consulted by the *Galadima* in the event that severe punishments were to be administered to members of the aristocracy. Constitutionally, she had the power to recommend to the state council the countermanding of the *sarkin*'s orders including the right to argue for his deposition since she was not required to take an oath of allegiance to the king nor could she be removed from office by him. Since the *Magajiya* had the power to reprieve offenders, she was much sought after as a patron and maintained clientage relations of the sworn allegiance type with numerous persons throughout the state. Lesser ranks of female office-holders had control of appointments and functions related to court life, and many were taken by the king and other senior officials as wives.

Alongside these aristocratic offices at the top levels of state authority were those reserved for Muslim officials. The most senior among them was that of the *Limamin Juma'a* who had direct access to the ruler and sat on the various high councils of state. He presided at the main Friday prayers in the city and was generally responsible for all the members of the clerical community. The next ranking office reserved for Muslims was that of the *Alkali,* the chief judge who presided over court cases involving civil matters (debt, inheritance, marriage, bridewealth, and the like). Interestingly, he pledged his loyalty not to the *sarkin,* but to the *shari^ca* (written Islamic law). Severe punishments (execution, banishment, mutilation, etc.) lay outside his province, for the council of state reserved for itself the sole right to apply these strictures. A third Islamic office was that of the *Dan Sanwai,* also represented by membership on the state council. It was he who acted as the chief among the ruler's scribes and confidential assistants and was the key figure in those matters that touched the economic activities of the long-distance trading community: he acted as host and protector of foreign merchants, and served, too, as purchasing agent for the court and the royal courtiers. The offices described here were those identified as existing in the Daura state in the eighteenth century; however, in varying configurations they were to be found in all the other states as well.[15] In most cases, the Islamic title-holders successfully converted appointive positions into hereditary office at these higher levels, while the lesser positions tended to remain open to members of the free Muslim citizenry.

Among the free population there were many other titled positions, some of which were reserved to lineages of free commoners and others which were filled without regard to the hereditary principle. The functions they served ranged from collecting tolls on caravans to the command of specialized military units, such as the light cavalry; from acting as the provincial tax collectors of the required grain tithe (*zakka*) to insuring the proper performance of protocol at the court; to overseeing the salt trade and making collections from the merchants specialized in it; and from the supervision of the transport of slaves to regulating the affairs of magicians, musicians, dancers, and the craft guilds.

The highest hereditary offices, including those reserved for *mallanci* (the Muslim intelligentsia), were in most cases secured by bonds of allegiance and pledges of loyalty (with the exceptions noted above). But for the vastly more extensive ranks of junior *sarauta,* the title had also to be purchased (*kudin sarauta*). In the city-state period, prices were reckoned in cowrie shells—the most universal form of currency throughout the *bīlad al-Sūdān*—and an office such as the *Dan Barau,* collector of the grain tax, might cost as much as 500,000 cowries. As can be imagined, access to office by a wealthy patron who could obtain the appointment and also pay the *kudin sarauta* for a client constituted one of the main ways of acquiring power.

Although they performed immensely important functions in the states, the titled offices of the heads of guilds carried with them relatively little political power. The *Sarkin Pawa* (head of the butchers) also served as the chief official of the main market. The *Korama* led the grain-sellers; the *Sarkin Dillalai* was the chief of commission brokers; the *Sarkin Makera, Bulkacima, Sarkin Marina,* and *Magajin Aska* respectively headed and collected the taxes from the blacksmiths, well-diggers, cloth-dyers, and barber-surgeons. Each in turn was linked to one or the other of the senior administrative officials to whom he owed loyalty in the overall hierarchical system. Here again, the problem of reconciling the functions of government and the specialized office-holders who administered them to the Hausa kinship principle was accomplished through the application of the institutions of clientship.

Lying alongside the structure of offices held by aristocratic and free commoner occupants was the other component of the system, the appointment of slaves as both senior throne officials and palace slaves assigned to important duties. First among the senior slave officials was the *Sarkin Yara* who presided over the administration of the *birane.* He was responsible for the maintenance of public buildings and could commission labor (*corvée*) to see that necessary tasks such as wall maintenance were done. He settled market disputes referred to him by the *Sarkin Pawa,* received the king's taxes collected by the various guild heads, and relayed the ruler's instructions to specific groups. Beyond that, the *Sarkin Yara* had responsibility for administering the provincial towns, which he accomplished through a system of agents (noble, commoner, and slave) who received royal commissions. He presided over the lesser council of state on matters that concerned the entire free population below the level of the noble lineages. Finally, this important slave official served as the *vizier* (roughly, comptroller) who helped establish the actual fees (*kudin sarauta*) required for appointment to titled office. Though he remained a slave by status, his links to his master, the king, were assured by his preferential marriage to one of the king's sisters.

Others among the senior throne slaves had similar, if less sweeping, administrative responsibilities and powers. The *Turaki* was charged with collection of the cattle tax. The *Sarkin Bai* was placed in charge of the palace and the city guards (slaves were always the guardians of the city gates). The *Sarkin Ruwa* supervised and collected taxes on water wells. Lesser throne slaves commanded slave military units, served as police chiefs in the cities, carried out the role of executioner, and managed the prisons. As in the case of Muslim title-holders, these offices of slaves tended to become, over time, hereditary even while slave status remained attached to their occupants.

Palace slaves had correspondingly important ranks with various titled officials who performed guard service, messenger duties, maintenance of the royal treasury, and certain tax collection functions. Eunuchs supervised the royal harems. And craftsmen groups that fabricated the quilted armor (called *lifida*) used to protect both warriors and their horses were under the supervision of a palace slave official.

As can be seen in the foregoing brief description of Hausa political institutions, the main state functions—executive, legislative, judicial—were not presided over by a single, privileged class drawn exclusively from Hausa descent groups. It would appear, to the contrary, that the Hausa rulers managed to craft an enormously complex system of internal checks and balances which included all the major elements of settled rural and urban society (but not the pastoral Fulani) at some level of the system.

Kinship and hereditary privilege stood as the main route to high office; but the complementary systems of clientship and slavery were successfully grafted upon it thus guaranteeing an important avenue of upward mobility for the foreign, commoner, and slave components of society. Since such a system might be regarded as having maximum limits (of both scale and complexity) beyond which it would cease to function efficiently, it is tempting to speculate that the political system described here was beautifully tailored to the city-state form. The scale remained manageable. The ruler and his officials could know at first hand even the most intimate affairs of the kingdom. And, every citizen and subject could regard him or herself as playing a part in the political life of the state through the networks of clientship that bound every person to another, superior patron. But this speculation implies that the city-state form ceased to function efficiently because, perhaps, it had begun to expand beyond its "natural" size. Instead, we know the system came to an end as the consequence of a great Islamic revolutionary upheaval led by the Fulani intellectuals, supported by their non-Muslim pastoral kinsmen, and joined by disaffected elements among the orthodox Hausa Muslims.

It is therefore appropriate to take note, briefly, of the growth of Islamic cultural institutions in city-state Hausaland.

Religion and State in the Hausa City-States

Except for the lengthy record of interstate warfare and the struggles of the Hausa states to preserve their autonomy in face of foreign threats, the growth and spread of Islam is the best known feature of the period from sixteenth through eighteenth centuries. The written accounts were mainly those produced by Muslims, both foreign travelers and members of the resident Muslim intelligentsia. It is hardly surprising, therefore, that the history of Islam in Hausaland has often served as the *leitmotif* for its historians, both contemporaneous and modern. However, it should also be remembered that Hausa traditional religion was never entirely displaced by Islam—especially in the countryside and in many of the smaller states—even in the period following the Fulani *jihad*. Just as important, as long as the old dynastic system of noble lineages drawn from traditional Hausa descent groups remained strong—as it did throughout the city-state period—it would continue to bind the Muslim ruling groups to their pagan kinsmen. Thus, the history of Islam in Hausaland should be regarded as the gradual appearance of an important new influence, imported initially by foreigners and adopted selectively by rulers as an added element of their authority, that functioned as a militant threat to the old Hausa systems of society and government only at the end of the eighteenth century.

Islamic influences reached into Hausaland from three directions and its agents were, for the most part, merchants and preachers rather than warriors and armies.[16] The *Kano Chronicle*, the surviving written record with the greatest time depth, refers to the first Muslims as *Wangara*, traders in gold and kola nuts from the lands of the Niger Mali empire in the west, who settled in Kano and converted its rulers. The Sarkin Yaji (1349–85), it is reported, adopted the faith as a consequence of the advice, prayers, and assistance given him by the Wangara as he prepared to embark on a military campaign. His successors, especially Kano's greatest early monarch, Muhammed Runfa (1463–99), vigorously pursued a policy of Islamization during that same time when the great market center was established, the major walls constructed, and successful military campaigns were undertaken to enlarge the state itself.

It was in the course of Runfa's reign that the second avenue of Muslim influence was also noted: the arrival of Muslim teachers and preachers from the North African Arab lands who carried with them written texts on Islamic law and religious instruction which were adopted by the local literati both as the basis for institutionalizing the *sharica* as a judicial standard for members of the Islamic community and for instructing new recruits to their ranks. Although many examples of the growing interest of Hausa rulers in Islamic principles of government might be cited, the most famous occurred during the reign of Runfa when he consulted an internationally famous Muslim jurist, Al-Maghili of Tlemcen (modern Algeria), on what steps a prince should take in expanding the faith. In a treatise entitled *The Obligations of Princes* Al-Maghili first wrote to Runfa setting down those practices which a rightly guided ruler should adhere to; and, subsequently, this great authority came with followers to settle permanently in Kano where they became leading members of the *mallanci*. A similar receptivity to the preaching and instructional writing of North African Muslim literary figures appears in the records of the Katsina and Gobir states as well.

The third direction from which Islamic influence made its appearance was the east. It is associated with the political and economic expansion of the Kanuri state in the Hausa arena. Initially this was indicated in the Abayajidda tradition in which the putative founder of the "legitimate Hausa Seven" was identified as a descendant of the ruling house of the Arab empire at Baghdad, arriving at Daura via Bornu. But, clearly, both the trade and political connections which sustained strong ties between Bornu and Hausaland meant that a regular source of Muslim influence continued to be felt from that direction.

Until the *jihad,* however, Islamic influence remained largely confined to two areas. First and foremost, that large segment of the population devoted to commercial enterprise adopted Islam. While it was initially the culture of the foreign merchant communities, increasingly it became the culture of Hausa merchants as well. As the latter began to spread as groups of traders far beyond Hausaland—south toward what are today the Nigerian forest lands and southwest into the Voltaic regions of present-day Ghana—they in turn became major agents of Islamic diffusion in West Africa. Certainly by the eighteenth century Islamic institutions and practices (the saying of daily prayers, celebration of the major Muslim festivals, use of Muslim jurists, obedience to *Qur'anic* strictures in the conduct of business, and so forth) had come to represent the basic flavor of life in the Hausa capital cities. It barely requires repeating that the leaders of the Muslim merchant and learned communities were thoroughly assimilated to the titled office structure of Hausa political life.

It was in the evolving Hausa forms of government that the second main thread of Muslim influence can be detected. From the time of Sarkin Yaji down to the present day, the majority of the rulers professed adherence to Islam. At the same time, as the disgruntled Muslim literati continuously noted in their writings, the *sarki* remained very tolerant of pagan (Hausa traditional) religious practices among the majority of their subjects while perfecting Islamic forms as the cult of the ruling classes. This religious dualism, as it has been called, was characteristic of religious life in the city-states right up to the very moment of the Fulani *jihad*'s outbreak. Unhappiness with such an impure state of affairs was the major ideological basis upon which the call to *jihad* was proclaimed.

Islam served to reinforce the powers of the autonomous rulers while it helped to organize and expand the growing networks of international commerce. All the while this gradual set of developments was taking place, a rather different set of problems constituted the main issues faced by the rulers of the individual states. These were the problems created by the intense competition between them and by the meddling and invasions of foreign powers. The strenuous efforts put forth to preserve state sovereignty and to enlarge the wealth and power of the state in competition with all the others—foreign relations, in effect—consumed the main energies and attention of Hausaland's rulers.

Warfare and Alliance—Foreign Relations of the Hausa States

While much of the work of internal consolidation remained to be done in at least two of the city-states—Zauzau in the south and Gobir in the north—those of the core region had emerged as full-blown sovereign entities pursuing aggressively expansionist policies by the beginning of the sixteenth century. This was especially true of Kano and Katsina whose rivalry to rank first among the states in power and control over the lucrative international commerce produced a nearly continuous set of armed conflicts between them until the mid-seventeenth century. But on various occasions other states, particularly Zamfara in the early seventeenth century, also entered the fray by trying to assert a military hegemony over the Western Hausa area. Among the non-Hausa powers whose armies entered Hausaland in the effort to make the states become tribute-paying vassals were the ever-present imperial Bornu (which frequently claimed suzerainty over both the eastern border states such as Daura and the larger core states of Kano and Katsina), the Songhay empire of the middle Niger region (in the early sixteenth century), followed by the break-away Songhay state of Kebbi (through the rest of the sixteenth and into the seventeenth centuries), and, a dimly-known but potent military state called Kwararafa whose raiding armies entered and occasionally devastated large territories belonging to both the Hausa and Kanuri (Bornu) states up through the seventeenth century.[17]

These internecine struggles and the conflicts with foreign powers stimulated the growth of military institutions designed for both defensive and offensive uses. The defensive wall systems were enlarged in the main *birane,* more modest earthworks constructed and maintained in the lesser towns, and regular guard forces recruited (frequently from among the slave populations) to man them. The titled ranks of warrior chiefs also grew proportionately: the *Kano Chronicle* recorded the presence of only eight major military commanders during the reign of Muhammed Kisoki (ca. 1582–1618) whereas their numbers had grown to fifty-two in Kano by the middle of the eighteenth century. The danger was always that a particularly strong commander might challenge the authority of the *sarkin* and the written records reflect periods of rebellion and attempted usurpation leading to civil war in many of the states. Kano, again, provides detailed evidence of the challenge presented to its legitimate rulers by a strong military faction during a civil struggle that raged within the state between the early 1640s and 1652 when the civilian party finally succeeded in suppressing a faction of warlord usurpers.

This need to maintain large and well-equipped military forces, and the consequent enlargement of the class of commanders, who in their turn might become the main disturbers of civil order, may have been responsible for the increasing use of slave generals and lieutenants—officers of the state who owed their loyalty directly to the ruler rather than to the kinship branch from which the ruler was selected. In any case, the state chronicles constantly stress slave-raiding as a major aim of warfare, the incorporation of slaves as one of the large elements making up the armies, and the rise of gifted slave war chiefs to high state office.

However, it was the cavalry that constituted the central military institution charged with carrying out the states' aggressive policies. The cavalry had necessarily to be recruited from among the wealthiest orders of society since horses were acquired more through trade than by local breeding. The commonest currency used to purchase horses (especially from merchants plying the trade to North Africa) was slaves, thus completing the circle of economic interconnectedness that linked slave-raiding to the overall military situation. As indicated in the discussion of the Hausa political structure, one of the strongest ties that bound high status clients to their lord was the obligation to provide military service. This meant, in effect, providing a horse (arrayed in cotton quilted armor), the grooms and attendants to maintain it, as well as the weapons and personal armor of the warrior himself. Together these represented a heavy tax burden on members of the Hausa nobility.

This system of "feudal" military service remained basically unchanged through the end of the city-state period. It has struck many historians as curious that none of the states experienced a shift in military organization from their basic reliance on cavalry forces to the use of infantry armed with firearms.

Muskets and cannon were known in this region of Africa from at least the beginning of the seventeenth century. Neighboring Bornu, through its connections with Ottoman-ruled North Africa, had even imported Turkish instructors to teach the use of such weapons.[18] Yet the horse-mounted warrior continued to exercise the most important aggressive military functions for the city-states: the opening up and protection of trade routes, slave-raiding, and attacks launched against competitors. The infantry forces were employed for defensive purposes: to defend the cities and to suppress rebellions. Unlike the cavalry, its membership was recruited from the commoner orders and the slave groups. Thus the Hausa, like most societies, mirrored in their military forms their social and political organizations. So long as lineage hierarchies remained at the top of the political order and so long as one of the principal obligations owed by noble and wealthy men was to provide their ruler with military service, the role of the *chevalier* held firm. So important was this institution that not even the Fulani, in their turn, did much in the way of substituting musket, cannon, and infantryman for the prestigious occupation of horse-mounted warrior.

Even the barest summary of the military fortunes of the individual states is beyond the scope of this chapter. However, certain main features can be described which help identify shifts in power that resulted from interstate rivalries and periods when foreign influence became pronounced.

The oldest, fiercest rivalry between city-states plunged Katsina and Kano into a series of conflicts and wars which lasted from the late fourteenth through the mid-seventeenth centuries. During the earlier part of this period Katsina seemed to have the upper hand. As that state lying nearest the major Saharan trade center of Agades—itself recently having emerged from contests with other rivals as the most important staging location on the trans-Saharan route to North Africa—Katsina made strenuous efforts to control all the import traffic to the south. Kano, whose growing prosperity was derived from the expansion of its manufacturing industries and its reasonably successful slave-raiding campaigns into the stateless regions, came to resent the key commercial role which Katsina had assumed. On repeated occasions the armies of the two competitors took to the field with the obvious objective of achieving more complete sway over the trade routes. Although Katsina's forces more than once came up to the very gates of Kano, the city was never taken. Kano's campaigns against the Katsinawa had equally limited success. The stalemate reached by the inability of either to dominate its competitor was finally recognized in 1652 when the two states reached a diplomatic accord that prevented open warfare between them until the end of the city-state period. By that time Kano had replaced Katsina as the largest and most prosperous of the two, a position it never subsequently relinquished.

While the two major rivals were locked in their struggle to achieve mastery over the core lands and the international trade routes, the most important states of the peripheral areas were absorbed with their efforts to achieve stable systems of rule at home and to resist foreign meddling. Zaria entered upon a long age of civil conflict during which rival lineages fought to achieve exclusive rights of *sarauta*. What finally emerged was a complex system of power-sharing between the noble competitors, which made its political system, at least, rather more open to disruption than the others. The capital itself was shifted frequently and became fixed at its modern location only in the eighteenth century. The armies of the Kwararafa and of Bornu continued to raid across the state and to exact tribute from the Zauzau kings, a situation which may have inspired the dramatic spurt of defensive wall-building there under the sixteenth century queen Amina. But Zaria lay too far south of the contact zone between Hausaland and the Saharan trade routes to vie for place as a premier commercial *entrepôt*. It therefore turned its attention to servicing the international trade by supplying slaves to the Kano and Katsina markets for which it received such precious commodities as salt, metals, and horses. By the eighteenth century the stability of the state had been secured and foreigners were kept sufficiently at bay to have made Zaria an independent power the equal to Kano itself.

Gobir faced problems different from those of Zaria, but at the same time, ones to which the solutions welded together a strong state in the late part of the pre-Fulani period.

The towns of the Gobirawa originally extended up to the Ahir region of the Tuareg. They were the last of the farming populations to abandon the marginal Sahelian zone. By the same token, the Gobir Hausa also occupied strategic locations which each of the great imperial powers—Songhay in the sixteenth century and Bornu throughout—tried to control. Inevitably Gobir was forced to pay tribute to, or if possible, strike up an alliance with one or another of the competing parties. This situation changed after the first third of the sixteenth century when Kebbi, a small state that successfully rebelled against the Songhay overlordship, entered the picture as an important buffer between Songhay and the Hausa states. For nearly a century Kebbi proved strong enough to demand tribute from most of its Hausa neighbors and acted as the virtual suzerain over Gobir. However, Kebbi's rule was challenged in the seventeenth century by Zamfara, which strove in its turn for mastery over western Hausaland including all of Gobir and important districts of Katsina. The effort finally collapsed since the technique of alliance was never successfully employed.

Gobir, by the beginning of the eighteenth century, was beginning to enter upon a period of stability and growth.[19] Its military structures developed in response to the various foreign powers which had attempted to rule it. As it increasingly came to be the guardian state to which fell the responsibilities of protecting the whole region from the desert nomadic warrior groups, as well as keeping the trade routes open and safe for Hausa and North African merchants, Gobir became the Hausa crucible within which so many of the contradictory elements of the city-state were forced to work themselves out in the direction of new solutions. As perhaps the most ethnically pluralistic of all the states, Gobir had constantly to contend with the presence of Tuareg, Fulani, and other non-Hausa groups within its borders all of which were attempting to define their own structures in an independent fashion. This had the effect of stimulating the development of strong military institutions which, geared at first toward the tasks of defense and political consolidation, might subsequently be turned toward more aggressive, expansionist policies. Not itself a major Hausa market and craft production center on the scale of Kano, it nonetheless occupied one of the key roles in facilitating Hausa commerce by protecting the northern trade routes. And, finally, Gobir became the scene of significant proselytizing efforts by Muslim propagandists and reformers. In retrospect, it is not surprising that, when the ultimate challenge to the city-state system did appear in the early nineteenth century, it struck first in Gobir state.

Conclusion—Strengths and Weaknesses of the Hausa City-States

CUthman dan Fodio, a Fulani *mallam* who resided in Gobir and may have tutored its crown prince in the ways of Islamic learning, appeared in the late eighteenth century as the Muslim "Sword of Truth."[20] He became increasingly disaffected from his patron, the Sarkin Gobir, whose levy of unjust taxes upon his fellow Fulani and coreligionists and whose willingness to tolerate many traditional Hausa customs and practices that varied significantly from the laws set forth in the *shariCa* caused CUthman to preach and to write against such abuses. He withdrew from the *birane* to establish a new settlement where followers and disciples came to receive instruction from the master teacher. The disciples soon organized their forces to resist the *sarkin*'s efforts to compel obedience to the state authorities. Military conflict erupted between the two factions; and, while reaching indecisive conclusions at first, news of this rebellion quickly spread throughout Hausaland and was received by many members of the Muslim community and by merchants and even non-Muslim Fulani as a welcome message of hope that they, too, might free themselves from the unjust demands of their rulers. With astonishing rapidity rebellious leaders appeared in all the city-states and each in turn journeyed to CUthman's fortified camp to receive the great teacher's blessing to carry the *jihad* back to their homes. At the same time they pledged their formal allegiance to what was clearly a new patron, the *amir al-muminun,* Chief of the Believers. In 1804 the *jihad* had been carried inside the walls of Gobir and its rulers were forced to flee. In 1807 Kano fell. By 1812, all the main *birane* had fallen under the sway of CUthman's authority. His sons became the actual administrators of a new empire, the Caliphate, with a new capital, Sokoto. The age of the Hausa city-states had definitively ended.

What appears as most striking in this story is not that the city-states finally succumbed to the power of a superior, imperial order of rulers. What is surprising is that they endured for so long. For at least three hundred and fifty years the independent Hausa polities had managed not only to withstand the efforts of neighboring imperial powers such as Songhay and Bornu to dictate their affairs and exact tribute from them, but they also managed to grow large, prosperous, and largely powerful in their own right. To do so they crafted

systems of government and society which skillfully drew from the majority of
ethnic Hausa obedience to a highly structured and complexly interlinked
authority system which was repeated in each of the states. Perhaps of even
greater significance was the fact that this fundamentally Hausa system which
had evolved from the earliest groups of kin-related farmers was able to assimilate and adapt so many non-Hausa peoples and ideas to it: foreign merchants,
Muslims, and pastoral Fulani.

The proof that this process did succeed is made the more convincing by what
the Fulani rulers set about to accomplish upon their accession to power: they
grafted an imperial structure on top of the Hausa city-state system but were
largely content to leave the social and political orders intact. Hausa titled offices
were given Muslim names (for example, the imperial ruler came to be referred
to as the *Sarkin Musulmi*), while the Fulani and some of their Hausa allies came
to monopolize the highest of those offices.

The main strengths of the Hausa city-states derived from at least three
sources. First, the region where they took root was relatively rich in resources.
Rainfall and fertile soil were adequate to sustain successful agriculture and
widespread animal husbandry. Their food surpluses permitted large numbers of
the population to take up specialized full-time tasks: craft manufactures, commerce, warfare, government, and religious occupations. Furthermore, in the
pre-city-state period this complex Hausa economic base was allowed to develop
in reasonable isolation from the tumultuous imperial politics of its western and
eastern neighbors. Indigenous, localized economic growth was an important
precondition for the city-state form. When, after the Hausa were drawn fully
into a wider, international economic world—as was the case from the sixteenth
century onward—the individual polities easily accommodated themselves to
the new economic opportunities without necessarily having to abandon their
political form. Competition was waged between some of them, such as Kano
and Katsina, to gain a larger share of the wealth from commerce and the sale of
their own economic surplus. But no state became essentially predatory upon
that commerce and sought to disrupt it. Otherwise, some of the states found
themselves in a favorable position of economic symbiosis with the others—
such as Zaria, supplier of slaves to the large northern market cities.

The second great pillar upon which the successful Hausa city-state system
was built was its elaborate socio-political system. The core of each state was
represented by the population of ethnic Hausa, each of whom had his or her
identity as a full citizen affirmed by ties of blood that linked the humblest to the
most mighty. Clientage reinforced this linkage, and titled office-holding gave it
concrete expression. So long as the scale of any polity remained manageable—
that is, so long as the kinship ties could retain the appearance of direct contacts
between rulers and ruled—the city-state served its people well.

But the Hausa city-states comprised much more than successful export-
oriented economies presided over by large kin-related groups. They were, all of

them, plural societies containing large non-Hausa elements. Perhaps the greatest strength of all was therefore represented by the capacity of the basic system to assimilate new features and outsiders. The largest such group, the pastoral Fulani, were allowed to remain outside the rigorously hierarchical socio-political system so long as they continued to maintain peaceful relations of economic exchange with the agricultural society. Foreign traders, too, represented an opportunity rather than a threat to the city-states and were suitably linked to the Hausa rulers through the system of clientage. The need for more workers, warriors, and loyal government servants increased as the city-states expanded, and the institution of slavery developed to satisfy that need. As these were either captives or purchased persons and not a submerged class of ethnic Hausa, they, too, could gradually be assimilated into the social and political systems. And finally, Islam first appeared in Hausaland not as a dangerous foreign ideology but as the religion and culture of the merchants. Since it posed no immediate threat in the political sense, its obvious values (literacy, refined legal codes, positive connections to the great centers of international commerce) could be adopted selectively without creating un-wanted disruptions in the basic political institutions. Until such time as the religious reformers began preaching against such tolerant practices, Islam served to support and clarify the character of city-state life, not to undermine its institutions.

The weaknesses embodied in the city-state form are equally apparent in the Hausa case. While the Hausa states succeeded for the most part in maintaining their independence from foreign rule, they never ceased to wage struggles among themselves. Too great a proportion of state wealth was spent on defen-sive requirements: walls are virtually the hallmark of city-states, but they are enormously costly to build and more expensive still to maintain and garrison. Furthermore, in a region where the presence of tse-tse fly makes the breeding of horses difficult, the excessive reliance upon cavalry (with its accompanying requirement of purchasing horses) drained off enormous wealth. Yet military service of the "feudal" type constituted a central feature of the political order without which the system of clientage at the highest levels would have pos-sessed significantly less substance. War booty, especially slaves, did add to the revenues of states that developed strong armies. But the need to use those same armies in the internecine struggles probably neutralized such benefits. Central, then, among the weaknesses of the Hausa city-states was the endemic military rivalry between them occasioned by the determined efforts of each to remain independent of the others.

The other principal weakness was probably inherent in the very concept of the city-state. That was the problem of scale. If a single state appeared to grow so successful as to enlarge the extent of its territory, it could only do so by encroaching on the territories of other states. When such policies were pursued, either alliances had to be formed or conquests firmly secured by the imposition of the successful ruler's agents as governors of the new lands. Zamfara, among others, sought to accomplish this type of forceful expansion and consolidation and failed in the effort, for other than its military strengths it lacked a secure home base to which the new possessions could be attached. Other city-states in other cultures finally lost their independence through just such a process in which the strongest among them finally imposed its rule over traditional rivals and created the basis for either a territorial state or an empire. In Hausaland a different result followed.

It was neither through foreign conquest nor through the triumph of one state that the Hausa city-state period was brought to an end. Perhaps no greater testament to the vitality and durability of the Hausa city-states can be made than to state that the Fulani reformers and their Hausa allies retained the basic features of life and organization within the states when they deprived them, finally, of their cherished local independence.

Notes

1. Historians have relied mainly on two sorts of literary sources to document the establishment and growth of the Hausa city-states. The first of these consist of local traditions, written mostly in Arabic by members of the resident Muslim communities. Many of these records are compiled in the work of the British colonial administrator H. R. Palmer, *Sudanese Memoirs,* 3 volumes (Lagos: The Government Printer, 1928). The second variety of written documentation consists of North African travelers' accounts of which Ibn Khaldun's fourteenth century chronicle *Histoire des Berbères* (nineteenth century French translation by M. G. de Slane [Paris: P. Guenther 1925–26]) and Leo Africanus's sixteenth century account *The History and Description of Africa* (translated into English by John Pory [Paris: A. Epaulard translation and edition, 1956]) contain critically important evidence. Currently, scholars are working intensively with other written documents and collected oral traditions to sketch in a more detailed picture than is available in the standard accounts. Serious archeological research has barely begun in Hausaland.

2. Over the past twenty years the Fulani *jihad* has received deep and careful study. Perhaps the best account to date of the foundation of the Caliphate is to be found in M. Last's *The Sokoto Caliphate* (London: Longmans, 1967).

3. The best example of this perspective may be found in S. J. Trimingham's *History of Islam in West Africa* (London: Oxford University Press, 1962) which continues to retain its place as the best study of West African Islamic history now available.

4. J. E. G. Sutton, "Towards a less orthodox history of Hausaland," *Journal of African History* 20, no. 2 (1979), 179–201. The earlier views may be found in M. G. Smith, "The beginnings of Hausa society," in J. Vansina, R. Mauny and L. V. Thomas, eds., *The Historian in Tropical Africa* (London: Oxford University Press, 1964), 339–357; and Abdullahi Smith, "The early states of the Central Sudan," in J. F. A. Ajayi and M. Crowder, eds., *The History of West Africa,* 2nd ed., vol. I (New York: Columbia University Press, 1976), 158–164, 183–201.

5. Sutton, "Towards a less orthodox history," 201.

6. The version of the legend presented here is drawn from H. R. Palmer's *Sudanese Memoirs*, vol. III, 132–134. Modern scholarly commentary on this text and many other centrally important documents of Northern Nigerian history may be found in Thomas Hodgkin's magnificent anthology, *Nigerian Perspectives*, 2nd ed. (London: Oxford University Press, 1975).

7. "The Kano Chronicle," in Palmer, *Sudanese Memoirs*, vol. III.

8. On traditional Hausa religion, the best work continues to be Joseph H. Greenberg's classic monograph, *The Influence of Islam on a Sudanese Religion* (New York: J. J. Augustin, 1946).

9. Dixon Denham, H. Clapperton, and W. Oudney, *Narrative of Travels and Discoveries in Northern and Central Africa in the Years 1822, 1823, and 1824* (London: John Murray, 1826) is the first thorough European travel account of Hausaland. It contains a wealth of ink drawings, including sketches and surveys of the Kano *birni*.

10. This section on Hausa society and economy as well as the following section on political organization draw heavily upon the work of Professor M. G. Smith, perhaps the outstanding contemporary authority. Although Smith writes as an anthropologist, he takes great effort to preserve an historical perspective especially where distinctions are drawn between pre-Fulani and post-*jihad* Hausa social and political organization. Smith has provided a very terse set of descriptions in "The Hausa of Northern Nigeria," in J. Gibbs, ed., *Peoples of Africa* (New York: Holt, Rinehart, Winston, 1965), 119–155. Detailed, full-scale treatments of two Hausa states may be found in M. G. Smith's *Government in Zauzau 1800–1950* (London: Oxford University Press, 1960) and *The Affairs of Daura* (Berkeley: University of California Press, 1978). On Hausa as a plural society, see M. G. Smith's "Pluralism in Precolonial African Societies," in L. Kuper and M. G. Smith, eds., *Pluralism in Africa* (Berkeley: University of California Press, 1969), 91–151.

11. On the vast expansion of Hausa long-distance trade communities, see various contributions in C. Meillassoux, ed., *The Development of African Trade and Markets in West Africa* (London: Oxford University Press, 1971).

12. A. G. B. Fisher and H. J. Fisher, *Slavery and Muslim Society in Africa* (Garden City, N.Y.: Doubleday, 1971).

13. M. G. Smith, "The Hausa of Northern Nigeria," 135.

14. Certainly the best-studied case of Hausa state politics and factional competition is to be found in M. G. Smith's *Government in Zauzau*. Office-holding slaves are described in the earliest texts, such as "The Kano Chronicle."

15. Consult the *Affairs of Daura* for a complete breakdown of the titled office structure and the relations of offices to each other.

16. Two chapters of Ajayi and Crowder, *History of West Africa*, vol. I, present good surveys of Islamic influence in Hausaland during the city-state period. They are: J. O. Hunwick, "Songhay, Bornu and Hausaland in the sixteenth century," and R. A. Adeleye, "Hausaland and Bornu 1600–1800." The earlier work of S. J. Trimingham, *A History of Islam in West Africa*, regards the seventeenth and eighteenth centuries as a period of Islamic regression in Hausaland.

17. The main outlines of these struggles are presented in the chapters by Hunwick and by Adeleye, see n. 16.

18. Ahmad ibn Fartuwa, *History of the First Twelve Years of the Reign of Mai Idris Alooma of Bornu*, an Arabic Text translated by H. R. Palmer (Lagos: The Government Printer, 1926).

19. The tangled histories of Gobir, Kebbi, and Zamfara have been partly straightened out by J. Sutton's reassessment of Hausa cultural origins. See especially 192–195 of his "Towards a less orthodox history of Hausaland."

20. M. Hiskett, *The Sword of Truth: The life and times of the Shehu Usuman dan Fodio* (New York: Oxford University Press, 1973).

Chapter Six

FIVE CITY-STATE CULTURES COMPARED

Robert Griffeth and Carol G. Thomas

As the past five chapters show, city-states have existed in many places from the Bronze Age into the modern period. If the five city-states examined in these pages have more in common than coincidence, some attention must be paid to the issue of causation. In this instance the problem might be stated as follows: what *caused* the city-state form to prevail in the five cases studied here over other possible forms of political, social, and spatial organization? Are common sets of historical, geographical, and economic circumstances essential preconditions for city-states to take shape?

The sampling from the evidence we present in these five cases is surely too small to generalize on the highest levels of social science theory. We do not pretend to offer a general theoretical model to explain why city-states appeared under some presumably governing set of circumstances. Nor do we assume that the factors we regard as having been most important in all the cases we studied are necessarily those that were present in other instances not examined. Social science theory has made great advances—particularly in the work of geographers, economic historians, and specialists in the study of urbanization and political centralization—which have contributed importantly to each of our studies in varying ways. Where rigorous (mathematical) analysis of substantial concrete data has been possible, the definition of key factors that contributed to a particular set of city-states has been enriched and deepened. For example, the crucial question of how city cores evolve in intricate interrelationship with the territories that surround them was first explored in that very south German area analyzed in this volume by Christopher Friedrichs.[1] Central places theory and the models (with many subsequent refinements) that it inspired have given historians a major tool as they have attempted to relate particular historical developments to the physical and economic settings in which they occurred.[2] Beyond that, the usefulness of central places models in examining the city-state form is obvious: the nature of the city-state consisted of *a* central place and the immediate hinterland or territory that was intricately bound to it in politics, social relations, and economic interdependency. In a different vein, Gordon

Griffiths' study of the Italian city-state was able to draw upon the exquisitely detailed analysis of the Florentine economy in which the conceptual tools and methods of modern economic analysis were thoroughly employed.[3] On the other hand, the application of such sophisticated analytical methods to our other three case studies could not produce the same enviable results since the concrete data on Sumer, Greece, and Hausaland are not even remotely so plentiful.

Thus, while the temptation to refine a basic model of "*the* city-state" seems alluring, the data necessary to embark on such a task are not available. Our quest for meaningful comparisons will therefore take the form of comparing and contrasting those features of the city-states studied where sufficient information is available. While this necessarily is well short of a major theoretical statement, we feel that we make a substantial contribution to ongoing efforts by social scientists generally, and historians in particular, who attempt to see the common themes that knit their individual work into grander patterns.

Returning to the issue of causation, our point of departure rests upon the simple historical observation that city-states require a fairly long period of gestation. All five of the cases examined in this study developed in circumstances where no complex administrative state was firmly established in their near vicinities. Certainly there are gradations in the applicability of this general formula ranging from total absence of major polities, as in the case of Sumer, to a temporary weakness of an existing power, as in Germany and Switzerland in the late Middle Ages. In each instance, however, the development of city-states was due in large part to the relative weakness of all polities in the geographical region where the city-state culture arose.

Sumerian civilization was a primary civilization; that is, it grew from prehistoric roots. To employ a useful, conventional distinction, it is the level of complexity achieved that distinguishes a "civilization" from relatively less complex "cultures." In the well chosen words of Colin Renfrew, civilization is "the self-made environment of man, which he has fashioned to insulate himself from the primeval environment of nature alone . . . a web of culture so complex and dense that most of his activities now relate to this artificial environment rather than directly to the fundamentally natural one."[4]

By this definition, all city-states are products of what is called civilization. But Sumer may be regarded as its first expression. In southern Mesopotamia the two great revolutions associated with the passage from prehistoric beginnings of human society to settled civilization occurred. The first of these was the revolution in food production during which plant and animal domestication, permanent village community settlement, and great diversification of labor functions slowly evolved from 10,000 to 7,000 B.C. There also the agricultural revolution was followed by a second fundamental transformation in human society, the urban revolution which produced the first cities in the ancient Near East in the fourth millennium B.C. Economic and political developments occurred on a restricted, regional basis giving rise to approximately a dozen independent polities. In each Sumerian city-state, a few hundred square miles were organized and exploited to support a population numbering in the tens of thousands.

In the primary civilization of Sumer, then, the rise of city-states was the first stage of development in a process of growing centralization of political authority. The rather startling demographic growth in so constricted a space obviously evoked the need for greater social control and efficient use of specialized labor. The subsequent history of the ancient Near East was marked in turn by the growth of great territorial states which, commanding greater coercive powers, came to exercise sovereignty over the smaller polities such as the Sumerian city-states.

The Hausa states are most analogous to the Sumerian of the four other cultures examined. Hausa civilization was not primary; there were influences from other complex cultures in West Africa in the formative period of the city-states in the fourteenth and fifteenth centuries. However, within Hausaland there had occurred a gradual increase in complexity of the societies of farming peoples throughout the first millennium of the African Iron Age. From individual, widely dispersed agricultural settlements villages (*gari*) developed which, in some instances, grew into cities (*birane*). Given their degree of relative isolation from more powerful states—e.g., Bornu, Songhay, Kwararafa—certain of the cities were able to exercise control over the territory surrounding the urban center.[5] Hence the process of formation of these polities shares many of the features found in Sumer.

Greece and Renaissance Italy are somewhat different in that larger territorial states had once dominated the land of the city-states. As an integral part of the eastern Mediterranean world during the Bronze Age from 3000 to 1000 B.C., the Aegean region developed several distinct civilizations in which palace centers governed lesser sites in the near vicinity. While not on the scale of the ancient Near Eastern kingdoms, the Greek states of the Bronze Age were larger and, in some ways, more complex than the city-states of the later Classical period.

Italy, too, was the seat of a formerly great political entity. Indeed, the Roman Empire marked a new height of imperial control in the Mediterranean region. Earlier city-states—Greek, Italian, Etruscan—as well as other political entities were steadily drawn together by Rome into a single unit from the fourth century B.C. The final imperial form of government was so solidly grounded that it survived the collapse of the empire itself, persisting under invaders such as Lombards and Franks to reemerge in altered form as the Holy Roman Empire.

There were, then, traditions of political centralization based upon large territorial and imperial models in both Greece and Italy. However, the actual institutions had dimmed if not disappeared altogether by the time of the city-states of the Classical period of Greek history, on the one hand, and of the late medieval period of Italian history, on the other. At the end of the Bronze Age there was a sudden collapse of the established civilizations. The eastern

Mediterranean was altered from the seat of flourishing international civilizations to impoverished, localized villages. So severe were the difficulties that the next four centuries are termed Dark Ages. Reorganization of larger states was a slow process, especially in Greece. By the end of the Dark Age, regionalism was so engrained in the Greek way of life and view of man's nature that unity among the hundreds of tiny city-states could not be achieved for another three and a half centuries. Large territorial states had been fashioned once again by 750 B.C. in the Near East, but they did not and could not threaten Greece until the city-states had taken firm root. When those city-states were finally caught in the embrace of a potent ruler, that ruler came from within the Greek cultural orbit rather than from a great Eastern empire.

In contrast to the emergence of the Greek *poleis* from the ashes of the Bronze Age kingdoms, the demise of the Roman Empire and the growth of city-states within its formerly extensive European domains was neither so sudden nor so complete. As late as the sixteenth century Leonardo Bruni could state that Florence "uses the Roman law, and was indeed a Roman colony. For Sulla the dictator established this colony, with the best Roman stock, with the result that we have the same laws as the mother-city, except for such changes as have been brought about by time."[6] Nonetheless, the imperial structure underwent major alterations in late antiquity and then disappeared. The bishops' control of former Roman cities was of a different order altogether from the earlier powers exercised by procurators and praetors.

Central Europe shares several features with medieval Italy. Many of its largest cities and towns had been founded by Rome when the might of the Empire had extended into southern Germany. Yet the situation was different in one major respect: a new imperial power arose in Germany and claimed suzerainty over the cities of the region. Those German and Swiss cities that ultimately became states in their own right did so despite the presence of an imperial authority which claimed to rule over them. Indeed, the emperor was often forced to grant extraordinary privileges to certain city-states in order to strengthen his position vis-à-vis feudal lords of the realm. Still, it is clear even in the case of the German city-states where the imperial presence was most directly felt that the forces of the empire were not sufficient to overwhelm the *de facto* autonomy of the strongest polities. When imperial rulers succeeded in expanding their powers in the eighteenth century, the city-states were reduced to the role of mere cities, i.e., urban entities governed from above.

The most characteristic set of circumstances that allowed for city-state growth were those in which political authority was diffused. Small, localized polities were free to perfect their individual forms of government and to extend their control over neighboring territory. However, the absence of centralized power in itself did not necessarily promote the city-state form. In much of Western Europe after the decline of Rome, feudalism became the characteristic order. Elsewhere, major population shifts away from the old core regions resulted in the creation of mini-states which preserved the form of former monarchical or imperial systems on a lessened scale. In still other cases, the foundation of new centralized political units by either nomadic conquerors or groups of agricultural settlers more often than not assumed kingly or imperial shapes rather than the city-state type of organization.

However, the continued neutralization of strong central authority was absolutely essential to insuring the continuity of city-state systems. The obvious defect of this situation lay in the fact that each individual state found its political raison d'être in its claim to independence. Cooperation between them directed toward building a larger polity was thereby precluded. This remained true even when a city-state culture was faced with a serious outside threat. Alliances were not unknown but they were usually regarded as temporary and apart from the preferred way of acting.

As a general rule, therefore, city-states—even when they exist as anomalies within larger political and economic systems—require that such systems be weak or absent altogether.[7] Proof of this generalization may be sought in the examination of other instances not discussed here. The Philistine, Aramaean, Phoenician, and Syro-Hittite city-states which flourished during the early Dark Age from roughly 1150 to 800 B.C. were quickly absorbed by the expanding might of the Assyrians in the eighth century and, two centuries later, by that of the Persians. The Etruscan states of Tuscany suffered a similar fate through the growth of Rome. The northern European commercial city-states, such as Danzig, and the maritime towns of Italy, such as Amalfi and Pisa, also fell victim to a larger power when the mechanisms which might have assisted them to retain their independent status proved inadequate.

Bearing in mind these general conditions that appear to have been present in order for city-states to emerge, we now turn to an assessment of the similarities and differences that can be detected in the cases that serve as our basic examples.

A Comparison of Similarities and Differences

Scale, measured both in territory and population, is the most apparent likeness among the five city-states cultures examined in this study. In each case studied the average size of a city-state was rarely more than a few hundred square miles. There were exceptional instances where the territory of one city-state grew to far greater proportions but this most often occurred as one state incorporated the land of a previously autonomous neighbor and held it for a temporary period. Florence and Milan, Sparta and Athens, Kano and Zaria are examples of enlargement through military expansion. Where open or waste lands supporting very small populations were located in territory contiguous to the core state, these too might be added to the city-state domain. The Hausa states provide evidence of such a process and the growth of population in the Mesopotamian city-states probably engendered a similar form of limited expansion. But the geographical setting in Greece and Europe limited the availability of lightly-populated lands adjacent to the city-states; thus any campaign of expansion must necessarily be undertaken at the expense of a neighbor. In these ways, constraints placed upon overall size remained a key factor in every case.

Another common feature among city-state cultures is the distinction between the urban center and its rural environs. In the sense that city denotes the political central point and state represents the hinterland necessary for the economic survival of the whole, city-state is a useful single term for all these polities whether they are precisely defined as *poleis* or *Reichsstädte* or *birane*. The focal point of the state was small: Sumerian Erech was under two square miles; Athens' center encompassed just under one square mile; Florence's walls in the early fourteenth century enclosed about two and one half square miles; Nuremberg was typical of the extent of German free cities in that it measured less than three quarters of a mile from one end to the other; the great earthen walls of the Hausa cities, enclosing both farmland and urban dwellings, were larger than the others but still contained no more than ten to twelve square miles.

Although the central space was narrowly confined, it was from that core that the life of the city-state was directed. In modern terms, this center would be known as the capital city inasmuch as the machinery of government was concentrated within the walls separating city from countryside. In all five cultures, walls were a normal feature serving to define the center of the city-state. They delimited and protected the central institutions from threat of attack and, during periods when the state might come under siege from an enemy, they served as a secure place for many of the rural dwellers who sought refuge behind them. Residence within the walls might also confer social and political status. In the Italian and German city-states only those who permanently lived within the urban center could exercise full rights of citizenship and this may have been the case in Sumer as well although the evidence does not allow certainty on the point. Yet, city residence did not confer special privilege in all of our cases: no situation similar to that in Italy and Germany existed for Greeks and Hausa. Thus, the free peasant farmers dwelling in the countryside of Attica made up at least fifty percent of the citizenry of Athens in the fifth century, for instance, and the preponderance of Hausa citizens lived outside the city walls.

Just as space was limited, so too was the population. There are variations in numbers between the five cultures but this variety is as much a factor of the structure of the economy as it is of basic difference among the states: economies that are essentially agrarian require more land to support their populations than do diversified economies which trade regularly with external economic units to sustain an adequate level of foodstuffs. In other words, a specific maximum or minimum size of population seems not to be a crucial factor in determining whether or not the city-state form of organization is adopted. Sumerian Uruk had a population of approximately 50,000; in the early part of the fifth century Athens had an estimated total population of between 120,000 and 150,000; high population figures for Florence indicate 120,000 persons in 1338; the totals for the German cities were in the 20,000 to 30,000 range, but this counted only those residents living within the walls; by the end of the eighteenth century, large Hausa states such as Kano may have numbered populations as great as a quarter of a million but most of the others had less than 50,000 souls.

For the Greeks it was a given rule that each citizen should know his fellows and this same value was shared by other cultures including all those studied here. Although population figures are in the hundreds of thousands, the actual citizenry was much smaller and of the citizens only a small fraction exercised full political rights on a regular basis. In this respect all city-states were oligarchic—even Athens, which is credited with the birth of democracy. Sumerian cities may well have been directed originally by an assembly of all free adult males, but gradually the power of the *ensi* rose submerging the power of the assembly. In spite of the incorporation of the free peasantry into government, most Greek *poleis* remained oligarchic. Athens was exceptional in including as much of her population in the management of state affairs as she did. Yet, even in the fifth century, Athenian policy was largely determined by one man, like Pericles, for years at a time. Lineage determined those capable of high office both in Italy and in the Hausa states. Leading families dominated the Grand Council in Venice just as the aristocratic families kept control of the Florentine polity through its many political changes. The consuls of the early commune were precursors of the Medici near the end of Florentine city-state independence. Among the Hausa, noble lineage membership provided the principal access to the highest titled offices. At the apex was the kingly family and beneath that extended a ladder of administrative positions from the *Kaura* (senior military commander) to the heads of the various guilds. Office in the German *Reichsstädte* was determined on truly oligarchic and timocratic grounds. Although in theory all male citizens, heirs of the original commune, had an equal right to participate in the political life of the city-state, in actuality all the German and Swiss city-states were ruled by a narrow elite, the most wealthy and prestigious members of the cities' guilds.

This tendency toward oligarchy illustrates an even more fundamental similarity in city-state cultures: the claims of those who made up the ruling groups, living in close proximity to each other, to regulate the affairs of state encouraged a particularist form of government. Even the German and Swiss cities, while nominally under the sovereignty of the emperor, had managed to establish their autonomy by the fourteenth century. As a result of their *de facto* independence, the city-states governed themselves in most matters that really counted. Moreover, their small size fostered a direct, rather than representative, form of ruling authority. While rights of citizenship were shared by many—those related by kinship ties, heirs of the commune, members of certain guilds—effective direction demanded concentration of power in the hands of a few officials. The various forms of political and social control which we identify here as oligarchic in character appear to have become the most typical form for the exercise of authority. And, above all, that authority was focused on preserving the cherished independence of the city-state from outside interference.

In addition to political autonomy, city-states have also striven to create for themselves conditions of economic independence, i.e., autarchy. The Sumerian states were the final product of the early revolution in food production as it was adapted to a river-valley environment. Hand in hand with urbanization came central direction of irrigation projects, regularization of an increasingly diversified labor force, and control over trade, especially in those goods not available locally. The Greek city-states were the products of small Dark Age settlements located in naturally defensible regions which were largely self-sufficient, that is, capable of providing the bare necessities of life for the inhabitants of the immediate region. Their attempts to provide the same degree of self-sufficiency as they grew larger continued throughout the independent life of the Greek city-states, although it was impossible for any one *polis* to meet its basic needs entirely. Consequently, the state assumed some control over the economic order and financial institutions of the *polis*. However, because the goal of autarchy and the means at its disposal to meet that goal were incompatible in the Greek state, the need to devise an effective state mechanism to supervise economic life was not perceived.

There was not the same contradiction in the later city-state cultures largely because they admitted to a need for extensive trade and commerce and, hence, the state assumed some degree of active direction over the economic life of its citizens even though the mechanism may not have been efficient or successful. Guilds were a regular feature of the Italian, German, Swiss, and Hausa economic systems. The chief members of the major guilds generally had a key voice in the affairs of state. The Calimala guild of Florence is an especially notable example of the interaction between economic and political authority; the guilds in the Swiss and German free cities possessed the right of selecting a given number of the council members of the city and it was the councils that enjoyed almost complete authority over both citizens and subjects. Hausa guild members, though accorded low social status within the ruling system, nevertheless exercised key roles—frequently associated with ritual performances—in the social and cultural spheres of Hausa life as well as in their primary occupational functions. In order to meet its charge of economic well-being, the Hausa city-state found a means of incorporating even the foreign elements— particularly long-distance traders—whose activities were so vital.

In every instance, a rural hinterland provided the essential foodstuffs for the population of the region, urban and rural residents alike. More specialized occupations came to be centered in the city where regulation of the whole economic structure was focused.[8] There were various degrees of regulation, to be sure, with the Greek *poleis* standing at the extreme end of the scale. Yet even for the Greeks who argued that the citizen should be a political animal freed from banausic pursuits of gaining a livelihood, there was a realization that the polity had economic responsibilities to its members. In every other instance of city-state culture examined here, the state openly, rather than grudgingly, acknowledged an active economic role.

Part of the necessary business of the state, then, involved interstate economic activity in addition to local production and exchange. Every city-state was compelled to carry on commerce beyond its own borders and in all cases the patterns of such trade links remained vital for its continued existence. Sumerian states sent merchants far afield, into central Asia to places like Tepe Yahyeh for steatite. Greek *poleis* were forced to trade for metals, at the very least, and many Greek states came to rely on trade for the supply of essential foodstuffs. Major guilds of Florence and other Italian city-states were critically linked to networks of international commerce. The German and Swiss cities may well have been founded on the attempt to further the well-being of their citizens through commercial activities. One of their chief weaknesses by the end of the eighteenth century rested on the failure to sustain those very interests. Hausa territory came to occupy the crossroads of a lucrative international commercial network whose control influenced the internal politics and social structures of the individual states. Furthermore, it was important enough to be the major cause of contention between the key competitors especially in the sixteenth and seventeenth centuries.[9]

The rivalry was as intense as if it were between people who shared no common cultural bonds. However, the bonds between the individual states of each city-state culture were many and close. Sumerians, Greeks, Hausa, Italians, Germans, and Swiss all recognized that they shared features of ethnicity, language, religion, and inherited customs that distinguished them from other contemporary cultures. Perhaps the Greek view of the situation is most expressive: all others were barbarians. The Hausa, too, referred to the "stateless peoples" who occupied lands on their far hinterland regions as *habe* (pagan, without any glimmer of Islamic ways, barbarians). While the European polities did safeguard the memory of their imperial antecedents and lived within the institutional framework of a common religion, their city-states also drew basic distinctions between peoples that came remarkably close to cultural xenophobia. This was the case even where other Europeans were concerned but especially with respect to Muslims, for many centuries their key trading partners.

On the other hand, it appears to be inherent in the city-state form of organization that efforts to maintain political and economic independence exert a greater pull than do recognized features of a common culture. The result is that interstate warfare is a constant theme that more often than not overshadows feebler efforts made to band together in a common cause. Interstate rivalry, often leading to chronic strife with its attendant heavy outlays for military purposes, is likely to be one of the central causes which shortened the life spans of most city-states.

Despite this apparent structural defect, it is interesting that in all our five cases the city-state form managed to endure for periods of about four to five hundred years. While such a life span may be the average for any polity, it appears long in view of the tensions within and among city-states. The Early Dynastic Age of Sumerian history is coeval with the period of independent states, that is, from 2800–2350 B.C. The vigor of the Greek *polis* extended over the four hundred years from 750 to approximately 350 B.C., the Classical Age. From the organization of the early communes in the late eleventh century to the dominance of the Spanish and French at the end of the fifteenth century was the age of the thriving northern Italian city-states. The German and Swiss states flourished for much the same time span that the Hausa states remained independent and vigorous, from the fourteenth to the end of the eighteenth centuries. What general conclusion should be drawn from this chronological symmetry is not precisely clear. It may very well be that the tensions born of interstate rivalry can be controlled for a limited time only—even though those limits extend up to a half millennium. Or it might also be that the very success of the city-state form exerts a positive attraction upon would-be conquerors but that territorial and imperial rulers require a lengthy formative period in which to secure their power bases before they attain positions of strength adequate to challenge and overwhelm small neighboring polities. In either case, there is evidence from our case studies that city-state systems manage to sustain their "classical" form for about four hundred years.

Finally, even after they lost their effective claims to independent status, all the city-states continued to enjoy a half-life when they were incorporated into larger territorial units. They preserved much the same physical appearance, frequently continued to exercise the same economic roles, and even perpetuated forms of government that were the major achievement of the city-state period. Beyond that they often served as models for their conquerors. The Sumerian law codes were the model for most subsequent Mesopotamian codes, including the famous Code of Hammurabi. The city-states of the eastern Mediterranean became the bases of Roman provincial government. The Fulani rulers of the Hausa states grafted an imperial structure onto the earlier system but they left the social and political orders mostly intact. The European cities continued to exist but as parts of greater political entities. Indirectly, then, we can answer a question of definition: while city-states do share physical and other features, the true nature of a city-state is not its physical form. Shorn of its independence, it becomes something else.

So far we have stressed those features of the city-states studied in this volume that reveal similarities; that does not mean that they were identical in character. What is more, there were considerable differences between individual city-states within each particular culture. It has been noted, for example, that while most city-states were very small in size, certain of them grew exceptionally large—Kano, Milan, Sparta to name a few instances. Certain economies remained virtually agrarian while others added a high level of commercial enterprise, a difference readily visible in comparing Thebes and Corinth for example. Yet Thebans and Corinthians recognized that their polities were of the same order whereas the Persian state was not.

The most surprising variation is that of political organization. Earlier we suggested that the most typical political form can be identified as oligarchic rule, the sharing of power by an elite group of the wealthiest citizenry. Within this broad definition, however, every conceivable permutation occurred. The Sumerian and Hausa city-states were monarchies with elaborate systems of official positions. The early modern European city-states most closely conformed to the system of rule identified by the term oligarchy. In Greece it is possible to see every form of government functioning simultaneously: democracy in Athens, oligarchy in Corinth, kingly rule in Sparta. The one factor common to them all is that the governing bodies and officials were selected by local processes from among the citizenry of the particular state.[10] Even in the case where it is least expected this general rule obtains: the *Reichsstädte* were imperial cities but they had won the right of self-government.

When an individual state expanded into the territory of a neighboring city-state, thereby creating a larger territorial state, it infringed on the right of self-determination of political form. Such a violation was a key factor in the lack of permanence of any city-state "empire." A city-state system seemed to have the means of restoring the equilibrium required for the maintenance of dispersed centers of authority. For example, such a violation provoked the Peloponnesian War in Greece (431–404 B.C.) from which no large, permanent territorial state emerged victorious; it caused Sumerian cities to take up arms against a violating state; it brought on almost two centuries of warfare between Kano and Katsina; and it led to unexpected alliances between Italian states (the success of the Scaliger state produced an anti-Scaliger League) and led to friendships with foreign powers (Cremona welcomed the intervention of Frederick II and joined with his Hohenstaufen forces in the destruction of Milan in 1162).

The form of government mattered less to the existence of a city-state than did its concept of citizenship. On the surface there appear to be different criteria in our case studies—kinship, degree of wealth, place of residence, level of social standing. However, there is a basic similarity underlying the sense of belonging in every case, namely kinship. We do not mean to imply that our examples of city-states are the only political forms to share common bonds of blood and culture. The point is, rather, that all five examples share this characteristic.

The Sumerian state was the product of early farming village communities in which ties of kinship served as the basis of community membership. To be sure, the rise of civilized societies brought other forms of association—craft and place of residence—but nonetheless, it is likely that common blood continued to determine the right of membership in the political life of the state, that is, participation in the assemblies. The fact that it was outsiders captured in war who were the slaves of early Sumerian cities strengthens the view that kinship abided as the basis of community.

It is not necessary to conjecture about the importance of ties of blood in the Greek and the Hausa states. Both Greeks and Hausa explained their past in terms of family genealogies. Hellen was the ancestor of the Hellenes; his sons were Dorus and Aeolus and his grandsons, Ion and Achaeus—the eponyms of the four dialects of the Greek language. In a like fashion the Hausa states traced their foundation to the hero Abayajidda, his son Bawo and, in turn, Bawo's six sons. More than picturesque stories, the traditions embody the perceived common bonds of shared blood and culture over generations.

The concept of citizenship in the Italian and northern European city-states went back to the early communes—*coniurationes*—of the eleventh and twelfth centuries respectively. Inhabitants of a community bound themselves by oath to act collectively in pursuit of their economic and legal rights. Membership in the commune was carried on by inheritance in the male line from one generation to the next. While the members of the original communities may not have been kin in the strictest sense, they did possess bonds of common culture, tradition, and interests and many were directly blood-related. Certainly the kinship tie served as the operative force in perpetuating the community.

It is true that city-states could and did admit outsiders to rights of citizenship. The German and Hausa states are especially notable in their willingness to open the community to others. In Germany, outsiders were admitted to citizenship if they had sufficient wealth or skills to make them desirable permanent residents. The right of citizenship then passed to their descendants by inheritance in the male line. In the Hausa states a number of means developed whereby persons of non-Hausa origin who were socially useful could be grafted onto the kinship structure. The system of clientship, intermarriage, and grants of special rights were normal means of enlarging the communal membership. Even in these instances, however, the sense of uniformity of community was not undermined. A common language prevailed, there was a degree of religious uniformity which bound new members to the body of the community. An illustration of this sense of belonging can be found by examining the role of those people who did not belong to the common culture: Jews were never fully incorporated into the German city-states and, in many instances, they were rigidly segregated in ghettos. The nomadic pastoral Fulani were tolerated by the Hausa so long as the relationship between the two groups consisted primarily of a beneficial economic symbiosis; but Fulani were not reckoned among those who possessed rights of citizenship.

Citizenship conferred clear privileges: Athenians paid no regular direct taxes while all foreigners resident in the city-state paid for that privilege. Membership in the community secured legal rights to the Hausawa not available to outsiders. In the German cities, most crafts or retail activities could be carried out only by citizens. Consequently, the privileges were guarded carefully by the full members of the community. Indeed, it was only when a national citizenship replaced the importance of local citizenship that the framework of the city-state was irreparably weakened.

There was considerable variation in the nature of the social stratification of the city-states. The two criteria determining one's position were, as we have seen in another context, birth and wealth. Blood lines decided whether a person belonged to the full citizenry while wealth was responsible for establishing one's place in the hierarchy of members. In each city-state culture there was a considerable distance between those at the bottom and the top of the social hierarchy. The Sumerian cities placed a king (*ensi*) at the apex who served as lieutenant of the gods to whom the city truly belonged. Below this *ensi* were his peers who held the highest offices. A middle rank was larger in size, composed of specialists and merchants as well as the more successful farmers. The bulk of the population was the peasant farming class, probably free *de jure* but with little freedom of movement or rights of political participation. And, as in all ancient societies, slavery was an essential institution in the Sumerian city-states.

The Greek city-states had a similar appearance at the lower end of the social scale; the slave population of Athens in the mid-fifth century, for instance, is estimated at more than half the total population of 300,000. It was virtually impossible to gain admittance into the body of free members of society in the Greek *poleis* of the Classical period. The upper orders of society were not so remote or privileged as they were in Sumer. This was so not only because of a different system of values but also because there was not the opportunity to gain great wealth and even more because the ordinary peasantry were admitted into direct and regular participation in affairs of city-state. In other words, there was something of a leveling process.

The Italian cities were of just the opposite nature—extremely top-heavy with the weight of a few wealthy, privileged families who dominated political, economic, and intellectual life from the eleventh to the sixteenth centuries. Not slaves but rural peasants occupied the lowest rungs of the social ladder. In the mid-range were the full members of the minor and middling guilds. In Florence, for instance, there were partial members of guilds (*subpositi*) who did not enjoy the political rights of citizenship although they were integrated into the life of the community as the rural inhabitants were not.

The German and Swiss cities included more of their inhabitants among the *Bürgerschaft,* but there were clear lines of demarcation within the citizenry. For example, the citizens were divided into five official strata in seventeenth century Frankfurt: patricians, non-patrician magistrates and merchants, distinguished retailers and professionals, common retailers and craftsmen, and unskilled workers such as coachmen and day-laborers. At the bottom of the social scale of the city population were servants, beggars, casual laborers, alien apprentices, and journeymen. Outside the walls of the cities were the rural peasants usually occupying the status of subjects. There was little opportunity for the peasantry to be incorporated into the citizen body of any northern European state.

The Hausa social structure may be the most complex of all our case studies. It was rigorously hierarchical and yet managed to incorporate outsiders into the life of the state. Consequently, there were several parallel lines of linkage operating simultaneously. The most important was that created by blood ties that provided the kinship basis of full citizenship. From king to humble farmer by way of noble families, shared blood was the basis of membership in the community. The lowest order of citizens was the peasant-farming *talakawa*. Certain crafts and occupations, bound together through guild organization, were of equally low status while others—merchants, bankers, literate Muslims—conferred a higher social standing. These professions were not monopolized by a few great families, as was the case in Italy. Slavery was of central importance to the Hausa city-states as it had been to Sumer and Greece, but, unlike the ancient polities, it was possible for Hausa slaves to acquire their freedom or to attain high administrative office. Slaves served as both senior throne officials and as palace slaves with important duties. A system of clientship was also a major avenue of upward mobility for the foreign, commoner, and slave components of Hausa society.

The foregoing consideration of similarities and differences discovered in our comparisons is intended to give substance to the basic four-part definition in the introduction to this volume. By way of summary we can now define city-states as polities that were small in territorial size and citizen population. Each took root during times when strong territorial states were either absent or seriously weakened, a situation which enabled the small polities to win political autonomy and to preserve their independence for periods up to five centuries. Each city-state culture also developed within a distinctive geographical region that exhibited considerable internal uniformity (although major differences are to be found between the environmental settings of the five cultures). Whereas no one dominating factor can be singled out to explain why the city-state form developed in these circumstances rather than some alternative type of political organization, our comparisons do help establish certain key conditions that appear to have been essential to the foundation and growth of each of the systems.

On the level of specific structural comparisons, remarkable correspondences are apparent. The term city-state systems takes one major sense of its meaning from the fact that the individual polities within an area evolved a common cultural tradition best evidenced by the use of the same language. Thus there is a common tie between similar units since city-states do not normally spring up as unique phenomena within cultural areas.[11] The 1500 Greek *poleis,* the more than a dozen Sumerian and Hausa city-states, the numerous German and Italian polities all support this generalization. While economic complementarity helps to explain one of the mechanisms which sustains a common culture, it is not by any means a necessary precondition: the evidence of profoundly different cultures all forming a part of one integrated economic system is as easy to find as the reverse.[12] But this is not the case within the city-state systems.

The physical appearance of all city-states reveals an even greater common modality. All had walls that encircled and protected the core from which the vital life of the state was directed. All had, or made efforts to acquire, economic hinterlands whose systems of production were intended principally to serve the needs of the immediate territory of the state and whose residents were attached as either citizens or subjects. Such links do not require a particular form of political or social organization; however, a sense of shared kinship—actual or artificial—provided the basic bond of membership in the community. Finally, attempts to promote an economic self-sufficiency to accompany political autonomy so animated city-state life that useful outsiders were incorporated into the social structures of the states even if they were not accorded full rights of political participation.

Such, then, are the basic comparative conclusions drawn from our data on the rise, growth, and elaboration of the city-state form. But in the final analysis they all failed to endure beyond the five hundred year life spans that seem to have applied to all of them. Why?

The End of Autonomy: Decline of the City-States

The absence of a strong territorial or imperial power was the key ingredient that insured city-state survival. By the same token, most city-states came to the end of their existence as independent polities when such powers appeared on their doorsteps. Leaders like Sargon of Akkad, Philip of Macedon, cUthman dan Fodio of Sokoto, Napoleon, and Charles V succeeded in sweeping away the cherished independence of small polities which lay in the path of their conquering ambitions.

Yet neither foreign conquest and invasion nor the successful usurpation of power by a gifted military leader account wholly for the decline of well-established city-states. In some instances the small states were able to turn back the advance of far more powerful adversaries as the Greeks managed to do during the Persian Wars of 490 and 480/79 B.C. Likewise, the Hausa states were frequently besieged by neighboring imperial Bornu's armies. From the sixteenth century forward both Italian and German city-states had frequently to deal with the imperial claims of those European monarchs who would restore the grandeur of empire. Resistance sapped the energies of the city-states yet they all managed to delay the final day of reckoning for impressively long periods. Consequently, conquest must be viewed as only one of the causes of decline.

This larger view brings us back to the issue of scale. As a product of its development, the machinery of a city-state was adapted to a relatively restricted territory and to a limited population base. The five city-state systems we survey had individual polities whose usual size amounted to no more than a few hundred square miles. Populations of individual states numbered in the hundreds of thousands at most, not in millions.[13] As a result, the organization of the state was fundamentally tailored to its small size. Governance was direct; that is, through officials selected or elected from among the inhabitants of the polity (except for the Italian practice of securing a *podestà* of the commune from another state). Certainly political office was not open to all inhabitants of the city-state's territory, but officials were not imposed upon the polity by a foreign suzerain—a king, emperor, or appointed bureaucrat of another state. Even the decision to recruit a *podestà* from another state was the decision of the ruling orders of the respective Italian polities.

On the other hand, the consolidation of a political order adapted to a confined, compact territory and small population must be viewed in light of another feature of all city-states, namely their almost continuous efforts to expand. The histories of Sumer, ancient Greece, Hausaland, medieval Italy, and early modern Germany are stories of warfare between states of the same geographic region and of similar culture. Wars have weakened or destroyed polities of all types and sizes; we do not claim that city-states were unique in this regard but simply stress the frequency of warfare among states with common cultural and economic ties. The Early Dynastic Age of Sumer (2800–2350 B.C.) was marked by rivalry of a dozen city-states. Each state, usually within sight of its nearest neighbor and most powerful rival, endeavored to maintain an independent status while increasing its wealth and territorial holdings. Various of the cities held temporary supremacy over others but a permanent unified kingdom of all the area did not result.

The history of ancient Greece is also a tale of inter-*polis* wars. The first phase of the Classical period dawned with a struggle known as the Lelantine War. Originally a dispute between two neighboring states over control of the plain lying between them, it spread to include city-states of Asia Minor as well as city-states of the mainland of Greece. The historian Thucydides later recalled (I.15) that it was "The conflict in which the rest of Hellas was most divided, allying itself with one side or the other . . ." up to his own time. Three hundred years later the vigor of Classical Greece had been spent after twenty-seven years of struggle known as the Peloponnesian War fought to halt the imperialistic expansion of Athens.

States like Kano and Katsina were the Hausa counterparts of Athens and Sparta. A series of wars between the two lasted from the fourteenth through the mid-seventeenth centuries. Resentment of Katsina's key commercial role drove armies from Kano to take the field on repeated occasions. Both hoped to maintain or even enlarge their sway over trade routes. Equally fierce was the rivalry between Florence and Milan, both successful expansionist states that came to possess the greatest size of any of the Italian city-states through their control of weaker states. In Germany, too, the fourteenth and fifteenth centuries produced a period of unending intercity warfare. In 1312, for example, Esslingen occupied Stuttgart and several other neighboring cities although the occupation was short-lived.

In other words, constant, unresolved tension between a city-state's ambition to expand and its need to consolidate and protect its interests in the core area produced a situation that the city-state organization was not able to resolve without changing its fundamental character. The organization of the polity was not suited to great territorial size as its resources to conduct major expansionist campaigns were quite limited. The same brake applied to its ability to control huge populations or even to exercise indirect control over other states. It is interesting to note that in no one of the cultures examined here did a single state succeed in imposing a permanent empire while at the same time maintaining its basic political shape. All city-state cultures were eventually absorbed by greater territorial states, but the success belonged mainly to powers arriving from outside: Akkad, Macedon, France, Spain, and even to some extent the Fulani of pluralistic Hausaland.

It might be objected that there is at least one well-known case of a city-state that did create an empire—Rome. Yet, consider Rome's experience. She was dominated by a foreign, Etruscan dynasty during the formative period of development. Rome became a key member—and soon the dominant partner—in the Latin League in the early days of the Republic. And the state was willing to create additional societal units (tribes) even during its initial expansion. In other words, the Roman state abandoned its city-state form even before it acquired an empire.

Interstate warfare between city-states was so normal that it can be defined as a natural attribute even though it played a major role in the decline of individual states and whole city-state systems. The rivalry and open hostility made it unlikely that any one state would gain complete primacy over all others. A certain degree of preeminence usually provoked reaction on the part of other states and, in the process, not only were energies dissipated but the tension brought about a leveling of potentially powerful polities. Such a situation was not fatal to the continued health of the city-states so long as there was no more forceful state able to take advantage of the weakened status of the small and vulnerable polities. Perhaps we might be justified in considering this condition as a natural mechanism producing a localized balance of power which functioned to restore the equilibrium between potential competitors who wished to monopolize force. However, an exact description of that mechanism is elusive since the objects of competition vary from one city-state culture to another. Political hegemony seems to have been the object of aggressive expansion in the cases of Sumer and Greece whereas control of the wealth to be derived from mastery over commerce appears to have been the conscious aim of the main Hausa rivals. An intermingling of both factors characterizes the conflict in the European cases with the effort to exert economic primacy invariably forming a central concern.

In all five cultures, however, endemic conflict weakened the city-state systems and helped prepare the ground for outside intervention in their affairs. As Thebes, Athens, and Sparta prepared the path for Philip of Macedon, so did Milan and Florence open the way to Charles V.

The debilitating effects of interstate conflict and the capacity of stronger powers organized along different lines to capitalize on that situation form only a part of what caused the city-state cultures to falter. Internal tensions also existed within each city-state which contributed to its inability to meet and overcome foreign pressures. Perhaps the most serious problem for all five systems stemmed from the concept of citizenship or its equivalent. That is, not all residents of a city-state's territory were accorded full and equal participation in the political, social, and economic life of their homeland.

The Greeks and the Hausa came closest to inclusion of all social strata in active management of state affairs. In Greece, citizenship was not limited to certain urban residents but extended to all adult males who were qualified by birth whether their homes were in the city proper or in the rural countryside. Moreover, the early military reforms of Greece demonstrated the importance of the peasant farmer to the well-being of the state; hence, these peasant hoplites were accorded increasingly greater political privileges from the seventh to the fourth centuries B.C. Kinship also provided the base of citizenship in the Hausa city-states where the free citizenry of Hausawa was the largest segment of the population both in the cities and the countryside. Ethnicity remained the most important ingredient in conferring rights and privileges. Yet, even though the Hausa social order was rigidly defined, granting full rights to adult males who possessed common bloodlines, it was possible to assimilate non-Hausa to the ethnic social core, as we have seen.

The Sumerian cities appear to have begun life in much the same mold as the established Greek *poleis* or the Hausa states with kinship serving as a measure of incorporation into the ruling social order. Shared blood may well have determined the free citizenry who, in assembly, decided matters of policy. Gradually, however, the role of the elected leader—the *ensi*—assumed greater importance and, accompanying his rise, a system of bureaucratic officialdom grew more elaborate. The end product was the exercise of virtually all governmental functions from the palace and, concomitantly, the exclusion of the bulk of the population from the political direction of the state.

From the time of the creation of the commune in northern Italy, citizenship was limited to property-holders with the greatest powers exercised by noble families. Even "popular" government was in the hands of the wealthy merchants or lawyers who were not noble but equally were not plebeian. The association of political office with the major guilds of the city demonstrates the timocratic nature of established authority in the Italian city-states. In addition to a property qualification, citizenship was restricted to urban residents; inhabitants of the rural *contado* did not possess citizen rights.

Many of the same conditions prevailed in the German and Swiss cities. Only adult males resident within the city walls were full citizens. Rural dwellers were subjects. Tied closely to economic status, citizenship enabled one to practice a craft or carry out retail activities. Since the free cities promoted production and trade, citizenship was regularly granted to those outsiders possessing wealth or skills that made them desirable members of the community.

However citizenship was defined, there were certain persons in the state who were either subjects or possessed only partial rights. These, the semi- or wholly disenfranchised groups, obviously brought pressure to bear upon the classes of privileged citizens employing the time-honored techniques of revolt, riot, lackadaisical work habits, and association with rebellious factions. Throughout much of their histories the Hausa states stand at one end of the scale measuring class friction since so many techniques of cross-cutting the lines of rigid social hierarchy were available. Ancient Greece and medieval Italy with their increasingly class-stratified structures stand at the other end of the scale.

The divisive feature that led to uncontrollable internal conflict in the Hausa city-states was religious in nature: when Islam and its reformist protagonists became less tolerant of Hausa tradition, customs, and the exactions of rulers, who although Muslim were regarded as not abiding by the true canons of Islamic law, the fabric of the tolerant, religiously pluralistic city-state culture unraveled.

Religion was a factor promoting division in early modern Europe as well. The bond of religion and state was especially strong in Germany and Switzerland: God's grace enabled the city-state to retain its freedom and prosperity, in the most pronounced view of its leaders. Consequently, the fervor of the Reformation was strongly felt and, in many instances, social and economic issues fueled the religious fires especially on the part of the rural peasantry who were not granted the blessings of citizenship in their states. In Italy similar demands for reform created massive disruption within states dating from the efforts of Bishop Hildebrand in the eleventh century to the time of Savonarola in the fifteenth.

The sense of distance and rivalry between classes of citizens and subject represented only one aspect of internal strife. Discord occurred between full citizens quite as regularly, if not more so. Inasmuch as the political direction of the European city-states was generally timocratic, the greatest source of unrest was economic. Guild revolutions occurred in both Italy and the German free cities; the attempt to introduce a new tax could trigger expressions of citizen outrage and, more than that, could occasion a clean sweep of the existing leadership from office. While the wealthy regularly remained in firm control, different leaders from among the higher social and economic orders were thrust into official positions in such periods of confusion. As far as the evidence permits us to penetrate Sumerian state affairs, they were also prone to demands for correction of economic and social injustices. Not only change of leadership but change of constitutional form was a normal occurrence in the states of Classical Greece. At times the militia companies in the German city-states even developed into vehicles of political protest.

Quite obviously in these comparisons of social unrest and "class conflicts" within the five cultures we enter upon one of the main interpretive—perhaps even ideological—battlefields of modern social science. We have no special desire to tiptoe around this raging controversy. On the other hand, our data does not permit us to use the great debate between social, economic, and historical theorists as the centerpiece of our comparative analysis of change in city-state life and structure.[14] Much less are we in a position to argue that city-states were ultimately the victims of social revolutionary forces that developed naturally within them. Whatever transformations might owe their origins to such causes, most city-states came to an end as a result of foreign conquest and absorption into a large territorial state. This is not to say that social unrest and something resembling a dialectic of conflict between social classes were not the most visible signs of change within city-state life. Such strife clearly weakened the ability of most city-state ruling groups to secure permanently the typical oligarchical form of organization. But we do not believe that this factor alone should be made to account for the incapacity of small polities to resist forceful assaults upon their autonomy by better equipped outside powers. For us, social conflict remains one important but not sole factor among numerous causes that led to the final downfall of these city-state systems.

This qualification serves to underscore at least two other factors that contributed to the decline of specific city-state cultures. These we shall call either *natural* or *accidental* (historical) causes. Natural causes of decline stemmed from fundamental changes in and deterioration of the productive capacity of the physical environment. Most notable is the case of southern Mesopotamia where, during the latter third of the third millennium B.C., the land at the head of the Persian Gulf became increasingly silted. The resulting increase in soil salinity rendered food production vastly less efficient. Given the technology of the period, the decline in crop yields could be neither halted nor reversed. The final outcome was the slow erosion of Sumer's prime economic base. Similar processes of deterioration in the agricultural base stemming from soil erosion, lack of adequate means of restoring soil fertility through fertilization, and continued dependence on a limited number of staple crops played their parts in the other city-state systems.

What appears from this factor of natural causes of decline is that city-states, in an attempt to make up the deficits occasioned by declining agricultural productivity in the face of growing populations, took to participation in a wider world of commercial exchange with the intent of importing necessary basic commodities. In such circumstances any major shifts or dislocations in the pattern of trade routes could produce alarming and disastrous consequences. For example, Alexander the Great's conquest of the Persian Empire (334–323 B.C.) caused international trade to be redirected in such a manner that the Greek city-states of the mainland were left in an economic backwater. The relocation of the main centers of European commerce from southern to northwestern Europe had roughly similar effects upon the old commercial and financial centers largely dominated by the Italian and south German cities before 1600.[15] Hausaland would seem to be the exception here. The shift of the trans-Saharan trade routes from the Niger region eastward to the Hausa cities themselves was a key factor in promoting the city-state growth.

Finally, one cannot discount the seminal role of the spread of ideas and ideologies that sometimes promoted and on other occasions undermined the city-state form. For the traditional Hausa, the adoption of the universalistic civilization of Islam by their rulers produced extraordinarily positive influences on city-state growth for a number of centuries. But in the end, it served as the rallying point for those who overthrew the system. A world refashioned along lines of Hellenic civilization for which the Greek city-states had been responsible led to their downfall when embraced by an imperial conqueror. The classic case is, of course, the Protestant Reformation in which the princes and merchant burghers of northern European cities called for adherence to the new sectarian doctrines which they championed to assert claims to local political autonomy and, indeed, to build enthusiasm for political autonomy.[16] By the same token, those monarchs who directed the Catholic Counter-Reformation employed the ideology of that movement to attack the prized independence of the Italian cities and many of the German ones as well. For Europe after 1789, and for most of the rest of the world in the century following, the ideal of the nation-state became so firmly rooted that it has swept all other models of political organization brusquely to the side. The European city-states lost their locally expressed privileges with the triumph of the nationalist ideal. Even those territorially compact modern entities with their urban cores and directly attached hinterland areas—such as Singapore—regard themselves as the possessors of nationhood, smaller but maintaining an equality with other such nations many times their size.

In no case did notions of a greater polity created in the name of an idea such as Islam, Protestantism, or the French Revolution spring from the mechanisms that controlled the lives of the city-states; such notions were not part of their natures since the greatest emphasis lay on the preservation and strengthening of their individual and unique qualities, not on the spread of those characteristics as a model for others. This helps to explain why city-states were often the victims of purely accidental or natural factors that undermined their well-being. They seemed unable to cope with and adapt to sweeping ideas of structured change. Their ability to grapple with immediate disaster in the form of drastic changes in the environment—such as the salinization of farmlands—obviously depended upon their success at either introducing improved technologies or altering the ways in which an economic surplus was created. None proved very good at the task. The limited resources of a city-state have the effect of dwarfing its importance in the world economy of which it also is a part. The advantages of smallness of scale at one period became, invariably, the disadvantages of another.

In conclusion, it appears that the element that served to define the physical form and internal organization of the city-state is primarily responsible for its decline. The finite limits of its confined territory and the feebleness of its total population size absolutely required that there be no larger expanding power in the near vicinity. The pattern of endemic rivalry between states exacerbated their inherent weakness. Grander ideas of what they might become—allies in an imperial adventure, functioning parts of a territorial state, glorious cities of a nation—rubbed against the grain of cherished local independence. When that was lost, the city-state passed from the historical scene.

The City-State Form

We began this study by suggesting that the historical appearance of the city-state covers a range of examples widely distributed in time and space and across great cultural frontiers. Even though we go on to argue that the city-state form to which we address our attention largely disappears from view with the dawning of the modern age of the nation-states, our study falls far short of comprehensiveness. No examples from any part of Asia outside the ancient Near East are included. None of those remarkable polities whose birth was fashioned through the efforts of commercial colonists is covered. Nor have we dealt with the impressive civilizations of pre-Columbian America—whose scales were often small and whose forms, at certain stages, might be thought to conform to our notion of city-state organization. Others besides the Hausa created city-state cultures in precolonial Africa yet they, too, have been excluded from our comparative enterprise. We have not attempted to produce an encyclopedic inventory of the city-state in history, even within the narrower confines of the European-Mediterranean-African worlds.[17]

Yet the five examples which we have examined are found to share common features and it is reasonable to ask whether we can point to any larger conclusions with respect to the development of state forms. Stated another way, have we not—at the highest level of historical speculation—merely identified a stage or developmental phase in the overall history of many civilizations? Looked at from the perspective of a dynamic process of historical evolutionary development, are not city-states intermediate solutions to long-range problems of political and economic centralization in most human societies? Do they not, as in the cases of Sumer and Hausa, represent an imperfect phase of consolidation on the long march to the marriage of political and territorial authority in large, over-arching institutions of government which finally succeed in imposing their wills over the small, contentious polities? Or, conversely, are city-states not merely the representative units that appear in the first stage of the long, painful attempt to reconstruct lost imperial glories, such as the city-states encompassed within the debilitated Holy Roman Empire?

The short answer to these questions is yes; of course city-states, wherever they made their appearance, were products of the longer range processes of either political centralization or the break-up of an existing centralized authority. Indeed, we have stressed that an absolute precondition for any city-state is the absence of strong and efficient states of any kind in its vicinity. Whether the original impetus for city-state development is to be found in the need to introduce greater efficiency to the economic enterprise, to defend segmented populations within a common cultural zone, to focus attention on a sacred place, or to spread the range of activities from a core region to new locales (as in the cases of the maritime city-states), their longevity and basic form remained viable only so long as better organized, coercive authority was feeble. Yet this does not address itself to the central question of whether city-states are a regular, chartable stage in the affairs of any civilization. The correct answer to the question seems to be that the city-state form is only one of the possible responses that various peoples have made to grouping, or regrouping, their local societies during times when centralized authority was weak. In Europe, feudalism characterized a different response to the same situation. Elsewhere, the rise of a provincial nobility contesting the powers claimed by a grand monarch or emperor resulted in the creation not of city-states but of small territorial kingdoms. The growth and decline of imperial rule in China bears strong witness to this last process and the same might be said for Japan, India, and Southeast Asia at various points in the histories of those civilizations.

One might also argue that if city-states were not always, or even frequently, the preferred form taken by politically weakened societies at least they were products of human initiative that capitalized on favorable, and remarkably similar, geographical, economic, and cultural conditions. In other words, should not city-states be identified primarily with the phenomenon of urbanization? From the available evidence we find it difficult to establish an effective and testable correlation on these grounds. All city-states were, at base, products of the urbanization process. However, degree of urbanization does not define a city-state. Moreover, the urbanization process has produced the city-state form in only a minority of cases. The great civilizations of Asia as well as those of pre-Columbian America flourished in areas that offered conditions of economic opportunity similar to those found in the Mediterranean, European, and African lands where city-state systems developed most successfully. Yet even in these areas city-state cultures were the exception rather than the rule. Therefore, in the final analysis, only the historical study of the particular circumstances that promoted each city-state culture can be used to discover why the general process of urbanization was for lengthy periods in certain places cast in the form of our model.[18]

What, then, remains of a useful comparative model of the city-state? First, it seems clear that the combination of favorable geographical conditions coupled with the absence of strong territorial political authority enabled city-states to win political autonomy and to preserve it for a number of centuries—long enough to fashion both a common cultural tradition and a relatively secure economic base. Second, there is solid evidence that five city-state cultures widely separated in time and space, while originating from different primary causes, ultimately came to possess remarkably similar features. Each evolved as a system containing numerous independent polities built around city cores but sharing a common culture and language with each other. So long as their scales remained limited in total size of territory and population, the urban cores and the immediate hinterlands that came under their control provided an optimum form of efficient organization. The more successful among them developed increasingly complex socio-economic systems that reinforced and sustained the urban mode. If they reached out beyond the area directly under their control by forging trade links with distant areas, the benefits to be gained were appropriated and used by the city-states and not passed on to some higher authority.

Although we have treated but five examples in order to sketch the dimensions and main features of this form of political society, we are convinced that it could be appropriately extended to other examples. Surely the list would include many of the maritime city-state cultures not only of Europe and the Mediterranean but also of Asia. We suspect that the model may not apply so well to the great civilizations of the Asian mainland even though entities resembling city-states made their appearance there. We feel that we have only begun to explore the possibilities of identifying and describing the city-state in world history and stand happily ready to be corrected and instructed if any should feel that we are guilty of the great sin of omission.

Notes

1. W. Christaller, *Central Places in Southern Germany,* trans. C. W. Baskin (Englewood Cliffs, N.J.: Prentice-Hall, 1966).

2. R. Abler, J. S. Adams, and P. Gould, eds., *Spatial Organization: The Geographer's View of the World* (Englewood Cliffs, N.J.: Prentice-Hall, 1971).

3. David Herlihy and Christiane Klapisch-Zuber, *Les toscans et leurs familles* (Paris: Ecole des Hautes Etudes en Sciences Sociales, 1978).

4. C. Renfrew, *The Emergence of Civilisation* (London: Methuen, 1972), 11.

5. The extent to which the Hausa city-states are to be regarded as basically indigenous creations with very ancient prehistoric roots is now the subject of debate. Another view is that they are the products of more recent developments (since 1000 A.D.) fostered by immigrant populations from the East. On the issue see the article by J. G. Sutton, *op. cit.,* Chapter V.

6. Gordon Griffiths's translation of *Peri ten tōn Florentinōn Politeias,* unpublished.

7. A different sort of case could be made that city-states (or units that strongly resemble them) sometimes occur when they are felt to be useful intermediate zones nestled in between very strong polities, as for example Monaco, Liechtenstein, or Luxembourg in Europe; Zanzibar in East Africa; Singapore in Southeast Asia.

8. Attempts to discover and analyze the regularities perceived in the general process of urbanization have provided a major focus of study by geographers and economic historians. The sophisticated models that have been developed to account for those regularities have been termed central places theory. Undoubtedly, the city cores of the city-states discussed here show evidence of having developed along lines that central places models postulate, particularly in regard to the differentiation of economic functions within a growing, urban-centered economic system. The problem that we confront is not that central places theory does not apply; clearly it does. Rather, it rests upon the distinction between cities as both the economic and political governing centers of a perceived unit. In the city-state form, both functions must be served by the core. In other cases, the locus of political power in the state might be found elsewhere than at its economic hub. An example that springs to mind is France in the late medieval and early

modern period where Lyons served as the great commercial-financial center, far removed from Paris, the political center. Spain of the same period might also be regarded in the same light. In other cases where both functions do occur in the same urban location—such as London—one could hardly define England as a city-state. We do not offer a thoroughly refined definition of a city's functions. Instead, we wish to make the simple point that all city-states possess cores that direct (or attempt to direct) all the affairs of their citizenry—political, economic, social, and cultural. This direction becomes vastly more difficult for the larger territorial state with its varying regions, different sub-cultures, economic sub-systems and the like. For an empire, such direction is a virtual impossibility, especially with reference to its major non-capital cities.

9. The dynamic relationship between growing participation in interstate and international trade and the rise of centralized political authority is often cited to demonstrate how the former engenders the latter. This line of analysis has been pursued quite vigorously in recent years by historians of precolonial Africa. See, for example, R. Gray and D. Birmingham, eds., *Pre-Colonial African Trade in Central and Eastern Africa before 1900* (London: Cambridge University Press, 1970). In the context of our study, however, the issue is not whether interstate and international trade patterns themselves give birth to larger economic systems that in turn attract political powers that seek to monopolize them. With the city-states we are interested in such trade patterns, and the conflicts between states to hold a major share of the benefits to be derived from controlling commercial exchanges, in order to illuminate one of the difficulties experienced by the system.

10. See following, p. 195ff.

11. We believe that our broad definitional criteria possess general validity. However, the size of our sample is sufficiently limited to raise questions about this assertion. It is possible to imagine forms, that bear all the hallmarks of city-states as we define them, that do occur as isolated phenomena. The city-state of Benin, a West African rain forest kingdom contacted by the Portuguese in the late fifteenth century, was part of a widely distributed southern Nigerian cultural stratum that produced no other city-states until the nineteenth century. And surely other examples could be found.

12. The Mediterranean trade network which lasted from medieval times to the sixteenth century and which joined in an economic partnership the culturally antagonistic Muslim and Christian civilizations could be cited as a prime example.

13. See pp. 185ff. above for estimates of the territorial extent and population size of the various city-states.

14. There is a temptation to demonstrate our familiarity with this great theoretical controversy by discussing, at least summarily, the views of some of the major proponents of different interpretations. To cite merely one example, the enormously influential schema set forth by V. Gordon Childe, *What Happened in History?* (Harmondsworth: Penguin, 1964) takes Mesopotamian Sumer as its point of departure in arguing the primacy of the class dialectic in the emergence of the first city-state civilization. The European cases are ones which continue to serve as principal examples in the ongoing conflict between rival camps of theorists. Yet we feel justified in making only this passing reference, for in no case can it be clearly shown that social unrest and class conflict were the unquestionable factors that terminated city-state organization. On the contrary, it is possible to imagine an individual city-state experiencing thoroughgoing upheaval based on such conflict while still maintaining its political freedom from the domination of others.

15. This shift has been the subject of intense investigation since, at least, the appearance of the grand synthesis of Henri Pirenne. An admirable survey of the historical literature was provided recently in the work of I. Wallerstein, *The Modern World System: Capitalist Agriculture and the Origins of the European World-Economy in the Sixteenth Century* (New York: Academic Press, 1974), especially chapters 4 and 5.

16. Limits imposed on the scope of any single volume such as this one have meant that northwest European city-state polities have not been treated in detail. However, it is interesting to note that the term was employed in reference to them by none other than the great French historian Ferdinand Braudel who wrote that "Even if you have never thought of it in this way, Amsterdam was the last polis. Venice was not the last, although it would be romantic to say that, until the terrible Bonaparte arrived in 1797, Venice was a polis, a city-state. In fact, by then it was only a local power, with nothing left to dominate, while Amsterdam had for a long time dominated the whole world, which was a fantastic prowess. I would not say that Amsterdam could be held in the hollow of one hand, but we could, I think, hold it in two." H. L. Wesseling, ed., *Expansion and Reaction: Essays on European Expansion and Reactions in Asia and Africa* (Leiden: Leiden University Press, 1978), 23. Clearly Braudel is emphasizing the role which a well organized "city-state," such as Venice once was and Amsterdam became in the seventeenth century, might exercise over a far-flung commercial empire. We regard this usage of the term as valid although we do not pursue it with any vigor as an analytical theme.

Apart from this economic perspective, the other great theme of the same period involves the extent to which championship of the Protestant cause by a specific ruler or merchant-burgher class might not also produce the city-state form (as, for example, Calvin's Geneva). The attempt to resolve the acute political turmoil of the wars of the Reformation by institution of the principle that the religion of any state should be that adopted by its ruler (*cuius regio eius religio,* embodied in the Treaty of Augsburg in 1555) might likewise be seen as a charter enhancing the city-state form of government. With respect to the Netherlands, at least, this notion must be tempered by a different one arguing that the northwestern European Protestant city-states were really the first flowering of nationalism. On this issue consult Gordon Griffiths, "The Revolutionary Character of the Revolution of the Netherlands," *Comparative Studies in Society and History* 2, no. 4 (July, 1960), 454–472.

17. Lewis Mumford's sweeping historical analysis, *The City in History: Its History, Its Origins, Its Transformations, and Its Prospects* (London, 1961; Harmondsworth: Penguin, 1966) delves deeply into the character of city-states and at the same time is limited to the Mediterranean-European sequence. The author's emphasis upon the functions of cities does not directly compare city-states in a cross-cultural context. The same thing may be said of another important, historically-oriented survey, Frederick Hiorns, *Town-Building in History, An Outline Review of Conditions, Influences, Ideas, and Methods Affecting Planned Towns through Five Thousand Years* (London: G. G. Harrap, 1956).

18. A popular alternative explanation draws heavily upon the theories of cultural diffusion. In the present case, the argument would assert that the city-state form found outside the ancient Near East and Greece bore lines of direct descent from those two places, either by virtue of immigrant colonizers who founded states patterned on those of their parent cultures or through the diffusion of the idea about how such states should be

organized. The problem with this interpretation—as with most tightly-knit diffusionist theories—is to account for the many people who were well-placed to receive either immigrants or ideas about the city-state but who did not bother to adopt them. Consequently, we reject any diffusionist hypothesis which would universally assert that all city-states derived from a common source.

List of Contributors

CHRISTOPHER R. FRIEDRICHS is associate professor of history at the University of British Columbia. He is the author of two monographs on German urban history in the Reformation and post-Reformation eras and has published articles in various scholarly journals.

ROBERT GRIFFETH is assistant professor of history at the University of Washington. He has conducted extensive historical field research in West Africa and has written articles for scholarly books and journals on Muslim and traditional West African societies of the pre-colonial period.

GORDON G. GRIFFITHS is professor of history at the University of Washington. A distinguished scholar of the European Renaissance and Reformation, Professor Griffiths has made extensive contributions to the study of Dutch, French, and Italian history of that era.

SONG NAI RHEE is professor of archeology and Old Testament at Northwest Christian College. He specializes in Semitic studies, comparative history, and anthropology. Professor Rhee has been the deputy director of the major archeological excavation at Tel Lachish, Israel—one of antiquity's largest walled cities—since 1974.

CAROL G. THOMAS is professor of history at the University of Washington. She has published extensively in her principal fields, the Mycenaean period and the Dark Age of ancient Greek history.

Selected Bibliography

The bibliography is directed at the nonspecialist. We have assumed that many readers will have a background similar to that of the authors. Each of us claims specialized knowledge in one particular city-state culture but has only general acquaintance with the other areas examined in this study.

It was a paucity of materials examining city-states in several cultures that called forth our effort and, consequently, there is little available for general reading in the subject. For one perspective we suggest Frederick Hiorns's *Town-Building in History, An Outline Review of Conditions, Influences, Ideas, and Methods Affecting Planned Towns through Five Thousand Years*. London: G. G. Harrap, 1956. Another avenue of approach is that of Lewis Mumford's sweeping historical analysis *The City in History: Its History, Its Origins, Its Transformations, and Its Prospects*. Harmondsworth: Penguin, 1966.

Sumer

a. General Surveys of Early Civilizations

Braidwood, Robert J. *The Near East and the Foundations of Civilization*. Eugene: Oregon State System of Higher Education, 1952.

Burney, Charles. *The Ancient Near East*. Ithaca, N.Y.: Cornell University Press, 1977. Treats developments in the Near East from the Neolithic period to the end of the Assyrian Empire in 612.

Frankfort, Henri. *The Birth of Civilization in the Near East*. Bloomington: Indiana University Press, 1951.

Lloyd, Seton. *The Archeology of Mesopotamia*. London: Thames and Hudson, 1978. A study of the rise and decline of Mesopotamian civilizations. Relies heavily on archeological data.

Mallowan, M. E. L. *Early Mesopotamia and Iran*. New York: McGraw-Hill, 1965.

Mellaart, James. *The Earliest Civilizations of the Near East*. London: McGraw-Hill, 1965.

Moscati, Sabatino, ed. *L'alba della civilta: società, economia e pensiero nel Vicino Oriente antico*. 3 vols. Turin: Union Tipografico-Editrice Torinese, 1976. A major effort on the part of a number of modern Italian scholars to examine societal organization (vol. 1), economic order (vol. 2), and intellectual developments (vol. 3) in the ancient Near East.

Redman, Charles L. *The Rise of Civilization*. San Francisco: W. H. Freeman, 1978. A treatment of the developmental stages of Near Eastern society from the end of the Paleolithic period to the emergence of city-states in Sumer.

209

b. The First Revolution: Domestication

Braidwood, Robert J. "The Agricultural Revolution." *Scientific American* 203 (1960) 130–152.
Braidwood, Robert J., and Braidwood, Linda S. "The Earliest Village Communities of Southwestern Asia." *Journal of World History* 1 (1953) 278–310.
    Braidwood is a major authority on the subject of agricultural origins and the rise of farming villages.
Reed, Charles, ed. *Origins of Agriculture*. The Hague: Mouton, 1977.
    Treats the forces which stimulated the origin and diffusion of food production.
Ucko, Peter J., and Dimbley, G. W., eds. *The Domestication and Exploitation of Plants and Animals*. Chicago: Aldine, 1969.
Wright, Gary A. "Origins of Food Production in Southwestern Asia: A Survey of Ideas." *Current Anthropology* 12 (1971) 447–477.

c. The Second Revolution: Rise of Cities

Adams, Robert McC. *The Evolution of Urban Society*. Chicago: Aldine, 1966.
    A comparative analysis of the independent rise of urban centers in Mesopotamia and prehistoric Mesoamerica.
Braidwood, Robert J., and Willey, Gordon, eds. *Courses toward Urban Life*. Chicago: Aldine, 1962.
Carneiro, Robert. "A Theory of the Origin of the State." *Science* 169 (1970) 733–738.
    Examines the problems of population pressure, limited land, and conflicts within populations as the primary causes of the rise of states.
Childe, V. Gordon. *What Happened in History?* Reprint, rev. Harmondsworth: Penguin, 1964.
    Mesopotamia is the point of departure for the argument that class dialectic was of major importance in the emergence of the first city-states.
Flannery, Kent V. "The Cultural Evolution of Civilizations." *Annual Review of Ecology and Systematics* 3 (1972) 399–426.
    Stresses that urbanism and the state arose as a result of increasing internal differentiation and specialization within societies.
Hole, Frank. "Investigating the Origins of Mesopotamian Civilization." *Science* 153 (1966) 605–611.
    Investigates the interrelationship of environment, irrigation, population growth, temple elite, trade, and warfare in the rise of cities.
Steward, Julian, ed. *Irrigation Civilizations: A Comparative Study*. Washington, D.C.: Social Science Section, Pan American Union, 1955.
    The need for large-scale irrigation systems is seen as a major stimulus in the rise of urban centers.
Ucko, Peter J.; Tringham, Ruth; and Dimbley, G. W., eds. *Man, Settlement and Urbanism*. London: Duckworth, 1973.
Wittfogel, Karl. *Oriental Despotism: A Comparative Study of Total Power*. New Haven: Yale University Press, 1957.
    A classic statement of the role of irrigation in urbanism.
Wright, Henry T. "Recent Research on the Origin of the State." *Annual Review of Anthropology* 6 (1977) 379–398.
    A general overview.

Wright, Henry T., and Johnson, Greg. "Population, Exchange, and Early State Formation in Southwestern Iran." *American Anthropologist* 77 (1975) 267–289.
Argues that urban centers were a response to large-scale trade which demanded efficient administrative organization.

d. General Studies

Hamblin, Dora Jane. *The First Cities.* New York: Time-Life Books, 1973.
Reconstructs daily life in the early third millennium B.C.
Jastrow, Morris, Jr. *The Religions of Babylonia and Assyria.* Boston: Ginn, 1898.
Jones, Tom B., ed. *The Sumerian Problem.* New York: Wiley, 1969.
Sixteen articles on problems related to the identity of the Sumerians.
Kramer, Samuel Noah. *History Begins at Sumer.* 2d rev. ed. London: Thames and Hudson, 1956.
_____. *The Sumerians.* Chicago: University of Chicago Press, 1963.
Mallowan, M. E. L. "The Development of Cities: From Al Ubaid to the End of Uruk" and "The Early Dynastic Period in Mesopotamia." Chapters 8 and 15 in *Cambridge Ancient History.* Vol. 1. Rev. ed. Cambridge: University Press, 1970 and 1971.
Woolley, C. Leonard. *Excavations at Ur.* London: Benn, 1955.
_____. *The Sumerians.* New York: W. W. Norton, 1965.
_____. *Ur of the Chaldees.* London: Benn, 1929.

e. Specific Aspects of Sumerian City-States

Adams, Robert McC., and Nissen, Hans J. *The Uruk Countryside: The Natural Setting of Urban Society.* Chicago: University of Chicago Press, 1972.
A detailed study of demographic changes in the Uruk region.
Diakonoff, Igor M., ed. *Ancient Mesopotamia: A Socio-Economic History.* Moscow: Nauka Publishing House, 1969.
Especially important are two articles treating economic aspects of Sumerian city-states by A. I. Tyumenev.
Evans, Geoffrey. "Ancient Mesopotamian Assemblies." *Journal of the American Oriental Societies* 78 (1958) 1–11.
Falkenstein, Adam. *The Sumerian Temple City* translated by Maria deJ. Ellis. Los Angeles: Undena, 1974.
Jacobsen, Thorkild. "The Cosmos as a State" and "The Function of the State." In *The Intellectual Adventures of Ancient Man* edited by H. and H. A. Frankfort, J. A. Wilson, Th. Jacobsen, W. A. Irwin. Chicago: University of Chicago Press, 1946.
Treats the relationship between the Sumerian world view and the nature of the Sumerian political system.
_____. "Early Political Development in Mesopotamia." In *Toward the Image of Tammuz and Other Essays* edited by W. I. Moran. Cambridge, Mass.: Harvard University Press, 1970. Also in *Zeitschrift für Assyriologie und vorderasiatische Archäologie* 52 (1957) 91–140.
_____. "Primitive Democracy in Ancient Mesopotamia." *Journal of Near Eastern Studies* 2, no. 3 (1943) 159–172.
Jacobsen, Thorkild, and Adams, Robert McC. "Salt and Silt in Ancient Mesopotamian Agriculture." *Science* 128, no. 3334 (1958) 1251–1258.
Deals with the problem of salinization in Sumer which increasingly rendered the land unproductive and became a major cause of Sumerian decline.

Greece

a. General Studies

Busolt, G., and Swoboda, H. *Griechische Staatskunde*. 3d ed. 2 vols. Munich: Beck, 1920–1926.
Detailed information concerning specific states.

Doxiadis, C. A. *The Method for the Study of Ancient Greek Settlements*. Athens: Athens Center of Ekistics, 1972.
The general statement of a major project in which human settlements are related to specific territory within the present boundaries of Greece.

Ehrenberg, Victor. *The Greek State*. London: Basil Blackwell, 1960.
The most complete account of the *polis*. Its emphasis is on political form and institutions. Its two parts deal with the Classical world of the *polis* and the Hellenistic era of larger states.

Fustel de Coulanges, Numa Denis. *La Cité Antique*. Paris: Hachette, 1864. Published in English in 1873 as *The Ancient City: A Classic Study of the Religious and Civil Institutions of Ancient Greece and Rome*.
Demonstrates the importance of religion in all aspects of life.

Hammond, Mason. *The City in the Ancient World*. Cambridge, Mass.: Harvard University Press, 1972.
Examines the *polis* as well as other urban entities in antiquity. Its full bibliography extends from the time of the first cities to the early medieval and Byzantine periods.

Herodotus. *The Histories*. Translated by Aubrey de Selincourt. Harmondsworth: Penguin, 1954.
A readable translation of the account of the Father of History who is one of the best witnesses to the success and failure of the Greek *polis*.

Kirsten, E. *Die griechische Polis als historisch-geographisches Problem des Mittelmeerraumes*. Bonn: Dümmler, 1956.
The standard account of *polis* territory.

Martin, R. *L'Urbanisme dans la Grèce Antique*. Paris: Picard, 1956.
An excellent survey of the urban features of the *polis*.

Pausanias. *Guide to Greece* translated by Peter Levi. 2 vols. Harmondsworth: Penguin, 1971.
A traveller's account of Greece.

Schoder, Raymond. *Wings over Hellas: Ancient Greece from the Air*. New York: Oxford University Press, 1974.
A beautifully illustrated volume.

Tritsch, F. "Die Stadtbildungen des Altertums und die griechische Polis." *Klio* 22 (1928) 1–83.
Places the Greek state in a larger historical and geographical context.

Wycherley, R. E. *How the Greeks Built Cities*. London: Methuen, 1949.

b. Origin and Decline of the *Polis*

Ehrenberg, Victor. "When Did the *Polis* Rise?" *Journal of Hellenic Studies* 57 (1937) 147–159.
A general survey of the literary evidence for the origin of the *polis*.

Gomme, A. W. "The End of the City-State." In *Essays in Greek History and Literature*. Oxford: Basil Blackwell, 1937, 204–248.

A sensible overview of problems in interpreting *polis* decline.

Jones, A. H. M. *The Greek City from Alexander to Justinian*. Oxford: Clarendon, 1940.

Shows the transformation of city-states into cities incorporated in larger states.

Mossé, C. *Athens in Decline: 404–86 B.C.* London: Routledge and Kegan Paul, 1973.

A case study for the change in status of one *polis*.

Redfield, J. N. *Nature and Culture in the Iliad*. Chicago: University of Chicago Press, 1975.

A persuasive description of Homeric society which offers an understanding of the roots of the city-state.

Roebuck, C. A. "Some Aspects of Urbanization of Corinth." *Hesperia* 41 (1972) 96–127. Reprinted in *Economy and Society in the Early Greek World*. Chicago: Ares, 1979.

A case study of one emerging *polis*.

Snodgrass, A. M. *Archaeology and the Rise of the Greek State*. Cambridge: University Press, 1977.

A current overview of the origin of the *polis*.

c. Specific Aspects of *Polis* Organization

Adkins, A. W. H. *Merit and Responsibility: A Study in Greek Values*. Oxford: Oxford University Press, 1960.

———. *Moral and Political Behaviour in Ancient Greece*. London: Chatto and Windus, 1972.

A thorough, sensible investigation of the connection between Greek values and political organization.

Andreades, A. M. *A History of Greek Public Finance*. Cambridge, Mass.: Harvard University Press, 1933.

Aristotle. *Athenaion Politeia*. In *Aristotle's Constitution of Athens and Related Texts* translated by K. von Fritz and E. Kapp. New York and London: Hafner, 1950.

The only nearly complete example of some 158 constitutions attributed to Aristotle and his school.

Austin, M. M., and Vidal-Naquet, P. *Economic and Social History of Ancient Greece: An Introduction*. London: B. T. Batsford, 1977.

A general discussion of the subject forms the first half of the book, while ancient sources and additional bibliography constitute the second.

Bonner, R. J., and Smith, G. *The Administration of Justice from Homer to Aristotle*. 2 vols. Chicago: University of Chicago Press, 1930–1938.

Calhoun, G. M. *Athenian Clubs in Politics and Litigation*. Austin: University of Texas Press, 1913.

A study of the only ancient counterparts to political associations.

Ehrenberg, Victor. *The People of Aristophanes: A Sociology of Old Attic Comedy*. 2d ed., rev. Oxford: Basil Blackwell, 1951.

The characters of Old Comedy speak for themselves and for their societal roles.

Finley, M. I. *The Ancient Economy*. London: Chatto and Windus, 1973.

Emphasizes orders of society and their place within the state.

Garlan, Yvon. *War in the Ancient World: A Social History.* London: Chatto and Windus, 1975.
Takes the large view of military aspects of the state. Examines such subjects as truces, distribution of booty.

Gomme, A. W. *The Population of Athens in the Fifth and Fourth Centuries B.C.* Oxford: Basil Blackwell, 1933.
The standard attempt to come to grips with numbers.

Jones, J. W. *Law and Legal Theory of the Greeks.* Oxford: Clarendon, 1956.

Larsen, J. A. O. *Greek Federal States: Their Institutions and History.* Oxford: Clarendon, 1968.

————. *Representative Government in Greek and Roman History.* Berkeley and Los Angeles: University of California Press, 1955.

Martin, V. *La vie internationale dans la Grèce des cités.* Paris: Recueil Sirey, 1940.

Nilsson, M. P. *Cults, Myths, Oracles and Politics in Ancient Greece.* London: C. W. K. Gleerup, 1951. Reprint. New York: Cooper Square, 1972.
Examines the interaction of religion and political organization.

Starr, C. G. *The Economic and Social Growth of Early Greece 800–500 B.C.* Oxford: Oxford University Press, 1977.

————. *Political Intelligence in Classical Greece.* Mnemosyne Supplement 31. Leiden: E. J. Brill, 1974.

Whibley, L. *Greek Oligarchies: Their Character and Organization.* London: Methuen, 1896. Reprint. Chicago: Ares, 1975.

Italy

a. Italian City-States Generally

Bertelli, Sergio. *Il potere oligarchico nello stato-città medievale.* Florence: La Nuova Italia, 1978.
The author approaches the subject from the point of view of political science.

Burckhardt, Jacob. *The Civilization of the Renaissance in Italy.* 2d ed. rev. translated by S. G. C. Middlemore. Oxford: Phaidon, 1945. First German ed., 1860.
The place to begin a study of Italian city-states. The famous first part on "The State as a Work of Art" attempts to explain and describe the precocious attainment of sovereignty on the part of both the republican and the despotic states in the fourteenth and fifteenth centuries.

Hyde, J. K. *Society and Politics in Medieval Italy.* New York: St. Martin's, 1973.
Treats the city-states in the period of the eleventh to the early fourteenth centuries. Has an extensive analytical bibliography.

Jones, P. J. "Communes and Despots: The City-State in Late Medieval Italy." *Transactions of the Royal Historical Society,* ser. 5, 15 (1965) 71–96.

Pullan, Brian. *A History of Early Renaissance Italy.* London: Allen Lane, 1973.
A survey of the period from 1250–1450. The author distinguishes between city-states in the century 1250–1350 and territorial states, which he feels is a better designation for states in the century 1350–1450.

Renouard, Yves. *Les villes d' Italie de la fin du Xe siècle au début du XIVe siècle* edited by Philippe Braunstein. 2 vols. Regards sur l'histoire. Paris: Societé d'Edition d'Enseignement Supérieur, 1969.
Organized by city, the study is based upon lectures delivered at the Sorbonne shortly before the author's premature death in 1965.

Sismondi, J. C. L. *Histoire des republiques italiennes au moyen age.* 16 vols. 1807–
    1818. Published in English in 1832. Reprint (with an introduction by W. K. Fergu-
    son). New York: Doubleday, 1966.
Waley, Daniel. *Italian City-Republics.* New York: McGraw-Hill, 1969.
    An excellent introduction to the republican city-states in northern and central Italy
    between the eleventh and early fourteenth centuries.

b. Florence

Baron, Hans. *Crisis of the Early Italian Renaissance.* Rev. ed. Princeton: Princeton
    University Press, 1966.
    Relying especially on literary sources, the author explains the transition from the
    traditional ideology of Guelfism to "civic humanism."
Becker, Marvin. "Economic Change and the Emerging Florentine Territorial State."
    Studies in the Renaissance 13 (1966) 7–39.
    Discusses the importance of the fiscal system which enabled the rich to grow richer
    from investments in the consolidated public debt and facilitated the growth of the
    territorial state.
_____. *Florence in Transition.* 2 vols. Baltimore: Johns Hopkins, 1967–1968.
    Volume 1 treats the decline of the commune; volume 2 studies the rise of the territorial
    state.
Brucker, Gene. *Civic World of Early Renaissance Florence.* Princeton: Princeton
    University Press, 1977.
    Treats the period 1378–1430 and is based upon the political deliberations called the
    Consulte e Pratiche. The author's thesis is that this period marked the transformation
    from a polity guided by corporate interests to one governed by an elite of professional
    statesmen.
_____. *Florentine Politics and Society, 1343–1378.* Princeton: Princeton University
    Press, 1962.
    Demonstrates the techniques by which the Albizzi faction controlled the machinery of
    government during the greater part of the period.
Davidsohn, Robert. *Geschichte von Florenz.* 4 vols. Berlin: E. S. Mittler, 1896–1927.
    Published in Italian as *Storia di Firenze.* Florence: Sansoni, 1956–1967.
    The fundamental work on Florence up to approximately 1340.
Herlihy, David, and Klapisch-Zuber, Christiane. *Les toscans et leurs familles.* Paris:
    Ecole des Hautes Etudes en Sciences Sociales, 1978.
    A computerized analysis of the *catasto,* the great tax assessment of 1427.
Marines, Lauro. *Lawyers and Statecraft in Renaissance Florence.* Princeton: Princeton
    University Press, 1968.
    Examines how the legal profession contributed to the development of the territorial
    state and the strengthening of the oligarchy.
_____. *The Social World of the Florentine Humanists.* Princeton: Princeton University
    Press, 1963.
    Argues that humanism was an ideology of and for the elite.
Rubinstein, Nicolai. *The Government of Florence under the Medici, 1434 to 1494.*
    Oxford: Clarendon, 1966.
    Describes how the Medici were able to exert control behind the mask of republican
    forms of government.

Schevill, Ferdinand. *History of Florence*. New York: Harcourt Brace, 1936. Reprinted as *Medieval and Renaissance Florence*. 2 vols. New York: Harper and Row, 1963. Remains the only survey in English of the whole of Florentine history.

c. Other City-States

Blanshei, Sarah. *Perugia, 1260–1340: Conflict and Change in a Medieval Italian Urban Society*. Philadelphia: American Philosophical Society, 1976.
Bouwsma, William J. *Venice and the Defense of Republican Liberty in the Age of the Counter Reformation*. Berkeley and Los Angeles: University of California Press, 1968.
Political ideas are of particular interest to the author.
Bowsky, William M. "*Buon Governo* of Siena (1287–1355): A Medieval Italian Oligarchy." *Speculum* 37 (1962) 368–381.
Bueno de Mesquita, Daniel. *Gian Galeazzo Visconti, Duke of Milan, 1351–1402*. Cambridge: University Press, 1941.
Chambers, D. S. *Imperial Age of Venice, 1380–1580*. New York: Harcourt Brace, 1970. A short introduction.
Gregorovius, Ferdinand Adolf. *History of the City of Rome in the Middle Ages* translated by Annie Hamilton. Reprint (8 vols. in 13). London: G. Bell, 1900.
Gundersheiner, Werner L. *Ferrara, the Style of a Renaissance Despotism*. Princeton: Princeton University Press, 1973.
Heers, Jacques. *Gênes au XVᵉ siècle: activité économique et problèmes sociaux*. Paris: S.E.V.P.E.N., 1961.
Herlihy, David. *Medieval and Renaissance Pistoia . . . 1208–1438*. New Haven: Yale University Press, 1967.
_____. *Pisa in the Early Renaissance*. New Haven: Yale University Press, 1958.
Hyde, J. K. *Padua in the Age of Dante*. Manchester: Manchester University Press, 1966.
Lane, Frederic C. "Medieval Political Ideas and the Venetian Constitution." In *Venice and History* (collected papers). Baltimore: Johns Hopkins Press, 1966.
_____. *Venice, a Maritime Republic*. Baltimore: Johns Hopkins Press, 1973.
Lopez, Robert. *The Commercial Revolution of the Middle Ages, 950–1350*. Englewood Cliffs, N.J.: Prentice Hall, 1971.
The author's various writings emphasize Genoa and the role of economic factors.
McNeill, William H. *Venice, the Hinge of Europe, 1081–1797*. Chicago: University of Chicago Press, 1974.
Partner, Peter. *The Lands of St. Peter*. Berkeley and Los Angeles: University of California Press, 1972.
_____. *Renaissance Rome, 1500–1559: A Portrait of a Society*. Berkeley and Los Angeles: University of California Press, 1976.
A supplement to his earlier study.
Pullan, Brian. *Rich and Poor in Renaissance Venice*. Cambridge, Mass.: Harvard University Press, 1971.
Schevill, Ferdinand. *Siena, the History of a Medieval Commune*. 1909. Reprint. New York: Harper and Row, 1964.
Waley, Daniel. *Medieval Orvieto*. Cambridge: University Press, 1952.

Germany and Switzerland

a. Survey of German and Swiss History

Barraclough, Geoffrey. *The Origins of Modern Germany*. 2d ed. Oxford: Oxford University Press, 1947.
A survey of medieval German history.

Bonjour, E.; Offler, H. S.; and Potter, G. R. *A Short History of Switzerland*. Oxford: Oxford University Press, 1952.
General introduction to Swiss history.

Helbing, Hanno, et al. *Handbuch der Schweizer Geschichte*. 2 vols. Zurich: Berichthaus, 1972.
Factual data about Swiss cities.

Holborn, Hajo. *A History of Modern Germany*. 3 vols. New York: Alfred A. Knopf, 1959–1969.
General survey of German history since the late middle ages.

Keyser, Erich, ed. *Deutsches Städtebuch: Handbuch städtischer Geschichte*. 11 vols. Stuttgart: Kohlhammer, 1939–1974.
Contains factual data about every city in Germany.

Taddey, Gerhard, ed. *Lexikon der deutschen Geschichte*. Stuttgart: Kröner, 1977.
Best one-volume reference work for German history. Contains a separate entry for each German and Swiss free city.

Zophy, Jonathan W., ed. *The Holy Roman Empire: A Dictionary Handbook*. Westport, Conn.: Greenwood, 1980.
Full bibliographies.

b. German and Swiss Free Cities

Dollinger, Philippe. *The German Hansa* translated by D. S. Ault and S. H. Steinberg. Stanford: Stanford University Press, 1970.
A general study which gives considerable emphasis to the free cities of Germany.

Keyser, Erich, ed. *Bibliographie zur Städtegeschichte Deutschlands*. Cologne: Böhlau, 1969. A fuller second edition, edited by H. Stobb and W. Ehbrecht, is forthcoming.
A guide to the literature in the German language on Swiss and German city-states.

Mauersberg, Hans. *Wirtschafts- und Sozialgeschichte zentraleuropäischer Städte in neuerer Zeit, dargestellt an den Beispielen von Basel, Frankfurt a. M., Hamburg, Hannover und München*. Göttingen: Vandenhoeck und Ruprecht, 1960.
A comparative study of five early modern towns.

Mayer, Theodor, ed. *Untersuchungen zur gesellschaftlichen Struktur der mittelalterlichen Städte in Europa*. Vorträge und Forschungen, no. 11. Constance: Jan Thorbecke, 1966.
Reflects the growing interest in the social history of central European city-states. Includes essays on medieval Lübeck, Nuremberg, Regensburg, and Schwäbisch-Hall.

Moeller, Bernd. *Imperial Cities and the Reformation* translated by H. C. Erik Midelfort and Mark U. Edwards, Jr. Philadelphia: Fortress, 1972.
Treats a crucial moment in the history of the free cities.

Oestreich, Gerhard. "Reichs- und Landesstädte." In *Gebhardts Handbuch der deutschen Geschichte* edited by Herbert Grundmann. 9th ed. Stuttgart: Union Verlag, 1970, 2: 426–436.

Planitz, Hans. *Die deutsche Stadt im Mittelalter.* Cologne: Böhlau, 1954.
The standard scholarly survey of German cities up to 1350.

Rörig, Fritz. *The Medieval Town.* Berkeley and Los Angeles: University of California Press, 1967.
A general study that gives considerable emphasis to the free cities of Germany.

Sayn-Wittgenstein, Franz Prinz su. *Reichsstädte: Patrizisches Leben von Bern bis Lübeck.* Munich: Prestel-Verlag, 1965.
An informal, somewhat anecdotal treatment of the history and culture of seventeen free cities in Switzerland and Germany.

Walker, Mack. *German Home Towns: Community, State and General Estate, 1648–1871.* Ithaca, N.Y.: Cornell University Press, 1971.

c. Individual German and Swiss Cities

Bothe, Friedrich. *Geschichte der Stadt Frankfurt am Main.* Frankfurt: M. Diesterweg, 1913. Abridged ed. Frankfurt: Englert und Schlosser, 1929.
Survey history.

Brady, Thomas J., Jr. *Ruling Class, Regime and Reformation at Strasbourg, 1520–1555.* Studies in Medieval and Reformation Thought, 22. Leiden: E. J. Brill, 1978.

Chrisman, Miriam U. *Strasbourg and the Reform.* New Haven: Yale University Press, 1967.

Ford, Franklin L. *Strasbourg in Transition, 1648–1789.* Cambridge, Mass.: Harvard University Press, 1958.

Friedrichs, Christopher R. *Urban Society in an Age of War: Nördlingen, 1580–1720.* Princeton: Princeton University Press, 1979.

Guyer, Paul. *Die soziale Schichtung der Bürgerschaft Zürichs vom Augsgang des Mittelalters bis 1798.* Kleine Schriften des Stadtarchivs Zürich, no. 5. Zürich: Stadtarchiv, 1952.
A short but classic study of Zürich society.

Monter, E. William. *Calvin's Geneva.* New York: Wiley, 1967.
The best work in English on Swiss city-states.

Pfeiffer, Gerhard, ed. *Nürnberg: Geschichte einer europäischen Stadt.* Munich: Beck, 1971.

Rotz, Rhiman A. "The Lübeck Uprising of 1408 and the Decline of the Hanseatic League." *Proceedings of the American Philosophical Society* 121 (1977) 1–45.
Discussion of one Hansa town in the late Middle Ages.

Schramm, Percy. *Neun Generationen: Dreihundert Jahre deutscher 'Kulturgeschichte' im Lichte der Schicksale einer Hamburger Bürgerfamilie (1648–1948).* 2 vols. Göttingen: Vandenhoeck und Ruprecht, 1963–64.
Uses the records of one family to interpret the history of Hamburg from the seventeenth century onward.

Soliday, Gerald L. *A Community in Conflict: Frankfurt Society in the Seventeenth and Early Eighteenth Centuries.* Hanover, N.H.: University Press of New England, 1974.

Strait, Paul. *Cologne in the Twelfth Century.* Gainesville, Fla.: University Presses of Florida, 1974.

Strauss, Gerald. *Nuremberg in the Sixteenth Century.* New York: Wiley, 1966.
The best overall description of a representative German city-state.

Zorn, Wolfgang. *Augsburg: Geschichte einer deutschen Stadt.* 2d ed. Augsburg: Hieronymus Mühlberger, 1972.

d. Aspects of Administration

Brunner, Otto. "Souveränitätsproblem und Sozialstruktur in den deutschen Reichsstädten der frühen Neuzeit." *Vierteljahreschrift für Sozial- und Wirtschaftsgeschichte* 50 (1963) 329–360.

Buchstab, Günter. *Reichsstädte, Städtekurie und Westfälischer Friedenskongress: Zusammenhänge von Sozialstruktur, Rechtsstatus und Wirtschaftskraft.* Schriftenreihe der Vereinigung zur Erforschung der neueren Geschichte, no. 7. Münster: Aschendorff, 1976.
Treats the legal and economic status of each imperial city before and after the Peace of Westphalia.

Dannenbauer, Heinz. *Die Entstehung des Territoriums der Reichsstadt Nürnberg.* Stuttgart: Kohlhammer, 1928.
Describes the way in which one major city-state acquired its rural territory.

Neusser, Gerold. *Das Territorium der Reichsstadt Ulm im 18. Jahrhundert: Verwaltungsgeschichtliche Forschungen.* Ulm: Stadtarchiv, 1964.
Deals with the administration of rural territory of a city-state.

Hausaland

a. Local Traditions Recorded by Others

Barth, H. *Travels and Discoveries in North and Central Africa 1849–1855.* 4 vols. London: Longmans, Green, 1957.
The most thorough and detailed description of nineteenth century Hausaland from the writings of a German explorer.

Bivar, A. D. H., and Hiskett, M. "The Arabic Literature of Nigeria to 1804: A Provisional Account." University of London *Bulletin of the School of Oriental and African Studies* 25 (1962) 104–148.
Survey of pre-nineteenth century Arabic materials dealing with Hausaland.

Cuoq, J. M. *Recueil des sources Arabes concernant l'Afrique occidentale du VIIIe au XVIe siècle.* Paris: C.N.R.S., 1975.
Basically Arabic documentary material. Firsthand accounts or reports of North African Muslim travelers in the period 1000–1700.

Denham, Dixon; Clapperton, H.; and Oudney, W. *Narrative of Travels and Discoveries in Northern and Central Africa in the Years 1822, 1823, and 1824.* London: John Murray, 1826.
An invaluable source of evidence on the character of the city-states during the period when they were being transformed into imperial emirates as told by the first European visitors to Hausaland in the early nineteenth century.

Hodgkin, Thomas, ed. *Nigerian Perspectives.* 2d ed. London: Oxford University Press, 1975.
A splendid anthology containing a sampling from primary sources with a good bibliography.

Lewicki, T. *Arabic External Sources for the History of Africa to the South of the Sahara.* London: Curzon, 1954.
Reports of North African Muslim travelers as firsthand accounts or incorporated into geographical treatises.

Palmer, H. R. *The Bornu, Sahara and Sudan.* London: J. Murray, 1936.
Includes Hausa oral traditions.

————. *Sudanese Memoirs*. 3 vols. Lagos: Government Printer, 1928. Reprint (3 vols. in 1). 1967.

The compilations of a British colonial administrator.

b. Scholarly Treatments

Ajayi, J. F. A., and Crowder, M., eds. *History of West Africa*. 2 vols. New York: Columbia University Press, 1971–1974.

Three chapters in Volume 1 present an admirable survey of the city-state period: H. F. C. (Abdullahi) Smith, "The Early States of the Central Sudan," 158–201; J. O. Hunwick, "Songhay, Bornu and Hausaland in the Sixteenth Century," 202–239; and R. A. Adeleye, "Hausaland and Bornu 1600–1800," 484–530.

Crowder, M. *The Story of Nigeria*. London: Longmans, Green, 1966.

A popular account of the pre-Fulani Hausa era.

Greenberg, Joseph H. *The Influence of Islam on a Sudanese Religion* [Hausa]. New York: J. J. Augustin, 1946.

One of the best anthropological studies of the Hausa which has significant bearing on historical issues.

Last, M. *The Sokoto Caliphate*. London: Longmans, Green, 1967.

The most complete treatment of the demise of Hausa city-states.

Smith, H. F. C. (Abdullahi). "A Neglected Theme of West African History: The Islamic Revolutions of the Nineteenth Century." *Journal of the Historical Society of Nigeria* 2 (1961) 169–185.

Initiation of a systematic study of the demise of the Hausa city-states.

Smith, M. G. *The Affairs of Daura*. Berkeley and Los Angeles: University of California Press, 1978.

Discussion of issues relating to the pre-Fulani Hausa city-states and the efforts of the post-Caliphate rulers to preserve a large measure of their local autonomy along traditional lines of government.

————. *Government in Zauzau 1800–1950*. London: Oxford University Press, 1960.

The seminal study of Zaria.

————. "The Hausa of Northern Nigeria." In *Peoples of Africa* edited by J. Gibbs. New York: Holt, Rinehart, Winston, 1965, 119–155.

A good starting point for the beginning student.

Stenning, D. T. *Savannah Nomads*. London: Oxford University Press, 1959–1963.

The classical ethnographic study of the pastoral Fulani.

Sutton, J. E. G. "Toward a Less Orthodox History of Hausaland." *Journal of African History* 20, no. 2 (1979) 179–201.

A discussion of the antiquity of Hausa origins.

Trimingham, S. J. *A History of Islam in West Africa*. London: Oxford University Press, 1962.

The standard account of West African Islamic history and Hausaland's place within it prior to 1800.

Waldman, M. "The Fulani *Jihad*: A Reassessment." *Journal of African History* 6 (1965) 333–355.

A survey of interpretive controversies of the Fulani rise to power.

Index

221

Copyedited by Anne Lowenkopf. Composed in VIP Times by McAdams Type of Santa Barbara. Printed and bound by BookCrafters of Chelsea Michigan. Text and cover designed by Tom Reeg.

Comparative

Protoliterate Age
Sumer 3500–2800 B.C.

Early Dynastic Age
Sumer 2800–2350

Sargon of Akkad 2350

Mycenaean Civilization
Greece 1600–1150 B.C.

Greek Dark Ages 1150–750 B.C.

Classical Age 750–350 B.C.

Alexander's Conquests 334–323 B.C.

Hellenistic Period 323 B.C.